Music, Narrative and the Moving Image

Word and Music Studies

VOLUME 17

The book series WORD AND MUSIC STUDIES (WMS) is the central organ of the International Association for Word and Music Studies (WMA), an association founded in 1997 to promote transdisciplinary scholarly inquiry devoted to the relations between literature/verbal texts/language and music. WMA aims to provide an international forum for musicologists and literary scholars with an interest in intermediality studies and in crossing cultural as well as disciplinary boundaries.

WORD AND MUSIC STUDIES publishes, generally on an annual basis, themeoriented volumes, documenting and critically assessing the scope, theory, methodology, and the disciplinary and institutional dimensions and prospects of the field on an international scale: conference proceedings, collections of scholarly essays, and, occasionally, monographs on pertinent individual topics.

The titles published in this series are listed at *brill.com/wms*

Music, Narrative and the Moving Image

Varieties of Plurimedial Interrelations

Edited by

Walter Bernhart
David Francis Urrows

BRILL

RODOPI

LEIDEN | BOSTON

Library of Congress Cataloging-in-Publication Data

Names: Bernhart, Walter. | Urrows, David Francis.
Title: Music, narrative and the moving image : varieties of plurimedial
  interrelations / edited by Walter Bernhart, David Francis Urrows.
Description: Leiden ; Boston : Brill Rodopi, 2019. | Series: Word and music
  studies ; 17 | Includes bibliographical references.
Identifiers: LCCN 2019013188 (print) | LCCN 2019015676 (ebook) | ISBN
  9789004401310 (ebook) | ISBN 9789004399044 (hardback : alk. paper)
Subjects: LCSH: Motion picture music--History and criticism. | Motion
  pictures and music.
Classification: LCC ML2075 (ebook) | LCC ML2075 .M8792 2019 (print) | DDC
  781.5/4209--dc23
LC record available at http://lccn.loc.gov/2019013188

Typeface for the Latin, Greek, and Cyrillic scripts: "Brill". See and download: brill.com/brill-typeface.

ISSN 1566-0958
ISBN 978-90-04-39904-4 (hardback)
ISBN 978-90-04-40131-0 (e-book)

Contents

Preface

The essays collected in this volume are based on a conference that was held in August 2015 at Fordham University in New York City and organized by Professor Lawrence Kramer, who as a long-term member of its executive board had invited the International Association for Word and Music Studies (WMA) to participate in it. The topic of the conference was "Music, Narrative and the Moving Image", which implied an extension of subject area beyond WMA's customary concern with aural and linguistic phenomena. This extension took account of both the conspicuous dominance of visual perception in the present cultural climate and the fact that the contemporary media world is characterised by an increased variety of media active on the scene which enter into ever more lively intermedial interaction. Thus, in the conference proceedings here collected, besides the obvious leading multimedia artform of the time, film – which is covered from the silent cinema era to most recent cases –, there are television, music videos, book illustrations and woodcuts treated among the visual media and genres; theatrical forms discussed are plays, operas, including "revolutionary" Peking opera, ballet, and even such rare forms as cabaret spectacles with shadow plays; among the literary genres, narrative fiction and poetry are discussed, as is instrumental music in various formations; and among the musico-literary forms, an emphasis on songs is noticeable.

The great variety of subject areas treated in the papers read at the conference is a challenge for finding a convincing structure to present them in the collection at hand. Nonetheless, the structure chosen has hopefully sufficient inherent logic. The natural major area of interest covered in the essays is film music. In some of the cases discussed the emphasis is on theoretical issues, concentrating on the various functions of music in film (Part 1, Section 1: "Film Music: Reflections on Functions"); while others offer an interesting range of diversified case studies of the use of film music (Part 1, Section 2: "Film Music: Significant Intermedial Cases"); a third section deals with the interaction of words, music and the moving image in media other than film (Part 2: "Intermedial Varieties"); and the fourth and last section addresses cases of intermedial transpositions that involve visual, aural and verbal aspects (Part 3: "Remediations").

Nonetheless, alternative structures could have been found, as there are various other concerns that recur in several essays and may have formed separate groups. Thus a number of essays discuss narrative functions – on top of those found in Part 1, Section 1 by Werner Wolf, Saskia Jaszoltowski, and Jordan Stokes – and include contributions by Christopher Booth, Heidi Hart, Ruth

Jacobs, and Marion Recknagel. A special group of essays deal with the absence of music in film – by Saskia Jaszoltowski, Ruth Jacobs, Lawrence Kramer, and Werner Wolf – while others are concerned with the presence of classical music in film (by Lawrence Kramer, Christopher Booth, Heidi Hart, and Walter Bernhart). Another recurrent subject area is opera, discussed by Axel Englund, Michael Halliwell, Bernhard Kuhn, Marion Recknagel, and David Francis Urrows (on 'revolutionary' Peking opera). An interesting further issue addressed in several essays is the degree of coherence found among individual media in plurimedial works, where "fusionist" tendencies (discussed by Bernhard Kuhn, Walter Bernhart, and Emily Petermann) stand in contrast to "separatist" tendencies (as identified by Peter Dayan and Axel Englund).[1]

In the discussion of functions of music in film (Part 1, Section 1), *Lawrence Kramer*'s pivotal essay ("Music's Body and the Moving Image") assigns music in film the vital function of establishing body images, which are missing in moving images without sound, and thereby reflects a prevalent contemporary concern in musical scholarship with embodiment. In a similar direction, *Saskia Jaszoltowski*'s contribution ("Disturbing Silences and Open Narratives: Musical Gaps in Fictional and Documentary Moving Images") thematizes the "ghostly effect" of soundless cinema and discusses various functions of the presence or absence of the acoustic dimension in diversified – narrative and non-narrative – forms of moving images. *Werner Wolf* in his essay ("Traditional and Non-Traditional Uses of Film Music, and Musical Metalepsis in *The Truman Show*") contrasts traditional commercial Hollywood practices of establishing real-life illusions, including emotion-centred functions of music, with postmodernist practices that entail the blurring of ontological levels and the exceptional introduction of musical metalepsis. *Jordan Carmalt Stokes* ("Homer and the Springfield Orchestra Bus: Four Test Cases for Any Future Challenge to the Diegetic/Non-Diegetic Model") offers a well-balanced argument for how to meet the challenges repeatedly expressed against the so-called "narratological model" of the distinction between diegetic and non-diegetic music in film.

The earliest example discussed of "Significant Intermedial Cases" of film music (Part 1, Section 2) concerns early Italian cinema of the 1910s. *Bernhard Kuhn* ("Operatic Plurimediality in Italian Silent Cinema: Nino Oxilia and Pietro Mascagni's *Rapsodia Satanica* (1915)") analyses *Rapsodia Satanica* as a Wagner-related film with recognizable intermedial references to high-art and the purpose of enhancing the cultural status of cinema at the time. With a similar objective, as discussed by *Walter Bernhart* ("Humanized Documentary, 'Light'

---

1   For a discussion of these categories see Walter Bernhart (2017). "From Orpheus to Bob Dylan: The Story of 'Words and Music'". *Aletria: Revista de Estudos de Literatura* 27/2: 277–301.

Verse, and Music Made to Fit: G.P.O. Film Unit/Auden/Britten's *Night Mail*
(1936)"), the 1930s British propagandist documentary film *Night Mail* hired
Benjamin Britten and W.H. Auden to produce a "collaborative *Gesamtkunstwerk*" of significant standing. In *Ruth Jacobs*'s moving essay "An Incarnation
of Memory: Song as Absence in Claude Lanzmann's *Shoah*" on Lanzmann's
1970s/1980s film, the specific use and non-use of music is seen as an essential
element in manifesting the incomprehensibility of the Holocaust experience
and its traumatic memory. In a transmedially extended reflection on repetition in literature, film and music, *Heidi Hart*'s essay ("Accumulating Schubert:
Music and Narrative in Nuri Bilge Ceylan's *Winter Sleep*") demonstrates how
the repetitive use of a particular piece of classical music in a film can make a
critical statement about usurped cultural and patriarchal superiority. With a
related orientation, *Christopher Booth*, in his essay "Mise en Scène, Mozart, and
a Borrowed Chorale: Learned Style and Identity in Pawlikowski's *Ida*", traces
the impact the presence of specific pieces of music has on the narrative shaping of a film and the subtle influence it exerts on the development of characters in the story.

In the first essay of Part 2 ("Intermedial Varieties"), *Peter Dayan* ("Shadow
Images Moving to Music: *La Tentation de saint Antoine* in Montmartre") takes
the reader to the world of 1880s Parisian theatre and discusses an exceptional
case of the relationship between music, word and image in the spectacle and
book versions of a cabaret shadow play. *Marion Recknagel*'s essay "'The Big
Turnaround in the Middle': On the Silent Movie and the Film Music Interlude
in Alban Berg's Opera *Lulu*" analyses the various dramaturgical functions of
the silent film with accompanying music that Berg placed at a pivotal position in the middle of his unfinished 1930s opera *Lulu*. *Frieder von Ammon* ("All
the Pieces Matter: On Complex TV Music") investigates the use of music in
'Quality TV' since the 1980s and observes a decisive shift from earlier TV series
in terms of a significant enhancement of sophistication in 'Quality TV' series.
Emily Petermann's focus in her essay "The Music Videos of Alternative Rock
Band They Might Be Giants: Prolegomena for a Theory of Nonsense across Media" concentrates on nonsense as a phenomenon that finds coordinated parallel expression in some examples of the multimedial form of the American
music video since the 1980s.

In the initial essay of Part 3 ("Remediations") by Axel Englund ("Thrilling
Opera: Conflicts of the Mind and the Media in Kasper Holten's *Juan*"), a highly
creative transposition of Mozart/da Ponte's opera *Don Giovanni* into a complex
combination of filmed live opera and movie thriller demonstrates the hazards
of mixing media in the adaptive process. *Alla Bayramova*'s essay "Novel, Woodcuts, Film, Music ...: Pondering over the Title of Gara Garayev's *Symphony*

Engravings 'Don Quixote'" discusses the transposition of Cervantes's great novel first into a film and further into a symphonic work by an Azerbaijani composer and champions an intensified intermedial approach to analysis. Michael Halliwell's essay "Film *as* Opera: Three Perspectives on *Still Life* and *Brief Encounter*" follows the intermedial adaptive steps from a Noël Coward play to a David Lean film and further on to two operatic remediations and identifies in the transpositional processes media-specific differences in choosing material from the source work. The remediation part of the volume is rounded off by *David Francis Urrows*'s entertainingly instructive essay "On the Intertextual Docks, or, Whatever Happened to Shanghai Lil?", which traces the various incarnations of a popular Shanghai character in such diversified media as a Soviet ballet, an American musical film, and a 'revolutionary' Peking opera.

As is agreeably customary, thanks are due to be expressed in a preface of this kind. I gladly thank my co-editor David Urrows for being a helpful second pair of eyes and ever prudently critical co-evaluator. My gratitude also goes to Larry Kramer for making the whole project possible by inviting us to Fordham and guaranteeing the congenial atmosphere for successful academic performance and proficiency. Self-evidently thanks deserve to go to all the contributors who have shown exceptional patience and spirit of cooperation in the long editorial process of turning the essays into a publisher-suitable shape. Of the publishing company, it is above all Masja Horn, Brill Acquisitions Editor for Literature and Cultural Studies, who deserves high praise and lots of thanks for being a constant source of support and encouragement in making the book finally see the light of day. I wish the book a wide attentive and sympathetic readership.

Walter Bernhart
Graz, December 2018

PART 1

Film Music

∵

SECTION 1

Film Music: Reflections on Functions

∵

CHAPTER 1

Music's Body and the Moving Image

Lawrence Kramer

Abstract

Moving images without sound tend to lack the dimension of embodiment. Music fore-stalls or remedies this lack; it projects and specifies a lifelike effect of embodiment on behalf of the images. Classical music in particular tends to project an idealized body image characterized as smooth and closed (what Mikhail Bhaktin calls the "classical body"). But it does so only in relationship to a contrary, more porous, sometimes violent mode of embodiment, which may equally reveal itself through classical music. Examples in cinema include Mike Figgis's *The Loss of Sexual Innocence* and Jacques Audiard's *De battre mon coeur s'est arrêté* ('The Beat that my Heart Skipped').

•••

One of the small ironies of the present moment is that musical scholarship has become increasingly absorbed with the body while music has become ever more disembodied. Now that musical delivery systems are primarily digital, in a world where most music is not live, the material and corporeal experience of music has become more the exception than the rule. At the same time, the bodies most frequently found enveloped by music are purely virtual, mere moving images that travel across the screens that are more or less everywhere anyone goes. The body has to a great extent become a solidified cinematic image, complete with soundtrack. Of course we still have 'real' bodies, inescapably, bodies that still move to music while coping with the vulnerabilities of physical existence. People still dance and go to concerts; they work out with headphones on; some even still play instruments. And of course you cannot make live music without blowing, striking, fingering, swaying, and so on. But we cannot take it for granted that the natural body, if the term still applies, retains its traditional priority over its simulacra. Once images learned to move, the body changed. The invention of cinema was the watershed of this process, which, however, has only accelerated as time and other technologies have intervened.

Nonetheless, the longing to retain the natural body is stubborn, and it is not content to reserve a space for itself outside the virtual world. From the outset of animation, from the inception of the moving image as a token of life, there has been a countervailing effort to preserve the sense of human embodiment in the very arena of the image that renders that sense vulnerable. Music, and particularly a certain classical or classical-inspired music, has played a major role in that effort. If Gertrud Koch is right to claim that primary among cinematic "reality effects" is to "make life and ban death" (Koch 2009: 928), then such music is primary among cinema's life-giving resources, though it has not sufficiently been acknowledged as such, even today.[1]

The reality effects of the moving image include overcoming the 'still life', *nature morte*, character of the still image – or, where bodies in particular are concerned, of the stilled image. Beginning in the eighteenth century, western societies increasingly demanded that images should be able to move, and thus to come to life: that the myth of Pygmalion should become a technological reality. From magic lantern shows to moving panoramas to kinetoscopes to cinema, moving images called on music to enliven them the way Shakespeare's Prospero calls on Ariel to fill the island with song.

As media, then, music and moving images are each other's supplements in the field of animation. Both work by inserting the image in time. Music gives life to the body's motion; the body gives form to the music's life. Music relieves the image of silence; the image relieves music of invisibility. Each medium fills in a gap in the other, though the exchange is not perfectly symmetrical; the gap in the image is perhaps the wider.

The need to visualize music, to find what Richard Leppert has called the sight of sound, is persistent. It is one reason why the body of the performer traditionally played a key role is how music is heard, and why recorded sound, the dominant form in the modern era, was traditionally accompanied by visual supplements, most sumptuously in the LP era with the art on album covers. If the supplements are defective, as for example in many YouTube clips, they may provoke a reversal and diminish the sense of embodiment.

Nonetheless, music without visual supplements is typically disturbing only when it is acousmatic, set apart from a source impossible to locate. Music does not depend on images, much less on moving images, to project a sense of embodiment. On the other hand, the moving image without music or its acoustic substrate, the possibility of ambient sound, is defective, and defective in a way that still images are not. Bodies are noisy. Movement implies sound; movement in dead silence is uncanny. Like the notorious muteness of painting, the silence of mute cinema acts like a latent blot on the image, a distortion not seen but heard.

---

1   See also Kramer 2014.

Koch, following Deleuze, argues that the cinematic illusion of motion is not a mere epiphenomenon. As Deleuze observes, the fact that the impression of motion is generated mechanically does not mean that either the motion or the impression is mechanical (cf. 1986: 2; qtd. Koch 2009: 927). Cinematic movement is a positive quality of the image; the image is actually, not virtually, life-like. But as long as the image and its motion are silent, the 'like' outweighs the life. Moving images become fully animate only through sound. Without a sonorous world to move through, the images remain spectral. In a sense the history of so-called silent cinema is a quest for sound – sound, not speech, which was almost an afterthought. But since music and the moving image are now inseparable, since our culture is saturated with moving images saturated by music, hearing has become a means of seeing. The moving image is as much an effect of the ear as it is of the eye.

How then, does the music in question give body? How does this music give its body, its own body, to the moving image? How does the music come to give that moving body a sensory character? What problems does this course of embodiment pose, what limits does it confront, and what possibilities does it open – or close?

Before seeking for answers – some answers, anyway – it is important to narrow the scope of the questions. My concern here is not with moving images in general, but with moving images of human or animal bodies. Similarly, the present concern is not with music in general, but with classical instrumental music and its offshoots. The alignment between these concerns is historically specific; it is limited but influential; and it is both recurrent and persistent. The elements excluded from consideration here, including voice, non-classical genres, montage, natural forms in motion, and so on, require separate examination, though part of the discourse on embodiment may well radiate out to them. It is also worth noting that the logic of embodiment, as my eventual examples should show, operates regardless of whether one is dealing with linear or non-linear time, or what Deleuze famously called the movement-image and the time-image (see 1986, 1989). Music, for that matter, though the point cannot be developed here, may trouble the seeming stability of that distinction.

But a problem remains. Just how can we theorize about musical embodiment? There are few general guidelines available, however evocative certain particular accounts might be. There is no theory of the musical body. With the combination of music and moving images, moreover, we are not dealing with the performer's body or even with the listener's, but with a purely imaginary body that in some sense inheres in the sound of the music. In what follows I propose to take this difficulty as an opportunity. The focus of attention will be the implicit body-image projected by the music, on the assumption that virtually no musical event can avoid projecting a specific imaginary body. In varying degrees, the body image the music projects will either merge with or diverge from the bodies imaged on screen.

Body images come in so many varieties that there is little point in trying to catalogue them or form a typology of them. But they can be usefully positioned along a continuum suggested by Mikhail Bakhtin in his classic study of European carnival. At one end of this continuum stands what Bakhtin (see 1984) identified as the "classical" body: closed, smooth, totalized, idealized. At the other end stands the "grotesque" body: open, rough, fragmentary, visceral. There is nothing musical about these concepts, but they nonetheless afford the possibility of giving a nuanced account of how the music involved carries the weight it gives to bodies that move on screen.

Classical or classically inspired film music generally idealizes the relationship between its sound and the force of embodiment; it is music for closed bodies, even in the love scenes. An obvious, because blatant, example is the use of the slow movement of Mozart's Piano Concerto no. 21 to idealize the beautiful doomed bodies of the lovers in the 1967 film *Elvira Madigan*. The link thus forged has stuck to the music in the form of a regrettable nickname, but even more in a transference by which the music on its own has come to embody that particular pictorial, sub-erotic mode of embodiment, even for those who have never seen the film. Even a scene of vomiting (vomit being the one thing, according to Kant, that cannot be aestheticized) leaves the spell intact.

The first movement of Mozart's Clarinet Quintet works to much the same end in Agnes Varda's cinematic ode to cheerful philandering, *Le Bonheur* (1985); the music's sensory lushness even dissolves the aftereffects of suicide, apparently with little irony. And virtually the whole point of Miklos Forman's (and Peter Schaffer's) *Amadeus* is the dissonance between the refined and sensitive body imagined by Mozart's music and the supposedly obscene body of its composer. Mozart himself was well aware of the charged relationship between imagined and lived-in bodies, as the seduction scenes in *Così fan tutte* and the serenade in *Don Giovanni* make clearly audible. The music in these scenes gives desire, or passion, or charm free rein while letting their expression chafe uneasily against the audience's understanding that in each case the wooer is impersonating someone else. The more false the body, the more seductive its voice.

Two further filmic examples are no less revealing in their awareness of the closed body as a fiction, sometimes a knowing one, sometimes not. The 1949 film *Portrait of Jennie* takes the closure of the classical body within the confines of the portrait as its subject. The title character, a ghost, is literally a moving image within the diegesis: the moving image of the actress, Jennifer Jones, is an image of that image. Which one is primary is impossible to say. The musical underscore draws on several pieces by Debussy. The music's fluid textures and harmonies give auditory form to Jennie's half-embodied state while the sensuous lyricism of melodies from such scores as "Prelude to the Afternoon of a Faun" and "The Girl with the Flaxen Hair" halo her image with fetishistic charm. The painter-protagonist of the film confronts the same predicament as Debussy's and Mallarme's faun, whose question about the moving images of bodies he has seen during the afternoon is "Have I loved a dream?".

Better still, consider Hitchcock's *Vertigo* (1958), in which the sound and the sight of the moving image engage in a giddy spiral of mutual corruption. The idealization of the classical body is sometimes pretty to a fault, as we inexorably come to see, or rather to hear. The film – notoriously, to invoke another Hitchcock title – concerns a disgraced detective, subject to vertigo, who has fallen in love with a murdered woman. The effect is obsession; the cause is the woman's portrait. The detective, played against type by James Stewart, is a debased Tamino, but with an added touch of Pygmalion. He goes on to fashion another woman as the double of the first by means of cosmetics, hair coloring, and costume. Like a film director, he does a remake. He gives his leading lady a makeover. She becomes a kind of living sculpture with whom he falls in surrogate love.

Of course the two women are the same person. Scottie, the detective, has merely restored the masquerade figure he took for real. But this restored figure of an already corrupt 'original' is corrupted further by the voyeurism of her de facto creator. Bernard Hermann's score supplies the auditory form of this debasement by casting itself as a knowing corruption of the music to which it repeatedly alludes, Wagner's *Tristan und Isolde*. One false covering echoes another; the body becomes the artifice of its artifices. At the erotic climax of the film, a 360-degree tracking shot of the protagonists kissing makes explicit the classically Freudian displacement that turns sexuality to vertigo while the scene's musical underscore comes to the vertiginous brink of *almost* quoting from *Tristan*.

The corruption is less sumptuous and even more heartless in the first of my major examples, Mike Figgis's 1999 film *The Loss of Sexual Innocence*. The film is saturated with classical music, partly as an ironic relic of idealized high culture, partly as an ambivalent, unassimilated kernel of animation, something like what Lacan or Žižek would call the stain of the Real.[2] The narrative is alternately disturbing and ridiculous, a combination that may limit the film's aesthetic appeal but that has its own symptomatic value.

---

2   On the Real in music see Kramer 2012 and Klein 2015.

In one key scene, the film-maker protagonist (Julian Sands) imposes himself sexually on his wife as she does the dinner dishes. We see this from afar,
through a nocturnal window, the eternal rear window of voyeuristic peeping,
itself shown from a distance – a window on the window, half to alienate the
peeping eye of the audience, half to protect it from view. As Lacan notes in his
analysis of the erotics of vision, following Sartre, being seen seeing is shaming
(cf. 1998: 84). The Brechtian long shot places the viewer in a position of self-
punishing self-consciousness: watching this scene is shameful but one can't
stop. The wife does not exactly resist her husband's advances but she does not
welcome them, either. She seems impassive, as if the body being manhandled
were hardly her own. The manhandling goes on while the slow movement of
Beethoven's "Pathetique" Sonata plays on the radio. The movement, long associated with romantic desire, seems in part to prompt the sexual approach.

The scene contains no overt violence but it is extraordinarily brutal and
demeaning, both to the woman who suffers herself to be sexually coerced –
the husband's action is a soft rape – and to the audience which is forced to
watch. And the audience, though playing a part, is not merely playing a role.
(Were even the actors doing that during the filming?) The window is not only
the classical locus of voyeuristic intrusion, but also a surrogate for the movie
screen. The self-consciousness imposed on the audience is thus cinematic as
well as sexual. It should make the watchers squirm as they confront the brutal-
ity that attaches to whatever excitement they too might feel, whether willingly
or not, as they watch. And watch: it's a long scene. It is even a kind of primal
scene, for cinema, anyway: in the first instance a stripping bare of sexuality,
but, beyond that, the exposure of something we know should remain unseen
even as we cannot tear our eyes away.

The music heightens these effects. It makes them worse. From the perspective (literally the perspective) established by the scene, Beethoven's melody
sounds initially like a veil of romantic illusion drawn willfully over narcissistic
aggressiveness. Worse yet, the crude fumbling on the screen tends to suggest
an unmasking, to reveal the self-deceptive substitution of romantic idealism
for crude lust as intrinsic to the music itself and to the whole cultural apparatus that supports it.

Yet at the same time it is only the music that inhibits the complete loss of
sexual innocence. The scene may seek to betray something about the music
but in so doing it also betrays the music. The unmasking of the music more
radically unmasks itself as merely cynical; the revulsion we (may or should)
feel at the scene is in part fostered by the music, demanded by the music,
which forms the standard by which we judge the erotic debasement. The difference, the dissonance, between what we see and what we hear plays to the

music's benefit as well as to the characters' and spectators' discomfiture. The music's ethical content just is that discomfiture.

And this content is not an empty abstraction. It depends, rather, on the music's body, the imaginary body required to play and to listen. The famous theme is very simple and easy to play; its expressive depth comes in part from the delicacy, the tenderness, the care with which the pianist's hand has to caress the keys in order to play it. This is a theme that has to be played with a loving touch, the presence or absence of which is distinctly audible.

And there is more. The music projects an image of mutual absorption and mutual consent, the very things conspicuously missing from the film scene. The image takes shape in the understated mirror imaging of the melody in the bass. Steadily murmuring inner voices form a medium bringing the melodic strands into near-physical proximity, rippling between one and the other as if in response to their touch on the keyboard. (See Figure 1.1) This acoustic intertwining comes in waves as the mirrored lines separate and reunite. It intensifies toward the close as the motion of the inner voices rises from even sixteenth notes to sixteenth-note triplets. The musical texture is woven so tightly that the whole process is almost subliminal. It hovers right at the threshold of perception, perhaps felt most readily as an expressive quality of the melody. But the mirroring captures the ear by its very elusiveness; it makes you listen harder. If you play the music, you can feel the mirroring in the movement of your fingers even without hearing it as a contrapuntal texture.

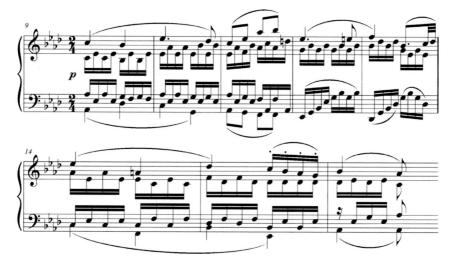

FIGURE 1.1 Ludwig van Beethoven, "Pathetique" Sonata, op. 13, opening of the 2nd movement

The two melodic bodies that grow attuned to each other in this mirroring process, moreover, are linked by the highly active middle voices, which form the locus of excitement without ever becoming heedless or overbearing. The minute one forgets oneself and plays effusively, the music sounds wrong. This music genuinely models romantic desire as a condition of mutuality, reciprocal pleasure, and the exchange of identity. Not to hear it that way, as the male character in the film scene does not, is to hear it wrongly. This failure of hearing is the most resonant element in the scene. It prefigures a disastrous failure of understanding that, at the climax of the film, will result in a woman's death.

The music is supposed to do the opposite, to impart a sense of life, though the fact that it goes awry here when it is heard or half heard over the radio insinuates a certain irony that cannot be confined to the dramatic situation. Music on the radio, and implicitly music in cinema, is no longer 'live'. Its mimicry of live sound is insufficient to shield it from narcissistic or aggressive appropriation. What saves the music, if anything does, is the viewer's unease in its presence.

Underlying the ironic, albeit still (almost unwillingly) idealizing depiction in *The Loss of Sexual Innocence*, is a fantasy of classical music as the correlate, the soundtrack, the acoustic substance of the intact body. That fantasy is the symptomatically revealing foundation of Jacques Audiard's *De battre mon coeur s'est arrêté* (The Beat that my Heart Skipped, 2005, a remake of an American film more aptly entitled *Fingers*). The film is a portrait of the artist as a young man caught between the life of a small-time gangster – an enforcer for his dissolute and manipulative father – and a career as a concert pianist in emulation of his late adored mother, who appears in the film only as a recorded voice expressing dissatisfaction with her performance of Chopin's E-minor Nocturne. The body of the protagonist, Tom, is a battlefield of conflicting impulses centered on his hands: to beat, strike, and maim in his father's service, and to play with skill and passion in his mother's.

The film rather crudely associates the two impulses with contrasting musical types. The gangster life goes with hard-driving, beat-driven techno; one climactic scene of visually disorganized violence, occurring the night before the audition for which Tom has been preparing throughout the film, occurs to the sounds of a cover version of "Do the Locomotion". The aesthetic life goes with classical music for solo keyboard, especially the toccatas of Bach, which as a genre exist precisely to both exercise and discipline the force of touch, as their name announces. The crucial audition involves Bach's Toccata in E minor, which we have heard and seen Tom practicing relentlessly. We know he can play this music well. But he cannot play it at the audition, from which he flees, because although he can privately indulge the fantasy that the music, Orpheus-like, has tamed his violent nature, part of him knows that it has done nothing of the sort, but only sublimated his furies. On the street afterwards, Tom puts on the large, heavy set of silvery headphones by which he listens to the techno beat, and then returns to his father's home – only to find the old man murdered, the victim of a Russian mobster whom the father has made the mistake of hounding for money.

That mobster figures in the last of the three pivotal sequences of the film (the audition being the second); to understand its role, however, the first of the three needs to be set in place. Tom is studying with a Chinese coach, an attractive young woman who at this point in the film speaks little French. As their work proceeds, their musical partnership takes on – this too a classic topos – an erotic tinge, but neither is willing to acknowledge the fact. Tom instead directs his desire to Aline, the wife of his partner, who has been flagrantly cheating on her. After Tom he sleeps with Aline, we see a sequence of brief scenes in which his playing of the toccata improves dramatically as he practices the music naked or near-naked. (Oedipus, please take note.) The sense of bodily fullness which Tom has previously experienced only in meting out violence now floods into him with the music.

But we already have reason to suspect that the experience is more fantasy than reality, something like a transposition of Oedipal turmoil to an ideal register. Tom's reformation of his body, especially his hands, is keyed to a video image of the strangely disembodied hands of Vladimir Horowitz floating over the keyboard. At one crucial point, preceding the audition, we see this moving image *as* fantasy, in slow motion and black-and-white. The fantasy of the intact body thus turns out to depend on the image of detached autonomous hands. Intactness is prosthesis. Coincidentally or not, the image closely resembles one singled out by Freud as a marker of the uncanny: a hand cut off at the wrist like the hands in the Horowitz video, and invoked in conjunction with feet that dance by themselves (cf. 1997: 225). The conjunction is bizarrely musical, as if the hand were playing the music to which the feet are dancing.

And that brings us to the final sequence with Mynskoff, the mobster. After the death of Tom's father, a scene that ends with Tom literally biting his trembling hands, an old-fashioned intertitle refers us two years later. Tom has now displaced his pianistic ambitions to become the coach or manager of his former coach, who is now his Romantic partner (and has learned fluent French). Dropping her off for a concert at the same auditorium where his audition ended in fiasco, he parks the car, only by chance to encounter Mynskoff in the street. Tom follows the mobster to a men's room where, after a few words, he attacks him, precipitating a highly violent struggle that ends when Tom squeezes the other man's genitals until the latter loses consciousness – and loses the gun which Tom then places in his mouth.

He cannot, however, pull the trigger. He doesn't have to. By reversing the positions of mouth and genitalia, sodomizing Mynskoff with a gun in the mouth and effectively castrating him, Tom has reduced the other man to a Bakhtinian grotesque body and nothing more: a breathing wound. Having done so he finds a washroom, cleans himself up as much as he can, and goes to the concert where his wife or partner is playing Brahms's G-minor Rhapsody. She plays

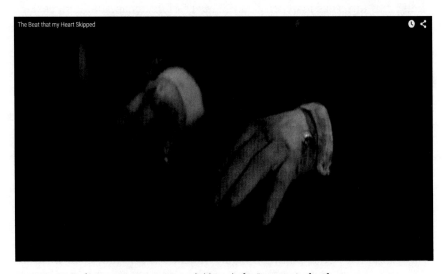

FIGURE 1.2 *De battre mon coeur s'est arrêté* (2005), dir. Jacques Audiard

with unusual restraint, almost placidity, at odds with the passionate thrust of the music. Importantly, we do not see her hands, only her calm face and still upper torso over the keys, the very antithesis of the image Tom has presented at the keyboard throughout the film. The only hands we see are Tom's. They fill the screen in closeup as they finger the music he is hearing: fingering, but almost twitching, seemingly unconscious in their motion and severed from the body whose wholeness they are seeking to grasp.

The hands are lacerated and bloody. They stand in stark contrast to the less glaring traces of violence that his efforts to make himself presentable in the house of culture have failed to wash away: the bruises on his face, the traces of blood on his shirt. (See Figure 1.2) The function of the music as a fantasy of bodily intactness, of creatively sublimated impulse, or of culture that transfigures barbarism, could not be rendered more literally – or more corporeally. The moving image of the body, the body of the moving image, is subject to defacement by the violence of its motion. The motion renders the body inherently porous, a leaky receptacle, even though the moving image lives only on a flat screen, without depth. Meanwhile the body of music, the musical body, is the other one, one never quite seen: the classical body of classical music, the body that may be deep, but does not bleed.

References

Bakhtin, Mikhail (1984). *Rabelais and his World*. Trans. Hélène Iswolksy. Bloomington, IN: Indiana Univ. Press.

Deleuze, Gilles (1986). *Cinema 1: The Movement-Image*. Trans. Hugh Tomlinson, Barbara Habberjam. Minneapolis, MN: Univ. of Minnesota Press.

Deleuze, Gilles (1989). *Cinema 2: The Time-Image*. Trans. Hugh Tomlinson, Robert Galeta. Minneapolis, MN: Univ. of Minnesota Press.

Freud, Sigmund (1997). "The Uncanny". *Writings on Art and Literature*. Trans. Alix Strachey. Stanford, CA: Stanford Univ. Press.

Klein, Michael (2015). *Music and the Crisis of the Modern Subject*. Bloomington, IN: Indiana Univ. Press.

Koch, Gertrud (2009). "Carnivore or Chameleon: The Fate of Cinema Studies". *Critical Inquiry* 34/4: 918–928.

Kramer, Lawrence (2012). *Expression and Truth: On the Music of Knowledge* Berkeley, CA/London: Univ. of California Press.

Kramer, Lawrence (2014). "Classical Music, Virtual Bodies, Narrative Film". David Neumeyer, ed. *Oxford Handbook of Film Music Studies*. New York, NY: OUP. 351–365.

Lacan, Jacques (1998). *The Seminar of Jacques Lacan: The Four Fundamental Concepts of Psychoanalysis*. Ed. Jacques-Alain Miller. Trans. Alan Sheridan. New York, NY: Norton.

Leppert, Richard (1993). *The Sight of Sound: Music, Representation, and the History of the Body*. Berkeley, CA /London: Univ. of California Press.

Žižek, Slavoj (1992). *Looking Awry: An Introduction to Jacques Lacan through Popular Culture*. Cambridge, MA: MIT Press.

CHAPTER 2

Disturbing Silences and Open Narratives: Musical Gaps in Fictional and Documentary Moving Images

Saskia Jaszoltowski

Abstract

Assuming that the interrelation between music and moving images was mainly defined in classical Hollywood cinema and that the degree of involvement with an audiovisually depicted narrative depends heavily on sound, the question is posed how the acoustic dimension in film may either enhance orientation or disturb the audience's perception. By considering recorded concert performances, documentaries, and fiction films, this examination aims at analyzing the absence of sound, vision, or narrative. Gaps in audiovisual texts are interpreted as well as intermedial transfers between word, architecture, and music.

•••

Gaps and pauses in speech are indispensable for understanding the content delivered by a narrator. Short silences between sentences or their grammatical parts structure the flow of verbal information. If the sound of the voice rests for a longer while, the listener might feel disturbed. The reason for falling silent might be, first, that the speaker has forgotten what he or she wanted to say; second, words fail to do so; third, the pause aims at provoking tension, expectation and the evocation of a particular meaning; or fourth, the speech has simply come to an end. If we listen to somebody speaking with only half an ear, our attention might suddenly be aroused when the narrator becomes mute. In this respect, an absent-minded listener may feel disturbed – in a subtle way – by silence, or in a rather radical way by its opposite, by a very loud sound event.

The soundtrack of a standard Hollywood movie works in a similar way. Film music might be considered as 'unheard' – to draw on the title of Claudia Gorbman's influential book on narrative film music (see 1987) – but it is 'heard' very well, that is, paid attention to, when it is either too loud or absent. Silence in a sound film can be extremely disturbing and is related to scenes that imply a very specific state of mind. As Gorbman has pointed out, silences are used in "dream sequences or other filmic depictions of intense mental activity" (ibid.: 18). It is possible that the supposedly uncanny effect of soundless moving images originates in the silent film era, where musical accompaniment seemed to be necessary to enliven the mute actors on the screen. Hanns Eisler and Theodor Adorno take up this position when they assume that the silent visuals had "a ghostly effect" (1947: 75) and retrospectively conclude that this was the reason for providing external sound during screening in theaters. Taking musical accompaniment in the silent film for granted, though, is thoroughly questioned by Rick Altman (see 1996). Without going into details on this matter, it can be established that not only did the use of music's illustrating function, but also its narrative function rose with the increasing tendency to tell a story through audiovisual means.[1] Consequently, this led to a more or less uninterrupted flow of music and sound accompaniment for silent films in the 1920s, and in the following decades to the familiar wall-to-wall scoring practice of such composers as Max Steiner. His music was never meant to disturb, but rather to unconsciously draw the spectator into the fiction. Only when music stops does one become aware of it and reality breaks into the fictional world. As mentioned, this might also happen during a rather uninteresting speech that only attracts the attention of an absent-minded listener, wakes him up from his dreams, and brings him back into the present time when the acoustic flow comes to a halt.

Not only do silences interrupt and disturb, but music itself also does so. This can be vividly experienced in everyday life while using public transport, for example. Involuntarily one might have to listen to a neighbor's musical taste, overhearing the sound through his or her earphones. Unaware of the disturbance, the neighbor is living in a 'different world' by acoustically silencing the 'real world'. In respect of music and film, the soundtrack similarly rules out realism and enhances the make-believe of the narration displayed on a two-dimensional screen. By comparing fiction films with documentaries, it is interesting to note that in the latter music is usually used sparingly. This oscillation between fiction and reality in moving images, with regard to the interplay between music and its dialectic counterpart, silence, is examined here by discussing the following five case studies.

---

1   This tendency holds true not only for live-action pictures but also for animated cartoons produced during Hollywood's Golden Age. There, the music takes on another function, that is, giving acoustic reality to an unreal world. Cartoon music enlivens the two-dimensional characters and enhances their emotional credibility. Further reading on the use of music in the animated genre is provided by Jaszoltowski (see 2013).

1   Framing the Gap

A very strict distinction between sound and its absence is experienced at symphony concerts with a standard repertoire program. In performances by, for example, the New York or the Berlin Philharmonic orchestras, the silence between movements or sections of a multi-part piece is filled with tension that is sometimes unbearable for a few and as a result is relieved by coughing. This eruptive bodily noise in return disturbs the silence in which someone else digests the music that has just faded away and who awaits the continuation of the work with suspense. Similarly, the silent gaps preceding and following the performance (or the individual pieces of a concert) are not empty but filled with tension, suspense, and reflection.

These gaps are usually left aside in musical analysis, and the music-filled space between silences is what is concentrated on. Traditionally, or at least relating to so-called absolute music, such an analysis is done by reading and analyzing the score which can, at first sight, be compared with reading a book: here, gaps occur when turning the page, chapters break up the narration and invite the reader to pause. On second thought, however, and in contrast to a conventional novel, the narrative character of music is generally widely questioned, and an understanding of music cannot be seen as originating only from reading the score – if there is one at all.

Whereas the gaps that occur while reading a narrative book can arguably be regarded as more or less meaningless, it is exactly this insignificance that is challenged by compositions like John Cage's silent piece entitled *4'33"* (1952). It contains three movements but not a single note. The only instruction for the performer is to keep quiet, to be silent, to 'say' nothing: "TACET". Reading the music signifies nothing but silence. When listening to an audio recording of the piece, it is impossible to distinguish the musical parts from the gaps between the movements. Only in a live or audiovisually recorded performance would this be possible depending on the interpretation, that is, the body-motion of the performers. Picked out of a countless number of YouTube videos that show performances of Cage's piece, the interpretation by a Berlin-based ensemble in a forest has been chosen to demonstrate that the distinction is first and foremost provided visually.[2] The musicians mark the beginning of each movement by exaggeratedly pretending to start blowing into their instruments (some of which are visible, others are substituted by mere twigs and branches of trees). Moreover, written words appear on the screen to announce the upcoming

---

2   The filmed performance by Zentralkapelle Berlin can be watched on www.youtube.com/watch?v=gjmVbTJzxXk [10/10/2015].

movement. The moving image is a very still picture: the camera stays static throughout the performance, taking the perspective of a spectator. What is heard is more or less the same throughout the whole performance. What is seen is distinguishable into the tacet parts and the surrounding non-musical parts. What is felt by the audience regarding tension, suspense, and reflection is yet another debatable issue. The question arises if the musical void, that is, the composed tacet, is in any respect more significant than the musical gaps that divide the composition into three movements. The answer may depend on the body-motions of the musicians, the way the moving images are composed and, not least, on the emotional and imaginative involvement of the audience, that is, the meaning ascribed to the piece by the listener. Alternatively, the question might be simply invalidated by a statement given by Edward Said: "There is no opposition between music and silence, nor between art and the unintended" (1997: s. p.). Without agreeing with Said, the perception, mindset, and attitude seem to change radically depending on an object's contextualization and its surrounding. Cage's piece sounds different depending on its site of performance because it incorporates the acoustic reality of its environment. In this respect, the silence of *4'33"* can be considered as a joke, as a challenge to traditional concert practice, or as a disturbing self-reflection on behalf of its listeners.

2   Forced to Silence – Falling Mute

A very different disturbing silence arises from the emptiness which is left at the end of an unfinished work of art – for example, the opera *Moses und Aron* that Arnold Schoenberg started to compose in 1930.[3] It ends in the second act with the words half-spoken by Moses: "O Wort, du Wort, das mir fehlt".[4] The third act remains a fragment because the music was never composed by Schoenberg after his flight from Nazi-Berlin into exile in the United States. Only the text exists – the narration carries on in silence because the music has ceased.

This is not the place to go into a textual or musical analysis of the composition itself, but the fact should be stressed that the opera's subject concerns the un-representable, and that Schoenberg's personal history inspired in turn

---

3   Initially planning on writing an oratorio, Schoenberg became engaged with the subject on Moses as early as 1923. After having completed the first and second acts in 1932, he thereafter worked only on the text part for the third act. For a more detailed overview of the genesis of the work cf. Schmidt, ed. 1998: 1–33 and Kerling 2002: 191.

4   This exclamation can be translated as: 'Oh, you word that is missing, that I cannot think of and speak out.' (Literally: 'O word, you word, that I lack.').

a work of architecture. In 1989, the unfinished work functioned as the musical model (cf. Kerling 2004: 270) for Daniel Libeskind's architectural concept
of the Jewish Museum in Berlin.[5] The silence of the third act was transferred
into architectural voids within the Museum as the un-representable in Jewish
history – "die Nicht-Darstellbarkeit" (ibid.: 272) – a link between the opera's
subject and Libeskind's concept. The building's ground plan consists of two
lines as a metaphor of the voices of Moses and Aron (cf. Willemeit 1998: 20f.).
The straight line is fragmented and cuts through the irregularly composed zig-
zag line with the voids at the intersection of the two. Libeskind points out that
the structure symbolizes Berlin's history of eliminating Jewish life and defines
the "[v]oid/invisible" as "these structural features [that] have been gathered
in the space of the city and laid bare in an architecture where the unnamed
remains in the name that keeps still" (1990: 24). After the opening of the museum he stated that the voids refer to "that which can never be exhibited when
it comes to Berlin's Jewish history: Humanity reduced to ashes".[6]

Libeskind's adjacent construction is divided into twelve segments, six voids
and six exhibition rooms. In the latter, Jewish history is told with words, written and spoken, displayed in visuals, moving and still, communicated through
music, recorded and depicted. With each item history is narrated but it is most
strongly presented by the architectural form itself, by the six voids that interrupt the exhibition. In these voids the Holocaust in all its cruelness, consequence, and incomprehensibility is supposed to be captured by representing
the un-representable. The voids arouse attention and depend on the exhibition
areas to achieve their significant impact. This dialectic interrelation of absence
and presence – comparable to silence and music – can only be fully perceived
by moving through and around the Museum. Studying the building's ground
plan is as insufficient as reading a score when it comes to the perception of
that which is not there. The visitor moving around the exhibition is challenged
by the topos of the un-representable and asked to complete history with her or

---

5   In 1989, the year that saw the fall of the Berlin Wall, Libeskind won the competition for ex-
    tending the Berlin Museum with the Jewish Museum. It was opened in 2001, two days af-
    ter the terrorist attacks on the World Trade Center in New York. The website of the Jewish
    Museum (www.jmberlin.de) provides detailed information about its history, its develop-
    ment, its political controversy and shows construction plans and photographs of the build-
    ing. Additional plans and models as well as Libeskind's essay "Between the Lines", which
    completed his competition entry, give further insight into his artistic inspiration and realiza-
    tion (see 1990).
6   This quote is taken from the Museum's website, www.jmberlin.de/main/EN/04-About-The
    -Museum/01-Architecture/01-libeskind-Building.php [10/10/2015].

his own narration – this might be what Libeskind had in mind when he called the Museum's space an "open narrative" (1990: 50).

Similar to Cage's *4'33"*, which asks for contextualizing the silences in (an audiovisual recording of) a performance, Libeskind's voids become visible and audible and, therefore, fully comprehensible only in moving images, as shown in a documentary on the Museum.[7] This film depicts the emptiness and quietness of the voids. The camera moves through the exhibition rooms, the visitors' mumbling voices as well as the narrator's voice-over are heard until one gets to the voids. Here, the camera stays still and the voices are muted.

3   Sound Designed for Orientation

In light of this, the metaphor of architecture as solidified or frozen music[8] contrasts to some degree with the observation that the perception of a building depends on moving one's body (or, as a substitute, the camera) through it. In this respect, the notion that music's matter is sound and body-motion[9] holds true for architecture as well. This is vividly proven by a documentary film entitled *Cathedrals of Culture* (2014). It consists of six separate episodes in which buildings assume the role of the main protagonist.

The first short film, directed by Wim Wenders, portrays Hans Scharoun's Berlin *Philharmonie*, opened in 1963. Shot in 3-D, it provides lively visuals of the building and captures Scharoun's concept of an organic architecture by moving through and around the *Philharmonie*. The documentary character of this episode is challenged in several ways. First, the architect himself comes to life in a few black-and-white scenes; second, a rudimentary story line of a schoolboy visiting his father at the sound and recording studio of the *Philharmonie* is presented; third, the voice-over of a narrator, pretending to be the voice of the building itself, retelling its own biography serves as a fictional element that anthropomorphizes the *Philharmonie*; fourth, the use of music enhances the fictional character of the story told, even though this is based solely upon facts.

The film not only delivers information about the history of the concert hall but also shows the orchestra at work. Just before the rehearsal for Claude

---

7   The film by Stan Neumann and Richard Copans can be accessed on www.youtube.com/watch?v=SUTktoz_NTU2 [10/10/2015]; the part referred to starts at 19'50".

8   This metaphor was probably formulated by Friedrich Wilhelm Joseph von Schelling at the beginning of the 19th century (cf. Pascha 2004 online: 22–43).

9   This notion stems from Aristides Quintilianus (cf. 1963: 5), who wrote three volumes on music between the first and fourth centuries B.C. His statement is cited and thoroughly explored by Albrecht Riethmüller (see 1994).

Debussy's *Jeux* (1912) is about to begin, the pretended building's voice starts whispering and the musicians, who are tuning up, stop their actions, which establishes a silent tension that is even more intensively felt later in the documentary when the beginning and end of the concert are shown. The end of the episode shows the silence between the last note of the piece and the sound of clapping hands in an audiovisually exaggerated way that suits the dramaturgy of the film.

In parallel with the smoothly moving visuals, a meticulous sound design captures the acoustics of the concert hall and its entrance hall; it stresses the sounds and silences surrounding the musical performances and rehearsals. Moreover, in several scenes the music played by the orchestra members is heard throughout and beyond the building, that is, when the visuals do not show the musicians. By doing so, the music serves as an emotionally moving underscore to the dynamic images of the architecture's organic structure. Throughout the documentary sounds and silences are organically interwoven, just as Scharoun's architectural concept was planned. Music and the voice-over bridge the gaps between visual cuts and narrative jumps from present-day material to historical footage and the fictional reanimation of the dead. Therefore, and unlike the afore-mentioned documentary on the Jewish Museum, *Cathedrals of Culture* aims at absorbing the audience soothingly into its diegetic world, just as classical Hollywood soundtracks do with their orchestral entrance and background music.

4   Stillness and Excess

The musical fanfares and overtures by Max Steiner or Erich Wolfgang Korngold, for example, draw the audience into the film narration. At the beginning of the sound era the opening music was often listened to while looking at a black screen, a closed curtain, or even at the written letters spelling out "overture" – at a picture devoid of movement.[10]

Without the opening music the audience has no time for attunement but is drawn straight away into the film's diegesis. In Lars von Trier's film *Nymphomaniac* (2014), the beginning is not only musically silent but also devoid of images that would define a narrative setting. Only by reading the letters of the

---

10   In this respect, the film overture functions not unlike the ballyhoo music of the silent era that was meant to attract the attention of a potential audience (cf. Altman 1996: 664). For the beginning of a classical Hollywood movie, *A Midsummer Night's Dream* (1935) and *Gone With the Wind* (1939) may, pars pro toto, be recalled.

title does the spectator know that the film is about to start. After a black screen with undefined and almost inaudible sounds, momentary scenes of falling snow, running water and dripping drops are visualized and the corresponding acoustic events of quietness, continuous flowing and disrupted noises, respectively, are heard. These snap-shots are sharply cut audiovisually, and assembled one after another without music as a binding element, resulting in a sequence that installs a rather realistic or documentary approach and one that at the same time establishes an unsettling atmosphere.

The first three minutes of the film serve as an introduction with an open narrative. Their quietness is harshly cut off by the loud and sudden beginning of Rammstein's song "Führe Mich" ('Lead Me'; 2009); their emptiness is opposed to the dense audiovisual depiction of the film's subject thereafter. The following five hours lack subtlety or abstraction and instead communicate, in a visually detailed and verbally direct manner, stories of sexual abuse and psychopathic self-destruction. The setting focusses on a nymphomaniac woman who confesses her fate to a seemingly trustworthy older man. By retelling her life in flashbacks with her own voice-over, a sense of realness is enhanced that aims at denying the fiction of the film. (This contrasts with the narrator in *Cathedrals of Culture*, in which the pretended building's voice rather fictionalizes the documentary.) Disturbance in *Nymph()maniac* emerges from the excess of sexual violence accompanied by human screams and groans, that is, from the avoidance of stillness in which the spectator would be able to reflect. Instead, the film delivers an abundance of straightforward signals, such as the bracketed ellipsis of the letter 'o' in the title's spelling, indicating in a platitudinous way the emotionally devoid anatomy of the protagonist's female genitals.

The ear is the sensory organ for both hearing and orientation. In *Cathedrals of Culture* orientation is established by a coherent combination of an organic sound design with 3-D cinematography. The audience is audiovisually drawn into the film and consequently guided through and around the Berlin *Philharmonie*. This is in contrast to *Nymph()maniac*, where orientation is denied by the abrupt editing of still or augmented sound events and empty or excessive images. At the beginning of the film the approach to capture a scene realistically results in a documentary and then disturbing effect, whereas the opening music in a standard Hollywood movie as well as the sound design of the film on the Berlin *Philharmonie* induces orientation in the sense of involvement and attunement. The non-fictional depiction of documentaries that usually refrain from using music as an additive is much more present in Lars von Trier's film than in Wim Wenders's short. In any case, even though the scenes and soundscapes of documentaries seem to be realistically captured, they nevertheless rely on exploiting the possibilities of audio recording. The degree of

technical enhancement may be responsible for the spectator's involvement
and the perception of the story as either realistic or fictional. In fiction films,
however, the absence of music or sound may accompany unrealistic, dream-
like, or mental situations, as stated above, but music disturbs with an even
stronger effect when it is almost inaudible.

5   At the Border of the Unreal

The oscillation between fiction and reality, as well as the loss of orientation, is
finally exemplified here by Stanley Kubrick's *The Shining* (1980). It is not surprising that the genre of horror film uses tension-filled silences to prepare for
loud outbursts of the unreal. Neither should one wonder why tonal music or
clear rhythmic structures, capable of ensuring orientation, are largely avoided.
About thirty minutes into this film the soundtrack consists of an acoustically
subtle composition of silences, voices, noises, and (very prominently) György
Ligeti's *Lontano* (1967). It leads to the first climax of the film and prepares a
turning point in the narration in which the deceptive family idyll at a quiet
and deserted, old but charming hotel is unmasked. The arrangement of the
soundtrack with the visuals hints at the intrusion of madness into the male
protagonist's obsessive brain and at the progress of the increasingly dangerous
seclusion of a mother and child.

The sequence begins with a muffled silence during a snow scene, in which
mother and son play together. Only their laughing voices can be heard faintly
before an undefined, flickering high noise starts creeping into the soundscape.
This is the beginning of an excerpt from Ligeti's *Lontano*. The scene might be
perceived as musically silent, but the high violins serve as an acoustic signi-
fier for the visually as-yet absent horror. Moreover, the music bridges the gap
between the playful snow scene and the following close-up of the father's face,
suggesting that he has exactly these images of his family on his mind. By cap-
turing the almost motionless facial expression, the moving picture seems to
freeze, while the absence of movement is filled with Ligeti's music. The sound
cluster increases the tension that is visible in the protagonist's facial expression and describes the psychological process (cf. Hentschel 2011: 25), that is, the
rise of insanity in his consciousness.

The musical quality of an eerie quietness originates from the instrumentation that leaves a gap between the low register (contrabass clarinet, double
bassoon, and double bass played sul ponticello) and the high register of the
violins. Such a meaningful emptiness in the orchestration of a piece of music is noticed by Zofia Lissa as one of the manifestations of musical silence

(cf. 1969: 180). The close-up is followed by a sudden black-out of the visuals in which only the word "Saturday" appears. This cut does not merely signify the time leap to the next day, which would be comparable to the pause between book chapters, but rather conveys the protagonist's process of becoming psychopathically obsessed overnight, due to the crescendo in the music that fluently bridges the gap and links the close-up of the man's face with the woman's awareness of the broken-down telephone line.

Lissa considers the failure of audio and communication facilities such as telephone or radio when depicted in a film as another significant case of silence on the soundtrack (cf. 1965: 244). The dead telephone line in this sequence signals the growing disconnection to the 'real' world outside of the hotel, while Ligeti's music signifies the intrusion of the invisible uncanny. Having realized that the telephone is no longer working because of the snowstorm, the woman tries to communicate with the outer world via radio – successfully. At this point, the music suddenly stops in order to emphasize the still existent connection to reality. The musical silence during the dialogue also bears a deceptive reassurance. The uncanny that was audible in the music but not yet visible in the image ceases in order to increase the audiovisual impact with which it is about to break into the narrative in the following scene. Here, the boy for the first time sees and hears the murdered twin sisters.

As Frank Hentschel correctly points out (cf. 2011: 22), the dramaturgy of the film is based on intensification, which is underlined by the build-up of the soundtrack. Musical cues enter more frequently for longer periods of time and become richer in acoustic texture. In other words, during the course of the film the space for musical silences, signifying reality, is reduced, whereas the space for musical quietness, signifying the invisible horror, is increased in the first half of the film and then replaced by powerful, loud, and accentuated music that accompanies the visual uncanny in the second half.

6   Coda

Silence is relative. There is no absolute silence. It is only perceptible within two points of reference – that is, inside music, as rests between notes, or as the gap between high and low registers. It is audible between movements of a work or in terms of the beginning and end of a performance. Musical silence in film is perceived in relation to the visuals and, drawing on Lissa (cf. 1965: 242), becomes meaningful only between two sections that feature an acoustic content. Conversely, visual absence in film is not absolute either. It becomes significant in relation to the sound and the surrounding moving images.

A disturbing effect emerges from the experience of almost nothing, of the almost inaudible, and the almost invisible. Disturbing it might be, because the attention of the audience, visitor, viewer, or listener is redirected from an object to one's inner self. Silence and absence, voids and gaps, receive their meaning only by their dialectic opposites.

To conclude and bridge the gap to the recorded performance in the forest of *4'33"*, Thomas Clifton may be quoted: "To focus on the phenomenon of musical silence is analogous to deliberately studying the space between trees in a forest" (1976: 163). It must be added, though, that the perception of a forest – whether it is creepy and dark, or light and peaceful, whether orientation or disturbance is established – depends on exactly these spaces. By moving through them (or being moved through them by the camera) and by listening to the sounds (authentic, augmented, or added) the image of a forest may vary between a realistic or a more fictional depiction.

References

Altman, Rick (1996). "The Silence of the Silents". *The Musical Quarterly* 80/4: 648–718.

Clifton, Thomas (1976). "The Poetics of Musical Silence". *The Musical Quarterly* 62/2: 163–181.

Eisler, Hanns [and Theodor Adorno] (1947). *Composing for the Films*. London: OUP.

Gorbman, Claudia (1987). *Unheard Melodies: Narrative Film Music*. Bloomington/ Indianapolis, IN: Indiana Univ. Press.

Hentschel, Frank (2011). *Töne der Angst: Die Musik im Horrorfilm*. Berlin: Bertz und Fischer.

Jaszoltowski, Saskia (2013). *Animierte Musik – Beseelte Zeichen: Tonspuren anthropomorpher Tiere in Animated Cartoons*. Beihefte zum Archiv für Musikwissenschaft 74. Stuttgart: Franz Steiner.

Kerling, Marc (2002). "Moses und Aron". Gerold W. Gruber, ed. *Arnold Schönberg: Interpretationen seiner Werke*. Laaber: Laaber. 191–231.

Kerling, Marc (2004). *"O Wort, du Wort, das mir fehlt": Die Gottesfrage in Arnold Schönbergs Oper* Moses und Aron. Mainz: Grünewald.

Libeskind, Daniel (1990). "Between the Lines: Extension to the Berlin Museum, with the Jewish Museum". *Assemblage* 12: 18–57.

Lissa, Zofia (1965). *Ästhetik der Filmmusik*. Berlin: Henschel.

Lissa, Zofia (1969). *Aufsätze zur Musikästhetik*. Berlin: Henschel.

Pascha, Khaled Saleh (2004 online). *"Gefrorene Musik": Das Verhältnis von Architektur und Musik in der ästhetischen Theorie*. PhD thesis. Technische Universität Berlin. https:// opus4.kobv.de/opus4tuberlin/frontdoor/index/index/docId/943. [10/10/2015].

Quintilianus, Aristides (1963). *De musica*. Vol. 1. R.P. Winnington-Ingram, ed. Leipzig: Teubner.

Riethmüller, Albrecht (1994). "The Matter of Music Is Sound and Body-Motion". Hans Ulrich Gumbrecht/K. Ludwig Pfeiffer, eds. *Materialities of Communication*. Stanford, CA: Stanford Univ. Press. 147–156.

Said, Edward (1997). "From Silence to Sound and Back Again: Music, Literature, and History". *Raritan* 17/2: 1–21.

Schmidt, Christian Martin, ed. (1998). *Arnold Schönberg. Sämtliche Werke*. Reihe B, Band 8, Teil 2: *Moses und Aron*. Mainz/Wien: Schott Musik International/Universal Edition.

Willemeit, Thomas (1998). "'O Wort, du Wort, das mir fehlt!': Musik und Architektur bei Daniel Libeskind". *Archithese* 5: 18–24.

Films

4'33" John Cage (2012). Bode Brodmüller, dir. Germany.

Cathedrals of Culture (2014). Wim Wenders et al., dirs. Germany.

Le musée juif de Berlin : Entre les lignes (2011). Neumann, Stan, Richard Copans, dirs. France.

Nymph()maniac (2013). von Trier, Lars, dir. Denmark.

The Shining (1980). Kubrick, Stanley, dir. USA.

CHAPTER 3

Traditional and Non-Traditional Uses of Film Music, and Musical Metalepsis in *The Truman Show*

Werner Wolf

Abstract

The present essay is a contribution to film (music) studies, showing the ambivalences postmodernist Hollywood films can produce, moreover a contribution to metalepsis research and intermediality studies. The film under discussion, *The Truman Show* (U.S.A., 1998), is a highly ambivalent film: it combines traditional Hollywood romance with a non-traditional critique of one of the most important tendencies of commercial (Hollywood) films, namely the creation of such a convincing illusion of reality that the resulting 'hyper-reality' (as in 'reality shows') begins to blur the boundaries between life and fiction. In *The Truman Show,* this ambivalence is mainly transmitted by the words and images of the filmic narrative. Yet film music also participates in the ambivalence owing to a remarkable combination of traditional and non-traditional uses. Among the former, the well-known functions of music as emotion-enhancer and bridge between frames play a role. Among the latter category, the (more or less conspicuous) absence of film music in certain scenes is noteworthy, moreover a phenomenon which has not yet found due attention in research: the existence of what in 'absolute' instrumental music would be impossible but which the plurimedial combination of music, narrative and the moving image in the sound film can produce, namely musical metalepsis. This is film music that paradoxically transgresses the boundaries of filmic levels both in a top-down and a bottom-up direction. Owing to the lack of attention usually paid to film music in the process of reception (a lack of awareness which, in *The Truman Show*, is exploited for a thematic purpose), musical metalepsis is not as overt and spectacular as 'ontological' metalepses would be in the fields of the verbal and visual channels. Yet it nevertheless enhances a major critical concern of *The Truman Show*, namely the blurring of ontological levels. In doing so, it participates in the film's fundamental ambivalence in a particularly noteworthy way: on the one hand, if perceived from a rational and 'expert' perspective, musical metalepsis contributes to the implied critique of the delusions of film-based hyper-reality; on the other hand its very covertness illustrates how easily most ('amateur') viewers tend to overlook certain filmic devices for the sake of an entertaining emotional immersion in filmic fake-reality and ultimately even hyper-reality.

...

1   Introduction: Topoi about Traditional Uses of Film Music's Relationship to Words and Images in Commercial Hollywood Movies, and Their Relativity

The relationship between film music and filmic narratives is a field where some topoi, dating from the 1930s (see Kalinak 2010: 16), have been firmly established, in particular when it comes to commercial Hollywood films. Film music is traditionally considered to be inconspicuous and plays, so to speak, second fiddle to the dominant narrative components, image and words. "[...] many in the audience do not even hear it" – is the opening statement of a recent introduction to film Music (ibid.: 1), and Claudia Gorbman's seminal study (see 1987) on *Narrative Film Music* (sub-title) bears the tell-tale main title *Unheard Melodies*. Indeed, film music is often even not consciously perceived (cf. ibid.: 6f.), since it acts as a merely passive support of the narrative flow.

As so frequently, topoi have their justification, but as sweeping generalizations they do not cover the entirety of the phenomena under discussion. Between the total inconspicuousness and "subordination" (ibid.: 31) of a mere background and the absolute 'visibility' or 'audibility' of foregrounded phenomena there are many nuances. After all, there are sound tracks which are particularly beautiful and so popular that they are reissued on separate CDs, thus obtaining some independence from the original film narrative. Even if one brackets off this special phenomenon, there is still some particularly rich film music that does indeed depart from the pole of inconspicuousness to a palpable degree, and some film music even shows features that – at least in other media – would be considered 'experimental'.

To what extent even commercial Hollywood productions can sport a relatively noteworthy film music that, for all its conventionality, also shows unconventional traits is in focus in the following discussion of a 1998 film which deserves more attention than is generally attributed to it, namely *The Truman Show* (directed by Peter Weir, film script written by Andrew Niccol). This is indeed a remarkable metareferential film owing to the profound ambivalence it shows in its exploration of the creation or transmission of filmic reality, but also with reference to some of its film music. While the majority of this music conforms to the aforementioned topoi of traditional uses, *The Truman Show* also contains some instances of non-traditional uses, in which film music can be shown to be a more active component in the represented narrative. Interestingly, in two cases, it even adopts features that allow it to be likened to an implicitly metareferential device termed 'metalepsis' in literature and other media (that is, a violation of the conventionally assumed autonomy of a represented world by a paradoxical transgression (in thought or deed) of the border that separates its inside from the outside (adapted from Thoss 2015: 177).[1] However, as we will see, its disruptive potential is more limited here – for reasons that enhance the movie's critical message.

2   Features of the Non-Musical Components of *The Truman Show*: the Frame Structure, and the Ambivalent Critique of Filmic Reality Simulation

The Truman Show is a meta-film, a film that reflects aspects of the production and reception of films, in particular with reference to (partially) scripted reality shows. This meta-reflection is transmitted through a frame structure, which complicates the diegetic levels of the movie. Drawing on Genettian terminology as adopted by Claudia Gorbman (cf. 1987: 3), one may say that here, as in all narrative films, there is a paratextual, an extradiegetic, and a diegetic (or intradiegetic) level; in addition, owing to the frame structure, there is also a hypodiegetic level, namely where the film portrays a world staged for TV transmission. The *paratextual* level is the level on which the (real) film credits are located (in the *Truman Show* they are part of the closing sequence).

The *extradiegetic* level is the space where a voice-over would be located (which does not exist here), and it is also the level which is responsible for non-diegetic music (which does exist here as it does elsewhere).

The *intradiegetic* level, in *The Truman Show*, is the world of a God-like film director named Christof, who has devised the embedded eponymous "Truman Show" and sold it to the fictional "multi-media giant [...] Omnicam" (Weir 1998: xii). This show is a hugely popular and profitable "reality show" (ibid.: xviii), which has run into its 10,909th day, that is, it has run continuously for almost 30 years. Parts of the profits also stem from international licences, "product placement" (ibid.: xiv) and what nowadays is termed "transmedia-storytelling" (Jenkins 2006: 4; Söller-Eckert 2013), the marketing of the Truman world and its commodities such as "board games, swap cards etc". through a "mail order department" (Weir 1998: xvii).

---

1   See also Genette 2004, Wolf 2005, and Wolf 2009: 50–56.

Owing to its meta-filmic frame structure, the intradiegetic level of the *The Truman Show* represents aspects of the production and reception of films as well as elements of the embedded show as a filmic production. The intradiegetic level thus recursively presents lower-level paratexts: peritextual credits of the embedded show and epitextual celebrity statements explaining some of its aspects. In addition, it consists of shots of Christof's control room located somewhere above the hypodiegetic world from which he and his crew look down upon their creation, and shots of various groups of TV viewers eagerly following Christof's "Truman Show".[2] One of these fictitious audience members is Silvia, a former extra in the show who has fallen in love with its eponymous hero and becomes part of the romance structure of the story.

The *hypodiegetic* level is the world of the hero Truman Burbank. He lives in an artificial sea-side town "Seahaven", a conservative fake world of small-town America, recalling the "small, close communities of nineteenth-century America" (Weir 1998: xvf.).[3] It has been constructed under a huge diorama-like dome complete with all imaginable details, including changing weather conditions and everything pertaining to a town, its inhabitants, and surroundings: offices, shops, streets, a radio and TV station, in which a hypo-hypodiegetic level is produced,[4] and natural peripheral borders including a forest, the beach

---

2   In the opening sequence of *The Truman Show,* all of this is presented in a bewildering mix of rapidly alternating shots from the intradiegetic level (celebrity statements and credits of "The Truman Show") and the hypodiegetic level (Truman's daydreaming about a mountaineering adventure in front of his bathroom mirror on the morning of day 10,909); the confusing effect thus produced is a good introduction to the blurring of ontological levels as one of the film's main themes and critical issues.

3   In his fictional account of the backstory of "The Truman Show", Weir also draws attention to the conservative clothing style adopted in this artificial word, a style recalling "the late 1930s and 1940s" (1998: xvi).

4   The intricacies of levels in *The Truman Show* alongside with the fact that not all films are fictional (but may be factual, as in documentaries) nor narrative (as opposed to descriptive) could give occasion for a general revision of Gorbman's film-musical terminology: on a first level a) one could differentiate between *extra-compositional* (quasi, in Genettian terminology, 'paratextual', or more precisely, 'peritextual') music (which, for instance, accompanies the logo of the film company and serves as a musical identity tag) and *intra-compositional* film music (that is, music specifically composed or arranged for the film in question); on a second level b) intra-compositional music could be further divided into *extra-representational* (or, in narrative films, 'extradiegetic') music (one could introduce here a further differentiation between epitextual music, that is, paratextual music that is specific to the film under consideration, and extra-representational/extradiegetic music in a narrow sense) vs. *intra-representational* (or, in narrative films, intradiegetic) music, that is, music pertaining to, and produced in, the represented world in which it is in principle audible (yet not necessarily by all characters); a further level would be *hypo-representational* (in narrative films: hypodiegetic) music, that is, music that is located on an embedded level of representation or

and the sea. In short, all of this is perfect virtual reality, except for Truman himself, a 'true man'. He is the only one in Seahaven who, for a considerable time, is not aware of the fake nature of the world he is made to inhabit, since he is not an actor but a person who, from his birth, has been set into this artificial creation of Christof's. In this world he, as a child, was made to lose his father during a sailing trip (a cruel psychological detail introduced by Christof in order to make Truman afraid of the 'sea' and thus prevent him from using it as a possible escape route). But this loss happened long ago. Truman's life since has been relatively happy: he has made friends, has married, and has a job in an insurance company. He has been spared tragedy and deep conflicts except for "low-key soap opera situations: [...] Just enough drama to make the viewer care about [him]" (Weir 1998: xiv). In spite of the relative happiness and security of his existence, Truman has started to question his world as a consequence of some accidents (e.g., a spotlight falling from the artificial sky, the initial event in the film) and also owing to some improbable coincidences (there is, for instance, the traffic in his neighbourhood that always follows the same pattern).

As we are made to understand, the whole show is based on the commercial exploitation of a human being – a fact which is used in this movie as part of a profound critique of the abuse of the power film has to simulate reality and make recipients become immersed in it. The recipients' sympathies, which are mostly produced by a kind of dramatic irony, elicited by the discrepancy of awareness between hero and (real as well as represented, fictitious) audience,[5] are increasingly geared towards Truman's curiosity (as a child he wanted to become an explorer), his dawning awareness that something is wrong about his world, his dreams about mountaineering and an – alas impossible – holiday on the Fiji Islands, and his eventual attempts at leaving his 'prison'. In the last scenes, we see Truman on board a small sailing boat: he has managed to outwit the all-present cameras and tries to escape by sailing to wherever he may land. When Christof realizes that his creation is attempting to abandon him, he becomes a punishing Old-Testament-like 'God' and raises a storm in which Truman all but drowns. All of this does, however, not prevent Truman from sailing on – until he reaches the end of the artificial sea, where his boat crashes into the illusionistically painted diorama-like wall. Christof, who has never

---

narration, e.g., music on a radio programme (and this embedding could continue and create *hypo-hypo-representational* music, and so on).

5   As opposed to traditional irony, which, as a rule, serves to distance the recipient from the 'victim' of irony, here the 'victim' elicits our pity, the dramatic irony thus producing both cognitive distance and affective closeness – one of the many ambivalences characterizing *The Truman Show*. (For the various kinds of irony that may elicit at least partial closeness see Wolf 2007.)

directly addressed Truman, is now prepared to enter into a dialogue with his 'creature'. He assures him of his love and warns him that he will find no more truth in the outside world than inside the safe cosmos of Seahaven:

> CHRISTOF:
> Truman, there's no more truth out there than in the world I created for you – the same lies and deceit. But in my world you have nothing to fear.
>   NICCOL/WEIR 1998: 106

Yet Truman decides otherwise, insisting on his autonomy as a human being – to the universal joy of the fictitious and arguably also the real audience. He salutes Christof with a final mock bow and disappears through a black door – behind which we surmise that he will finally be reunited with his Silvia, the girl he has fondly remembered since his teenage days. Christof is forced to "cease transmission" (film text missing from the published film script) – but some members of the fictitious audience, notably two members of a security staff, want a continuation of immersive TV amusement, and one of them reaches for a TV programme magazine to see what alternative shows are available.

This is an important concluding detail, since it adds to the movie's criticism, which is based on ideals such as pity, the grandeur of love, the value of leading an authentic, self-determined life and of being able to distinguish fiction from reality and thus of being able to escape the confusions elicited by a capitalist world of simulacra as described by Baudrillard (see 1978/1981/1984).

The precise objects of this criticism merit some further remarks. It is, first, directed at the incredible irresponsibility, hubris and greed of people like Christof, who, in the interest of quota, renown and financial profit, experiment with a human being and are ready to sacrifice a whole life to a show replete with product placements. It is, second, aimed at the almost totalitarian power of the media to create such perfect simulacra that reality and fiction become blurred (a confusion which starts with the opening sequence[6] and sometimes even extends to the fictional actors [cf. Weir 1998: xvii]). Third, the film's critique is also aimed at the tacit consent and complicity of both the fictitious and the real audiences who know about the problematic morals and the fake nature of the show and yet love to immerse themselves in it as voyeuristic witnesses of a life in all its intimate details.

The illusionism of the hypodiegetic world is in fact so strong that even though we are informed about the fake nature of Truman's world from the quasi-paratextual celebrity statements at the beginning of the film and the partly

---

6   See above, note 2.

grotesque reactions of the fictional audience, some of the reminders of its artificiality as experienced by Truman come as a shock. Most intense among these
is the crash with which Truman's boat comes to an unexpected standstill at
the limits of the fake world. This is part of the film's aesthetic strategy, namely
not only to *show* the power of filmic illusion with reference to the fictional
audience but also to allow the real audience to *experience* it for themselves.
This effect is achieved by making use of the typical devices of illusionist Hollywood movies: realistic decor; an emotionally engaging love romance; a nice
hero played by a well-known star (Jim Carrey), whose predicament and mortal
danger elicits deep emotions; and, last but not least, appropriate film music.

The aforementioned crash is thus all the more a shock if we become aware to
what extent we ourselves have been confused about the ontological difference
between (fictional) reality and (fictional) fake-world. At the end it remains
doubtful whether we are really able to escape the attractiveness of filmic illusion, and it remains an open question as to whether reality, a black box from
the perspective of the Truman world, is really so much better and authentic as
hoped for by Truman – and perhaps by ourselves. All of this gives the entire
film a remarkable ambiguity: it combines traditional Hollywood romance and
the realization of filmic illusionism with a non-traditional and anti-illusionist
critique of this very illusionism and ends up by allowing some doubt whether
the blurring of the boundaries of life and fiction by commercially driven media
and their 'hyper-realities' can really be resisted to the extent that we would like
to believe.

3 Traditional Uses of Film Music in *The Truman Show*: Music as an Inconspicuous, Passive Support of the Immersive Framed Story

Now that the ambivalences of the film as a whole have been established, let
us consider what role the film music plays in *The Truman Show* (it was mostly
composed by Burkhard Dallwitz and Philip Glass and is available on a separate
CD; see Figure 3.1). As will be shown, it takes part in the film's overall ambiguity, displaying a conventional and a less conventional side.

Let us consider the conventional uses of film music first. A recent introduction to film music contains an incomplete, yet impressive, list of the multifari-
ous functions of film music which is worthwhile quoting,[7] since many of them
are also relevant to *The Truman Show*:

---

7 For a similar list of functions see Davison 2007/2010: 212f.

FIGURE 3.1   *The Truman Show: Music from the Motion Picture*, CD-cover

> Film music [...] can establish setting, [...] it can fashion a mood and cre-
> ate atmosphere; it can call attention to elements onscreen or offscreen,
> thus clarifying matters of plot and narrative progression; it can rein-
> force or foreshadow narrative developments and contribute to the way
> we respond to them; it can elucidate characters' motivations and help
> us to know what they are thinking; it can contribute to the creation of
> emotions [...] [it] can unify a series of images [...] [and] encourages our
> absorption into the film by distracting us from its technological basis [...]"
>
> KALINAK 2010: 1

Some illustrations from the movie may establish the partially traditional
use of film music. There is, first, the conventional function of film music as
"unify[ing] a series of images", that is, as a bridge linking individual frames and

thus "distracting us from [the] technological basis" of slicing filmic information into separate frames divided by cuts. An example of this function may
be found in the concluding part of *The Truman Show* (Chap. 19, "Setting Sail",
soundtrack no. 15 on CD, "Truman Sets Sail", composed by Dallwitz), where
the music bridges several shots: first from the diegetic control room (where
Christof – first without music – is eagerly looking for his missing hero); the
second group of shots is of some of the viewers (a man in a bathtub, patrons
of a café, and two security guards), who are all happy that Truman has been
found; the third shot is of Truman on board his boat. Interestingly, the music
sets in a second before Christof's order, "resume transmission" (Niccol/Weir
1998: 97), and is heard throughout the following frames – it is thus in principle
extradiegetic music. However, if one does not listen carefully to the exact onset
of the music's fading in, one may get the impression that it is part of the hypodiegetic transmission and thus diegetic music – all of which creates a curious
ambiguity.

One of the most powerful functions of film music, namely to enhance
emotions and moods, can also be experienced in the same section of the film
(Truman's escape on a sailing boat, scene 20, "Cue The Storm"). Here the storm,
raised by Christof, is accompanied by the beating rhythms of an appropriate
'storm music' (soundtrack on CD no. 16, "Underground/Storm", composed by
Dallwitz), and is then followed – in time with the reappearing sun – by a quiet
adagio melody, an opposition reminiscent of Beethoven's juxtaposition of a
musical thunder storm and the regaining of serene pastoral bliss in his sixth
symphony (soundtrack on CD no. 17, "Raising the Sail", composed by Philip
Glass). This is music accompanying pictures with minimal sound effects; one
hears the hoisting of the sail and initially the lapping of the now calm waves –
no words are spoken; they would be unnecessary since the whole sequence of
shots is about relief from the previous tension (including the fictional audience, in this case Christof's crew, among which we see a woman who sighs).

This function of music as an emotion and "mood-enhancer" (Kramer 2008:
229) contributes in turn to the most important overall function of film music,
namely, on the one hand, to intensify the viewers' immersion or aesthetic illusion and, on the other hand, to gloss over possible elements of 'distraction'
or distance in the interest of the illusionist principle of 'celare artem' (cf. Wolf
2013: 50f.). To what extent such a support for the *celare artem* principle is helpful and efficiently glosses over an element of antirealist improbability may be
experienced by each viewer of the film who does *not* notice that Truman, who
has been soaked through seconds before, is displayed with dry hair and a dry
pullover in the very next shot, in which he is seen to blissfully sail on into the
seemingly endless distance.

A third traditional function of film music is paradoxically present when we do *not* hear any music in certain stretches of film. It operates on the principle of foregrounding through deviation from expectations in a film mostly accompanied by music and creates a meaningful or, in some cases, even conspicuous absence. This is what Kalinak summarizes under the phrase already quoted, "call[ing] attention to elements onscreen". This function could be observed in *The Truman Show* in the opening shots of the aforementioned Chapter 19, "Setting Sail". Here, the absence of music underlines the bustle in the control room during the search for Truman. Another, more conspicuous example occurs at the sudden end of Truman's voyage (Chap. 21, "The Sky's the Limit", beginning; the soundtrack on the CD is still no. 17, "Raising the Sail", composed by Glass). The soothing music here comes to an unexpected halt, when the collision of the boat with the wall of the diorama occurs, shockingly revealing the artificiality of the hypodiegetic world and jerking all those out of their illusion who – albeit only for moments – believed in the reality of this world (in view of the powerful emotions and immersion elicited by Truman's story, this is arguably the majority of the both the fictitious and the real audience!). Instead of film music we are here made to hear all but silence, with only the faint sound of the waves of the artificial ocean. Absent music operates here as shock enhancer.

So far, present and absent music composed or arranged specifically for this movie and fulfilling traditional functions of film music has been in focus. In contrast, one of the somewhat less traditional uses of *The Truman Show's* film music is the repeated insertion of classical music.[8] It occurs several times in this film, comprising extracts from Mozart's piano sonata in A major, K 331, and his horn concerto no. 1 in D Major (K 412), from Brahms's "Wiegenlied" ('Lullaby') and from the second movement of Chopin's first concerto for piano and orchestra, which accompanies the closing credits. As Lawrence Kramer has aptly remarked (although for diegetic music), the use of classical music is "especially likely" to "attract attention", as it "stands out" from the majority of non-classical film music, and therefore "the question of meaning will be in the air" (2008: 230).

What is the meaning, what are possible functions of entering recognizable music and thus music replete with pre-established connotations as a consequence of previous "ascriptions" (Kramer 2002, Chap. 7: 149) into *The Truman Show*? One possible function, derived from classical music's connotations, would be as a prestige marker; similarly, it may serve to give the movie, or parts

---

8   In addition, there is the replay of "Father Kolbe's Prayer", a previous composition by Wojciech Kilar. (This piece is played after Truman has found out about the limits of his world at the end of Chap. 21; soundtrack no. 18 on the CD.)

of it, a conservative aura: this is certainly important for *The Truman Show*, which, as we have seen, rests on conservative values. However, this conservatism is perhaps not wholehearted but may also play a role in the film's implicit critique of a traditional materialistic culture in which everything, including art and human beings, becomes a marketable commodity. After all, what the film illustrates is a world of 'disneyfication' and mock idealization, in which the reality status of the represented cosy, conservative life is doubtful, but ultimately irrelevant. The use of classical music as both marker and criticism of conservatism thus contributes to the general ambivalence of the film as a whole.

This ambivalence is also present in another function of classical film music in *The Truman Show*: when, at the outset of the plot, the lamp representing a star 'Sirius' from 'Canis major' accidentally falls from the dome's roof which represents the night sky,[9] Truman is understandably upset. This incident presents a danger for Christof, since it might indicate to Truman that his world is fake – with unforeseeable consequences for the show. Truman, after a visible moment of hesitation, enters his car in order to drive to his insurance office and listens to his car radio (Chap. 2, "Day 10,909", beginning). Suspiciously – seconds after the incident with the spotlight – the radio already reports the accident in the news, but the speaker tries to explain it away as an object lost by an aircraft (no aircraft sound was, however, to be heard during the accident). The jovial newsreader moreover seems to enter into an improbable conversation with Truman, who answers him in turn – a paradoxical, normally impossible, transgression of diegetic representational levels and thus a violation of the autonomy of Truman's world: a metalepsis. Yet Truman does not seem to notice, perhaps since something like that has occurred frequently when listening to Seahaven's radio. After this, the announcer fades in Mozart's march rondo "Alla turca" from his A Major piano sonata (K 331) and explicitly thematizes the function of this piece of well-known classical music: "sit back, and let this music calm you down" (Niccol/Weir 1998: 4). Classical music, and Mozart's music in particular, is here clearly used in one of the functions traditionally ascribed to it, namely as a nerve-soother.[10] However, this not yet all to this particular stretch of film music.

---

9   Ironically, this happens immediately after Truman has been 'attacked' by his neighbour's big, friendly Dalmatian.

10   From a musico-historical point of view it may come as a surprise that the march rondo "Alla turca" has been chosen of all classical compositions, a movement which, at least in its original version, can hardly be called "nerve-soothing"; yet since Mozart's time it has become somewhat of a staple of classical music and arguably has lost its original effect. Whether this clash between actual/original function and the function explicitly attributed to it by the (musically illiterate?) radio announcer must remain an open question.

4   Non-Traditional Uses of Film Music in *The Truman Show*: Music
       as Relatively Active and Conspicuous Disruption of the Narrative
       Flow? The Ambivalent Use of Musical Metalepsis

This brings us to the potentially non-traditional uses of film music in this
movie. A first instance of them can be experienced in the aforementioned
scene with the Mozart music. As the scene goes on, something unusual (at
least for the filmic genre at hand) occurs: hypo-hypodiegetic radio music can
be heard (and seen) to seamlessly change into (extra)diegetic music, for it is
not only heard inside the car both by Truman and the (fictitious as well as
the real) audience but continues outside of the vehicle, accompanying shots
showing the car's trajectory through a stretch of Seahaven, and even extends
through a scene in which Truman is buying a magazine – all settings in which
the hero can no longer hear the music (given the distance from the car, and the
likely fact that the music would be switched off, once Truman has left the car).
This is a musical metalepsis, more precisely a bottom-up metalepsis (one paradoxically transgressing the border of the hypodiegetic in the direction of the
diegetic level). It complements the adumbration of a verbal metalepsis which
we have witnessed in the impossible conversation between Truman and the
newsreader, who seem to be in dialogue with one another in spite of the medial boundary between hypodiegetic reality and a doubly mediated, hypo-hypodiegetic radio programme.[11]

    This initial musical metalepsis has a counterpart towards the end of the
film, in Chap. 23 ("Good Afternoon, Good Evening, & Good Night", soundtrack
on CD no. 19, "Opening", composed by Philip Glass), where extradiegetic music becomes diegetic. The extradiegetic status of the music during Truman's
last smile, following his mock farewell to Christof just before exiting through
a door of the diorama into a black space, is unmistakable, for it bridges shots
from different diegetic levels – which only extradiegetic music can do: first,

---

11   For the music in *The Truman Show*, the different levels are (for the corresponding termi-
      nology see above, note 4): a) extradiegetic music is music 'above' or 'outside' Christof's
      world; b) diegetic music is music produced and played inside Christof's world (for the
      sake of simplicity, and since this differentiation does not play a role in our film, one may
      here conflate 'real' music actually played in this world, and 'tinned'/represented music,
      i.e., the music used as fictitiously extradiegetic music for the embedded "Truman Show";
      c) hypodiegetic music would be 'real' music played by characters in Truman's world; and
      d) hypo-hypodiegetic music is 'tinned'/represented music in this world. Whether the leap
      from Truman's hypo-hypodiegetic car radio music to a higher level is one to the diegetic
      level or to the extradiegetic level is difficult to assess, but this does not affect the metalep-
      tic nature of this leap.

Truman's departure (in principle: hypodiegetic level, although no longer part of the scripted "Truman Show"); second, Christof's frustrated face (diegetic level); third, Truman's mock bow (again, in principle, hypodiegetic level, yet beginning to 'raise' to the diegetic level), fourth, Silvia's happy reaction (readable on her face; she is a viewer of the "Truman Show" and thus located on the diegetic level), followed by Truman rising from his bow; fifth, Silvia rushing down the stairs of her house, presumably in order to meet Truman (a meeting, where definitely the distinction between hypodiegetic and diegetic worlds becomes blurred); then various reactions from the fictitious (diegetic) audience (including cheers in the bar, the man in the bath tub and the security staff). All of these scenes are accompanied by the same happy music (another instance of a conventional use of film music, not only as a bridging device but also as an emotion enhancer). Yet this music suddenly comes to a stop, after one of Christof's staff members murmurs "cease transmission" (not in the film script), and we see a small video screen going blank – a clear indication that the music suddenly has, as it were, made a metaleptic top-down tumble from the extradiegetic to the diegetic level, for it is only diegetic music (the music produced for Christof's programme) that can react to a button pressed in Christof's studio.[12]

In literature and other media, metalepsis is highly unusual, therefore conspicuous, disruptive, disturbing and often illusion-breaking. A good example of this in the medium of film is the 'screen-passage' in Woody Allen's film *The Purple Rose of Cairo* (USA, 1984). There, a male hypodiegetic character of a black-and-white film within the film, which is on display in a cinema *mis en abyme*, becomes aware of a spectator (a woman admiring him) – this is what in research is termed an 'epistemological metalepsis' (cf. Wolf 2009: 52f.; Nelles 1992: 93–95); he then addresses her and leaves the screen, taking on colour and joins her in her diegetic world – to the dismay and horror of the cinema audience, whose reaction is a testimony to the shocking paradoxicality of this metalepsis, which has now become 'ontological'.

As opposed to this shocking metalepsis based on words and image, the musical metalepses in *The Truman Show* are far less spectacular and overt. Owing to the lack of attention usually paid to film music in the process of reception (a lack of awareness which, in *The Truman Show*, is exploited for a thematic purpose), they may even escape the awareness of inattentive 'amateur' members of the audience. The lack of attention may be reinforced by one of the

---

12   If one considers the ontology of the diegetic action only, one could also argue that the metalepsis operates bottom up, for the pressing of a diegetic button seemingly has an influence on an extradiegetic phenomenon.

traditional functions of extradiegetic music, namely to bridge gaps and hide unrealistic technical elements. Many film viewers may, in fact, be so used to these functions that they hardly notice that the gap in the metaleptic cases discussed is not one between frames located on the *same* level but between *different* levels, nor would they arguably notice another of the improbable and unrealistic effects of the editing of this film, namely the weird clarity with which Mozart's music is heard in a car: there are no engine or tire sound-effects to undercut or disturb the soundtrack.

Yet this is only one possible effect, which may be complemented, or even counteracted by another: for the film contains at least two clues for making us at least potentially aware of a certain disruption taking place. First, there is the generic or aesthetic frame of a pervading realism and illusionism (which dominates the film's metareferentiality, since in most cases the meta-aspects are 'naturalized', that is, they appear as probable effects of the plot). This frame does *not* allow to simply disregard the formal musical metalepsis as generically sanctioned (as would be the case in 'unrealistic' musical films, where extra – and intradiegetic music merge so frequently that no disruption is felt).[13] Second, there is a remarkable clash in the nature of the shots: in the earlier metalepsis, the hypo-hypodiegetic music which accompanies a close-up of Truman in his car (the camera is visibly located behind the dashboard), is immediately followed by a panoramic shot of a part of Seahaven, with no visual information being given about Truman having parked his car and alighted from it; rather, the next shot is a newsagents shop in which Truman eventually is shown to buy a magazine – to the ongoing accompaniment of the "Alla turca" music. The reverse happens in the concluding musical metalepsis, where we first see a total shot of Christof's control room and then a little screen which goes static. Thus the different nature of the shots (close-up vs. panoramic/total shot) may be said to be a visual counterpart to the transgression between different levels that occurs on the film musical level.

So, *if*, not least owing to these clues, the musical metalepses *are* noticed by the 'expert' viewer or listener,[14] they enhance a major critical concern of *The Truman Show*, namely the blurring of ontological levels. They achieve this enhancement by combining an in principle remarkable, unusual and potentially

---

13   Nor would classifying what happens here as merely 'transdiegetic' sound (*sensu* Jørgensen 2009: 97–99), that is, sound that conventionally transgresses diegetic levels, as is often the case in computer games, be appropriate: the metareferential foregrounding of filmic conventions is so frequent in *The Truman Show* that the 'migration' of music across diegetic levels does acquire an implicitly metareferential, metaleptic quality.

14   For the differentiation and in fact complementarity of amateur and expert reception see Kramer 2008.

illusion-breaking ontological paradoxicality with its acceptance as if it were the normal state of affairs: one and the same represented phenomenon cannot be hypodiegetic and diegetic, or extradiegetic and diegetic, at the same time – and yet the amateur viewer may hardly notice this paradoxicality, and what is more, most viewers will in all likelihood *not* have felt a disruption of their immersion in the filmic world or worlds.

In an ambivalent meta-film, such as *The Truman Show,* this ambivalence of the effect produced by the musical metalepses, which are both potentially disruptive and more or less smoothly integrated in the narrative flow of the film, is certainly not accidental – and it is arguably more than the effect of film music's traditional inconspicuousness and subordination to the verbal and pictorial narrative: on the one hand, if perceived from a rational 'expert' perspective as a paradox, the musical metalepses contribute to the implied critique of the delusions of film-based hyper-reality. On the other hand, their very covertness illustrates how easily the mass of viewers tend to overlook certain filmic devices for the sake of an entertaining emotional immersion in filmic fake-reality and ultimately even hyper-reality. It is a particular challenge for the expert viewer not only to listen to the musical metalepses from the distanced perspective of the connoisseur, but also from the perspective of the general viewer and see that *both* perspectives are important for the film's overall meaning. It is in fact illuminating to see this ambivalence rather than smooth it down in a one-sided way, as Melanie Lowe does (cf. 2007: 170); she describes the Mozart example as containing a "shift[...] from its original status as diegetic music to non-diegetic music" (forgetting in her terminology about the embedded, and hence hypodiegetic nature of the "Truman Show") but then reduces "Mozart's music" functionally to being "ultimately a passive backdrop to the artificially civilized world of *The Truman Show*" (ibid.). If one does not follow Lowe but perceives the ambivalence of the musical metalepses as such, they become *mises en abyme* of important facets of the film's message, or in Kramer's words, "a microcosm of the whole film" (2008: 237).

What contributes to the importance of perceiving the musical metalepses as such as well as their ambivalence, is the fact that they are not the only ones in this film: besides the aforementioned verbal metalepsis in the form of the 'impossible' conversation between listener and radio-announcer there is a visual one: one of the composers, the minimalist Philip Glass, figures as one of the 'keyboard artists' in Christof's control room and is also mentioned as such in the closing credits (a paradoxical conflation of authorial roles and filmic characters, which is traditionally avoided). However, this detail will go as unnoticed by most non-expert viewers and listeners as is the repeated, covertly metafilmic occurrence of Hitchcock as a semi-inconspicuous extra in his own films.

All of this, in principle, foregrounds one of the major thematic concerns of *The Truman Show*, which eminently aligns it to postmodernism, namely highlighting the precarious line between fiction and reality. If we realize the metalepses as such, this may enhance our will to resist this postmodernist blurring of ontological levels. If we do not – or only belatedly – become aware of the metalepses as a means of blurring this line, we thereby testify to the immersive pull even of critical films such as *The Truman Show* as attractive simulacra. And this immersive pull is intensified by the film music, which was apparently considered to possess a particularly appealing quality, for – as already mentioned and in line with the fictional market strategy of transmedial storytelling – it has been marketed as an independent commodity in the form of a CD.

The commodification of the very film music which contributes to laying bare the dangers of commodification in a film critically exposing the appeal of reality shows is a further and perhaps ironic ambivalence related to *The Truman Show*. Finally, a similar ambivalence can also come into play once the music is appreciated as such, for it will backfire when we watch the film a second time. In this case, the music will be both: mostly inconspicuous and conspicuous, subservient to the narrative and relatively independent from it.

5   Conclusion

With reference to the functions of film music in *The Truman Show,* the result of the foregoing discussion is equally ambivalent: film music – even in a critical meta-film such as *The Truman Show* – tends to conform to the topoi of inconspicuousness and subservience as mentioned in the introduction to this contribution. Yet it has been shown to have a potential that goes beyond these topoi – a potential of critique and disruption aimed at the filmic creation of virtual realities to which film music in general so efficiently contributes (as emotion enhancer, as a seal for the technical seams left by the medium and as lubricant for the narrative and immersive flow). This critical potential of non-traditional use also contributes to underlining music's ability to become a constituent in its own right in a filmic narrative next to language, pictures and non-musical sound. Yet it will appear as such only if we pay attention to it. Music may demand less of our attention than the more dominant components of filmic narratives, word and image, but it is certainly rewarding to pay more attention to the relationship between these components and film music.

Taking the film music in movies such as *The Truman Show* seriously may yield unexpected results. In our case, this is both a contribution to intermediality studies and to a branch of research which has recently found increasing attention, namely metalepsis research. In principle, since metalepses are bound to represented worlds and since (instrumental) music cannot represent possible worlds, metalepses ought to be excluded from music. I myself made this claim with reference to "instrumental music as a typically non-representational medium" (Wolf 2009: 51). Film music, however, teaches us that the combination of media in a plurimedial artefact such as the sound film can have a curious effect: it can expand the potential of the medial components and make them enter areas which would be inaccessible to them alone. As a consequence, the claim of an impossibility of musical metalepsis in instrumental music as such must be qualified: as we have seen, in film music, the plurimedial combination of music with the moving image and words, which allow for the differentiation of 'world'-levels, enables such an unusual thing as a musical metalepsis. Paying close attention to the film music in *The Truman Show* thus not only enriches our understanding of a particular film and of the ambivalences postmodern Hollywood movies can produce but also yields a noteworthy contribution to both metalepsis and intermediality studies.

References

Baudrillard, Jean (1978/1981/1984). "La Précession des simulacres". Jean Baudrillard. *Simulacre et simulation*. Débats. Paris: Editions galilée. 9–68. (Engl. trans.: "The Precession of Simulacra". Brian Wallis, ed. *Art after Modernism*. The New Museum of Contemporary Art, New York: Documentary Sources in Contemporary Art. New York, NY. 253–281).

Davison, Annette (2007/2010). "High Fidelity? Music in Screen Adaptations". Deborah Cartmell, Imelda Whelehan, eds. *The Cambridge Companion to Literature on Screen*. Cambridge: CUP. 212–225.

Genette, Gérard (2004). *Métalepse: De la figure à la fiction*. Collection Poétique. Paris: Éditions du Seuil.

Gorbman, Claudia (1987). *Unheard Melodies: Narrative Film Music*. London: BFI Publishing/Bloomington, IN: Indiana Univ. Press.

Jenkins, Henry (2006). *Convergence Culture: Where Old and New Media Collide*. New York, NY: New York Univ. Press.

Jørgensen, Kristine (2009). *A Comprehensive Study of Sound in Computer Games: How Audio Affects Player Action*. Lewiston, NY: Edwin Mellen Press.

Kalinak, Kathryn (2010). *Film Music: A Very Short Introduction.* New York, NY: OUP.

Kramer, Lawrence (2002). *Musical Meaning: Toward a Critical History.* Berkeley, CA: Univ. of California Press.

Kramer, Lawrence (2008). "Whose Classical Music? Reflection on Film Adaptation". David Francis Urrows, ed. *Essays on Word/Music Adaptation and on Surveying the Field.* Word and Music Studies 9. Amsterdam/New York, NY: Rodopi. 227–242.

Lowe, Melanie (2007). *Pleasure and Meaning in the Classical Symphony.* Bloomington, IN: Indiana Univ. Press.

Nelles, William (1992). "Stories within Stories: Narrative Levels and Embedded Narrative". *Studies in the Literary Imagination* 25/1: 79–96.

Niccol, Andrew, Peter Weir (1998). *The Truman Show: Screenplay, Foreword, and Notes by Andrew Niccol. Introduction by Peter Weir.* New York, NY: Newmarket Press.

Söller-Eckert, Claudia (2013). "Transmedia Storytelling and Participation Experience". Bernd Kracke, Marc Ries, eds. *Expanded Narration: Das neue Erzählen.* Bielefeld: Transcript. 321–339.

Thoss, Jeff (2015). *When Storyworlds Collide: Metalepsis in Popular Fiction, Film and Comics.* Studies in Intermediality 7. Leiden/Boston, MA: Brill/Rodopi.

Truman Show, The: Music from the Motion Picture (1998). Soundtrack Album by Burkhard Dallwitz and Philip Glass. CD released June 2. Milan Records.

Weir, Peter (1998). "Introduction". Niccol/Weir. xi–xviii.

Wolf, Werner (2005). "Metalepsis as a Transgeneric and Transmedial Phenomenon: A Case Study of the Possibilities of 'Exporting' Narratological Concepts". Jan Christoph Meister, ed. in cooperation with Tom Kindt and Wilhelm Schernus. *Narratology Beyond Literary Criticism: Mediality, Disciplinarity.* Narratologia 6. Berlin: de Gruyter. 83–107.

Wolf, Werner (2007). "'Schutzironie' als Akzeptanzstrategie für problematische Diskurse: Zu einer vernachlässigten Nähe erzeugenden Funktion von Ironie". Thomas Honegger, Eva-Maria Orth, Sandra Schwabe, eds. *Irony Revisited: Spurensuche in der englischsprachigen Literatur. Festschrift für Wolfgang G. Müller.* Würzburg: Königshausen & Neumann. 27–50.

Wolf, Werner (2009). "Metareference across Media: The Concept, its Transmedial Potentials and Problems, Main Forms and Functions". Werner Wolf, ed. in collaboration with Katharina Bantleon and Jeff Thoss. *Metareference across Media: Theory and Case Studies. Dedicated to Walter Bernhart on the Occasion of his Retirement.* Studies in Intermediality 4. Amsterdam/New York, NY: Rodopi. 1–85.

Wolf, Werner (2013). "Aesthetic Illusion". Walter Bernhart, Andreas Mahler, Werner Wolf, eds. *Immersion and Distance: Aesthetic Illusion in Literature and Other Media.* Studies in Intermediality 6. Amsterdam/New York, NY: Rodopi. 1–63.

CHAPTER 4

Homer and the Springfield Orchestra Bus: Four Test Cases for Any Future Challenge to the Diegetic/Non-Diegetic Model

Jordan Carmalt Stokes

Abstract

One of the most fundamental premises in the study of film music – the narratological distinction between diegetic and non-diegetic music – is also one of the most frequently challenged. This essay offers a defense of the diegetic/non-diegetic split by describing a series of scenes in which the distinction seems to be doing important work. A narratological reading of the scenes is contrasted with a reading that uses an alternative model recently advanced by Ben Winters, in order to show how these scenes can be used as test cases for the development of future theories.

•••

Since Claudia Gorbman's *Unheard Melodies: Narrative Film Music* (1987), film music scholars have made the distinction between diegetic music, which exists in the world of the story and can be heard by the characters, and non-diegetic music, which comes from somewhere outside of the story world, and which can only be heard by the audience. (In what follows, for brevity's sake, I will refer to this as "the Narratological Model".)

TABLE 1   *The Basic Narratological Model*

I)	Diegetic
II)	Non-diegetic

Under the Basic Narratological Model, all cues would fall into one of these categories.

As Robynn Stilwell has noted, students grasp the Narratological Model almost instantly, but are also quick to recognize that the neat split between diegetic and non-diegetic doesn't seem to capture every instance of film music (cf. 2007: 184). Indeed, the Basic Narratological Model has more often been described in the breach than in strict observance: I do not know that any scholar has ever used the simplified version of the model presented in Table 1. Gorbman certainly did not, for in the same book that popularized the terms diegetic and non-diegetic, she suggests a third label, "meta-diegetic", for music that is proper to a nested narrative such as a dream sequence or flashback (1987: 22f.). The film theorists David Bordwell and Kristin Thompson add the category of "internal" (as opposed to "external") diegetic music, which refers to music that is imagined, remembered, or hallucinated by one of the characters (1979/2001: 306). And Stilwell's already-classic 2007 essay, "The Fantastical Gap between Diegetic and Non-diegetic", points out that many cues move more or less freely (but not imperceptibly or arbitrarily) between any and all of the aforementioned categories. Our business as critics and analysts, Stilwell suggests, is not to squeeze each cue into the appropriate theoretical cubbyhole, but rather to attend to the ways in which any particular cue engages, or fails to engage, with the entire set of theoretical categories.

These are only a small sampling of the refinements and expansions that have been suggested, of course. But in my own writing and teaching, I have tended to use an expanded version of the Narratological Model that draws on the theorists listed above, as detailed in Table 2. To my mind, this model is both flexible and powerful, accounting for many striking musical effects without forcing any cue into a procrustean bed.

TABLE 2   *The Expanded Narratological Model*

I)	Diegetic
	A) Internal Diegetic
	B) External Diegetic
II)	Non-diegetic
III)	Meta-diegetic

All of these positions are separated by Stilwell's "Fantastical Gap". Not all cues fit neatly into a single category; cues may also move between multiple categories over time.

The Narratological Model is not universally admired, however, and in recent years a number of scholars have objected to it strenuously. My purpose in this essay is to mount a particular sort of defense of the Narratological Model by exploring a number of cases in which the model – or rather, the set of expectations that the model attempts to capture – does important cinematic work. I do not intend to prove once and for all that the Narratological Model is right.

(I have chosen some rather unusual scenes to make my case, and cherry-picking is fatal to any argument by induction.) However, I do think that any scholar who wishes to dispense with the Narratological Model needs to confront these examples, and explain, at least to his or her own private satisfaction, how these scenes achieve their various effects in the absence of the diegetic/non-diegetic split. What I offer is therefore a sort of proving ground or obstacle course for any future challenge to the Narratological Model, in hope that this will lead future challengers to more nuanced and powerful theories.

The remarks that follow are divided into three sections. First, I will say a few words about the different types of challenges that have been raised to the Narratological Model (only some of which are vulnerable to counter-critique that I am mounting here). Second, I will explain one of the most articulate and forceful of the recent challenges, that of Ben Winters, in some detail. And finally, I will walk Winters's theory through my four test cases, comparing the explanation offered by the Expanded Narratological Model to the alternative reading that Winters's model seems to offer. In this way, I will demonstrate the sort of intellectual engagement with the test cases that I hope to see from future theorists.

The reader will perhaps object that I am putting words in Winters's mouth. I answer with Falstaff: "I will answer it straight: I have done all this. That is now answered". (*Wiv.* 1.1.56) Winters was kind enough to clarify certain aspects of his theory for me by personal communication, and I have tried to present as faithful and sympathetic a reading of his theory as I am capable. Nevertheless, it should be stated firmly that the theory on trial here is my own reading of Winters's theory. The reader will decide whether I have erected a straw man.

In any case, the goal is not to prove Winters wrong. At the risk of giving the game away, I will say at the outset that his theory *can* pass all of the tests. But it does so only at some cost to its elegance and distinctiveness, and perhaps to certain of the scenes in question.

Before engaging with Winters's theory, however, I wish to offer a few brief remarks on the sorts of objections that have been raised to the Narratological Model. I detect three basic categories, of which only one is actually vulnerable to my counter-critique.

1 A Typology of Objections

The first sort of objection involves finding a particular scene in a particular film that doesn't quite fit, and making the claim that, while the Narratological

Model is fine in general, we need to expand or abandon it to understand such-and-such a particular score. Much of Stilwell's "Fantastical Gap" essay is taken up with a series of such examples. I am sure that Stilwell would describe her essay as a refinement of the model rather than an objection to it, and indeed we ought to think of such challenges as refinements even if their rhetoric is that of objection. I think of these theories as 'pragmatic', in that they are usually concerned with solving a problem of analysis. They build on the general rule rather than asking us to abandon it. The narratological model is a strict subset of the possibilities offered by any pragmatic objection, and therefore, obviously, these theories will be able to deal with any test case I can offer.

On the other hand, there are what I call 'visionary' objections. A visionary theorist would hold that, although the Narratological Model offers a good approximation of the way that we usually think about movies, the way we usually think about movies is *wrong*. We need to throw out our habits of perception and start afresh. Again the kind of defense I'm offering would be pointless: a visionary could look at all of the test cases described below and say that, indeed, all of these effects depend upon a clear intuitive distinction between the diegetic and non-diegetic; thankfully, come the revolution, such confused films will no longer be made. An example of this sort of thought can be found in Gregg Redner's *Deleuze and Film Music* (and in particular the chapter on Jean Vigo's *L'Atalante*), where we are asked to subsume not only the distinction between diegetic and non-diegetic, but even the distinction between sound and image under the rubric of Deleuzian "sensation" (2011: 25–46). A Deleuzian approach to anything involves a radical reframing of our usual experience. It is futile, therefore, to demand that a Deleuzian approach to film music explain our intuitive experience of that particular phenomenon.

There is a third category of objection, however, in which the theorists claim that the narratological model mischaracterizes both the way that scores are constructed and the way that we intuitively react to them. I call these theories 'dogmatic', and it is here that I am trying to make my intervention.

2   Winters's Model

The most articulate and thorough dogmatic theory in recent years is that of Ben Winters, which has been refined through a series of articles, including "Corporeality, Musical Heartbeats, and Cinematic Emotion" (2008), "The Non-diegetic Fallacy: Film, Music, and Narrative Space" (2010), and "Musical Wallpaper: Towards an Appreciation of Non-narrating Music in Film" (2012), as well as a chapter in Winter's monograph *Music, Performance, and the Realities of Film: Shared Concert Experiences in Screen Fiction* (2014). In an e-mail to the author, Professor Winters indicated that the monograph version was his definitive utterance on the subject and may be considered to supersede any contradictory statements that appear in the earlier articles (see 2015). To my mind, however, the clearest exposition of Winters's theory comes in "The Non-diegetic Fallacy", where he offers a version of the following table. (Winters no longer uses the terminology listed in the table, as his goal is to steer us altogether away from considering film music in terms of narrative levels. Nevertheless, I present the table here as an important stage in the development of his thought.)

TABLE 3   *Winters's Model from "The Non-Diegetic Fallacy"*

I.	Extra-fictional
II.	Fictional
	1) Extra-diegetic
	2) Intra-diegetic (including meta-diegetic)
	3) Diegetic

There are liminal boundary spaces, specifically described as 'fantastical gaps', between the Extra-fictional and the Fictional, between the Extra-diegetic and the Intra-diegetic, and the Intra-diegetic and the Diegetic (cf. 2010: 237). Some clarification of terms is probably required. Extra-fictional music is music that is outside of the film's running time: a designated overture cue, for instance, or perhaps the 20th Century Fox fanfare (cf. ibid.). The various fictional categories are more to our purpose. Diegetic music means here exactly what it does in the Narratological Model. Extra-diegetic music, which is "deliberately distanced from the here-and-now of the narrative space's everyday world" (ibid.), is more or less equivalent to non-diegetic music. In that the model seems to contain equivalents for both classic terms, it would seem at first blush to be what I have described above as a 'pragmatic' challenge to the Narratological Model. However, Winters describes extra-diegetic music very much as a special effect. It is rare and must be flagged as extra-diegetic by the film. Most underscoring, we are told, falls into the new category of 'intra-diegetic' music, which Winters recognizes as the most radical and interesting part of his model (cf. ibid.). This refers to music that – while having no apparent in-world source – is nevertheless a part of the diegesis, and can be heard by the characters. Just as with diegetic music, of course, the fact that it can in principle be heard by some character does not mean that it is in fact heard by all characters at all times. What matters is that there is nothing more unusual about a character hearing intra-diegetic music than there is about a character hearing diegetic music.

As noted above, Winters no longer uses this terminology, and we will follow his example. Drawing on Winters's writings on this topic as a whole, however, we can derive the following set of non-hierarchical categories, which clearly correspond to the categories listed in the table. For any given passage of film music, one of the following statements will probably be true:

A)   The music has an apparent in-world source; characters can hear the music.

B)   The music has no apparent in-world source; nevertheless, characters can hear the music, which either seems to emanate directly from the characters or to more or less literally come out of the woodwork.

C)   The music is associated with an omniscient and omnipresent narrating presence (as in a montage sequence); characters cannot hear the music. Category C is rare, and must be specifically signaled. (The conditions for this third possibility will be explained in due course.)

The reader will note that I have made no attempt to describe the argument through which Winters justifies his theory. This is intentional. Winters has very interesting reasons for thinking as he does (ultimately grounded on the sensible claim that fictional worlds need not, and in fact do not, behave like the factual world), and even readers who are ultimately unconvinced by his theory would benefit from grappling with his critique of the Narratological Model. But none of this is material to the intervention I am trying to make. My point is that even Winters (who is presumably convinced by his own logic) should have to reconcile his argument with the test cases offered in the final part of this essay.

Or at least, he should do this if his argument is dogmatic (in the sense introduced above). Winters occasionally hedges his bets, offering his theory as a speculation of possibility rather than an assertion of fact (cf. 2014: 158). A theory that was really intended as a thought experiment would be a visionary one, and thus not vulnerable to my critique. But this is not Winters's intent: the theory is meant to accurately convey his own intuitive experiences, and he asks his readers "to believe that such responses are genuine" (ibid.: 7). What is more, he enlists our own experiences and intuitions in support of his argument by making use of examples and counterexamples. "Trying to imagine the opening idol-stealing scenes of *Raiders of the Lost Ark* (Steven Spielberg, 1981) without John Williams's music, is, I would suggest, an unnerving experience". (Ibid.: 83) Whether one agrees with this claim or not is beside the point. What matters is the structure of the argument: we are implicitly asked to try to imagine the scene in question, and see what we think of it. That is, we are to appeal to our *intuitive understanding* of the scene. And Winters, for his part, *intuitively* rejects the possibility that ordinary pieces of underscoring are non-diegetic in the narratological sense. But the Narratological Model is nothing more than a formalized way of describing our intuitions. To say that the Narratological Model is non-intuitive is to say that it is deluded. (And as we shall see, the test cases described below have less to do with music than with expectations: do we *assume* that a certain cue is non-diegetic until we see evidence to the contrary? Are we *surprised* to hear the rhythm of the underscoring picked up by a character's vocalizations? And so on.)

It may of course be the case that the Narratological Model is deluded, and should be discarded. But how can the scenes described below achieve their various effects without it? This is the question that we must pose of Winters, and which we will address in the next and final section of the paper. The lines of battle, at last, are drawn. Let us see what becomes of Winters's theory upon first contact with the enemy.

3   Test Case One: Comedy

3.1   *Homer and the Springfield Orchestra Bus in "The Springfield Files"*
Our first test comes from "The Springfield Files" (1997), the tenth episode of the eighth season of *The Simpsons*. A drunken Homer Simpson wanders down an isolated road on the outskirts of town. Eerie electronic music plays in the background, while Homer – too drunk to notice at first – realizes that there is something menacing about his surroundings. Suddenly, an engine is heard, and Homer is caught in the headlights of an approaching vehicle. Shrieking violins enter on the soundtrack (playing the famous murder cue from *Psycho*), and Homer screams in alarm ... and then Homer steps back to let the vehicle pull past him, and we learn that it is a bus containing the Springfield Philharmonic Orchestra, and that the *Psycho* cue is being played by the musicians. The bus stops to let off one of the violinists, and then drives away. Homer stares in consternation while the violinist continues to play – solo – her part from *Psycho*.

Although the specific example comes from *The Simpsons*, jokes of this kind can be found in Woody Allen's *Bananas* (1971), and Mel Brooks's *Blazing Saddles*

(1974). What makes this funny? The precise nature of humor is of course a vast topic, but one widely-held explanation is that humor derives from incongruity: we laugh when something defies our expectations. In this particular case, one of those expectations concerns the status of the music that we have been hearing. When the strings from *Psycho* come in, we instinctively recognize them as non-diegetic. When the bus pulls into frame, we suddenly realize that the music was diegetic all along. Our expectations are overturned, and so we laugh.

Of course, this explanation depends on our accepting some version of the Narratological Model. The test for those who wish to abandon that theory is not to explain where the music in this scene is coming from, but rather to explain the joke. For the joke is powered less by the music itself and more by *our intuitions about the music*. If we are surprised to learn that the music comes from somewhere, it would seem to follow that we initially assumed that the music was coming from nowhere: i.e., that on some level we intuitively recognize the existence of non-diegetic music as a category.

But alternative explanations for the joke do exist, and Winters's theory is capable of providing one. When the *Psycho* strings appear in "The Springfield Files", Homer is recognizably afraid. For the Winters of the "Musical Heartbeats" article, this is decisive: because the emotion in the underscoring matches the emotional experience of the character, we are to assume that the music is emanating from the character, and thus a part of the diegesis: we are in Winters's category B. When it turns out to have a more quotidian source (that is, when it turns out that we are in category A), there is incongruity, and therefore comedy. But note the consequence for the theory: category A and category B are evidently distinct enough that confusing one for the other is literally laughable. (Falling back to the language of the "Non-diegetic Fallacy" article for a moment: although Winters assures us that intra-diegetic music is in some sense *inside* the diegesis, for this joke to be funny we must intuitively recognize that intra-diegetic music, if not quite *non*-diegetic, is at the very least *not* diegetic.)

4   Test Case Two: Uncanniness

4.1   *The Murderer's Rhythmical Laughter in* L'ucello dalle piume di cristallo

In comedic contexts, crossings of the 'fantastical gap' are comedic. In most other contexts, they are uncanny. Our second test is drawn from two scenes in Dario Argento's *giallo* thriller, *L'ucello dalle piume di cristallo* (1970). Our first scene is the lead-up to a murder. As it opens, a young woman walks into an apartment building and ascends a triangular art-deco staircase. On the soundtrack, there is a murmuring of eerie drones and bell-like sounds, and perhaps a faint sound of breathing. Halfway up the stair, the lights cut out. The woman pulls out a book of matches and nervously lights one, continuing to ascend the staircase. A swirling piano figure enters in the background, increasing the tension. But so far, the music consists only of atmosphere. The woman's match burns out. She strikes another, and as it lights, illuminating her face, a voice enters the musical texture, rapidly singing "la-la-la-la-la-la-la" on a single pitch, slowly dropping in volume and blending into the bell-like sounds in the musical background. (A bit later, the murderer pops out of the shadows and dispatches her.)

Ennio Morricone's music for *L'uccello* is a wonderful demonstration of the principle that a theme need not be a melody. A theme can by any graspable musical feature that stands out from its musical context. The eerie "la-la-la-la-la" gesture in *L'uccello* is the central theme of the score. It appears frequently, sometimes multiple times within a single cue, and because it is so sonically weird, audience members aren't likely to ignore it. What's more, most of the film's music is essentially athematic: the typical cue is a swirling soup of musical atmosphere, much like the stairwell cue prior to the appearance of the vocal theme. As minimal as the vocal theme is, it is the most clearly defined sonic element in the entire soundtrack, and so we cling to it like a life preserver in a heavy sea. Assuming that one pays any attention to the music at all, one becomes highly attuned to this theme while watching the film.

Now consider a second scene, in which the killer calls up the police to taunt them. A crowd has gathered in front of a store window where a TV is broadcasting a special message from the police. The detective is describing the progress that they have made in their investigation of the murders. The camera pulls away, gliding through the crowd to a phone booth, which it enters. A leather-gloved hand reaches out from behind the camera, picks up the receiver, and dials. We cut to the police station, where a detective answers the phone. Eerie music creeps into the background of the soundtrack. Chiming sounds, a swirling piano figure: it is essentially the same music as the beginning of the stairwell sequence. And then the killer laughs. It is an odd, percussive sort of laugh, flat, quick, and mechanically rhythmic, "Ha-ha-ha-ha-ha-ha-ha-ha-ha". The effect is subtle but definite. The killer's laughter has the same rhythm, the same monotone flatness, and essentially the same dynamic profile as the vocal theme. (Interestingly, this only applies to the English language dub of the film. The Italian version has the killer laughing, but the laughter is neither rhythmic nor monotone. Might it be that, of the two soundtracks, only the English version was prepared after the score was recorded?)

In the comedy example we were confused about where the music was coming from. Here there is no such confusion. The music is non-diegetic music, throughout, and the laughter is diegetic laughter. But *musical details* have somehow made their way from the non-diegetic underscoring into the diegesis. If we were to apply a very inflexible version of the Narratological Model, this would be a problem. Under the Expanded Narratological Model, however, the laughter's violation of the normal split between diegetic and non-diegetic music becomes the entire point. It is eerie precisely because it is transgressive. (This is how horror films work more generally: the werewolf moves between the categories of man and beast, here, the killer moves between categories on the soundtrack.)

Turning to Winters's theory, it would initially seem that this particular test poses no difficulty whatsoever. If anything, the killer's laughter makes more sense for Winters than it does for the Narratological Model: when we hear the killer's laugh, we realize that the killer has access to this sourceless music, and thus we are firmly in category B. The problem, however, is precisely that the music fits Winters's model so well. Under Winters's theory, category B should *always* be a possibility. (It should be the dominant possibility, in fact.) We ought to assume that any character might at any time start singing along with the underscoring. How, then, are we to account for the laughter's chilling and transgressive effect? I see only two ways out of this.[1] One is to say that most people would *not* feel that anything musically strange is happening in that phone call. (I tend to reject this, but perhaps my sensibility has been warped by my years of working with the Narratological Model.) The other would be to say that, indeed, the laugh is chilling, because, while the characters can *in principle* hear the underscoring, it is surprising and frightening, and suggestive of madness, for them to ever *actually* hear it. And if it comes as a surprise for a character to hear the underscoring in Winters's model, doesn't this suggest that, all else being equal, we have a strong tendency to assume that the characters have no more access to the music of Winters's category B than they would to classically non-diegetic music? On this account, Winters's theory is still structurally sound, in that it is possible to describe the scene through its

---

1   A third possibility (which occurred to me only after consulting with Professor Winters directly, although we did not discuss this specific clip), is to suppose that the characters can routinely hear the underscoring, but generally do not acknowledge that they can hear it. I have difficulty accepting this, however: it suggests that the characters operate under a taboo that is, on the one hand, literally inconceivable for us (since we cannot know what it feels like to hear this kind of music or understand why it would be unmentionable), but which, on the other hand, we grasp on a deep unconscious level (because without consciously thinking about it, we are still startled to see the taboo violated).

concepts. But for me, this test weakens (or perhaps even destroys) one of the theory's central features.

5 Test Case Three: Asynchronicity in Vertical Montage

5.1 *The Temporally Specific Moment of Recognition in* Penny Serenade

The third test is taken from George Stevens's *Penny Serenade* (1941). The film tells the story of Julie and her husband Roger, a newspaper reporter. Early in the film, Julie suffers a miscarriage, and is told that she can never again become pregnant. Our scene takes place immediately after this tragic reversal. Roger has always dreamed of starting his own newspaper, and he and Julie are being shown around the print shop that he has rented for his new business. Other than music, the scene takes place in complete silence. The real estate agent cheerfully points out features of the building to Roger, who nods enthusiastically. Julie, however, is entirely still, staring past the camera at something that we do not see. A descending sequential string figure plays (expressive of nothing save for a vague sense of emotional warmth), eventually coming to rest on a dominant harmony. Two things then happen simultaneously. The camera whips away from Julie to reveal what she has been staring at: a painting of a smiling infant. And on the soundtrack, we hear a melody – powerfully highlighted through its volume, voicing, and register – which throughout the film has served as a leitmotif for Julie's frustrated desire for a child.

This leitmotif tells us something about Julie's emotion, but the important point for our purposes here is not the content but the recipient of this message: the leitmotif tells *us*. It tells no one else. Significantly, there is no diegetic character who could share this experience of the music, because none of them share our temporal orientation to the painting. The leitmotif is synchronized with the moment of revelation, but it is only the audience to whom the painting is revealed.

Under the Narratological Model, this is trivially explained. The music in this scene is non-diegetic. (So too, in a sense, is the camera movement that reveals the painting, although the painting itself is diegetic.) It is foundational to the Narratological Model that non-diegetic music is directed to the audience. This is usually brought up in relation to the music's ability to shape emotional response (the music makes the audience sad, it doesn't make the characters sad), or the music's informational content (only the audience has heard the *Jaws* theme; only the audience knows not to go in the water), or the realistic consistency of the diegetic world (there is no orchestra on the surface of the moon). Less attention has been paid to the specifically temporal aspect of the music's 'for-us-ness', but I would argue that it is equally important. It is this aspect of the *Penny Serenade* sequence that I offer as my third test.

In that this example hinges on a precisely timed synchronization of music and image, the effect can be thought of as an aspect of montage (specifically, vertical montage).[2] Interestingly enough, Winters carves out an exception in his early theory for some types of montage, arguing in "The Non-diegetic Fallacy" that when confronted with something like the training montages from the *Rocky* franchise, we *do* have to think of something like non-diegetic music in Gorbman's sense: "Music that functions to unify a montage sequence might well be understood as 'narrating' from an external perspective the events we are witnessing, passing in a compressed time frame, and be labelled legitimately 'nondiegetic' or, perhaps more appropriately, 'extradiegetic'". (2010: 236) Winters's reasoning here is that the montage sequence "plays with cinematic time" (ibid.). We see what are evidently little snippets excerpted from several months' worth of time in the story-world, but we experience these as a continuous temporal flow of perhaps two or three minutes. In these sequences, musical time is aligned with audience time: it is continuous and brief, rather than discontinuous and long.

In his later monograph, Winters offers an alternative explanation according to which the characters actually experience the time of cinematic montage just as the audience does. Of a montage sequence in *The Best Years of Our Lives* (William Wyler, 1946), he writes that the characters "do not experience [the sequence] as a fractured series of images [...] because the music lends it the same sense of continuity for them as it does for us" (2014: 192). But I find his earlier argument far more convincing. Indeed, Winters's reasoning on this point in "The Non-diegetic Fallacy" strikes me as entirely persuasive, and constitutes a valuable contribution to our understanding of montage. However, the effect is more general than he seems to recognize. Suppose that, rather than an extended montage sequence, we limit ourselves to a single instant of montage, cutting from a shot of a ship leaving New York to a shot of the same ship pulling into Liverpool, ten days later. During this transition, five seconds pass for the audience, and five seconds of continuous music are played. Surely, this too plays with time? Surely, this music too is linked to the temporal experience

---

2   Vertical montage is a concept developed by Sergei Eisenstein. It follows from Eisenstein's broader theory of montage, in which any juxtaposition of two ideas – paradigmatically through the editing together of two strips of film – will give rise to a third idea in the mind of the audience. Vertical montage is Eisenstein's term for juxtapositions that are simultaneous rather than concurrent. Although the concept was developed to account for sound-image relationships, Eisenstein specifically notes that it is applicable to any simultaneous juxtaposition whatsoever (cf. 1942/1975: 74–80).

of the audience (and removed from the temporal experience of the characters)? How do we explain montages of the type that Sergei Eisenstein specialized in, where, rather than compressing large stretches of time, the montage *expands* time while juxtaposing facets of a single dramatic event? How do we even explain D.W. Griffith's montage of crosscutting? All of these are examples of montage, and all of them create the same problem: the music stays in a single time and place while the images jump about between two or more. And as the *Penny Serenade* example shows, similar effects can appear even in the vertical montage of a single shot. The components of the montage, in this particular case, are the camera movement, the painting, the leitmotif, and – crucially – Julie's emotional state. Three of these are synchronized, but not the fourth.

In that Winters's early theory carves out an exception for the more extravagant varieties of montage, there is no difficulty in using that same exception to account for all of the montage effects described above. But this does not leave the theory unscathed. In principle, under Winters's theory, the music in the *Penny Serenade* sequence has two potential sources: it could be category B, emanating from the bereaved mother, whose emotion it seems to express (or perhaps from the painting itself), or it could be category C, music that arises from an omniscient and omnipresent narrator. Category C is supposed to be an exceptional case, reserved for special effects such as large-scale montage sequences. But only category C aligns with the temporality of the sequence. The mother was already aggrieved, and the painting already present, well before the leitmotif became audible. (And note that even under Winters's later theory, in which characters are supposed to experience montages just as the audience does, this scene would be a problem. To avoid category C, we would have to believe Julie does not see the painting while she is staring at it, but that she sees it as soon as it is shown to the audience – by which point she is no longer looking!) Montage poses no problem for Winters's theory in that he recognizes it as an exceptional case. But montage is an inescapable aspect of film grammar – and therefore we may find ourselves falling back on this exception more often than is strictly comfortable. (And let us recall that category C is functionally identical with the traditional category of non-diegetic music.)

6   Test Case Four: MERM implies MURM

6.1   *The Laughable Snare Drum Tattoo in* Lagaan

Nothing in Gorbman's theorization of the Narratological Model demands that it always apply to every sort of film. What she describes is the classical

Hollywood style. Other film traditions may have other filmic grammars, and even within Hollywood we may detect alternative traditions. I use the term 'traditions' advisedly: what matters, again, is less the specific filmic text than the *expectations* which audience members bring to bear on that text. Are there categories of films within the Hollywood tradition that invite a different model of spectatorship? That is, are there films to which the Narratological Model does not intuitively apply?

There is at least one: the musical. When characters burst into song, accompanied by an invisible orchestral accompaniment to the beat of which they dance and sway, audiences intuitively accept this as a generically determined feature of the musical. This requires us to hold two apparently contradictory facts as true: the characters are aware of the music, and the music has no source within the world of the film. This violates physical laws, of course. But then, musicals frequently demonstrate a certain contempt for the laws, not only of physics, but even of logic and causality. Characters dance on ceilings, instantaneously change their costumes and location, and levitate out of swimming pools on sparkler-bedecked scaffolds. Raymond Knapp describes this aspect of the musical as "MERM: Musically Enhanced Reality Mode" (2010: 67). While MERM is in operation we do not question any of the bizarreries that the musical genre habitually gives rise to.

We should distinguish between the physical violations that are features of MERM and the physical violations that appear in science fiction and fantasy. When Fred Astaire starts dancing on the ceiling, we don't expect him to ever be able to do it again once the sequence is over. (The next time he needs to change a lightbulb, he'll break out a stepladder.) When Yoda levitates a spaceship, however, this feat goes into our list of Yoda's attributes. In a sense, it is only Astaire who violates the laws of physics. Yoda merely reveals that the laws of physics in *Star Wars* are different than we had heretofore supposed. MERM is a consequence-free zone: events that transpire within it do not require us to update our understanding of the nature of the cinematic world.

But as Knapp and others have noted, it is not the case that musicals are always in MERM. Indeed, as musical sequences begin, they often slip into MERM gradually: a song begins with diegetic piano accompaniment in a songwriter's garret apartment, and then the (non-diegetic) orchestra takes over, and then there is a flourish in the strings, and suddenly the characters are dancing atop the Eiffel tower. We are now in MERM. What were we in before?

Knapp contrasts MERM with reality. In a few unusual musicals, he notes, "no one steps out of the film's real world for even a moment's worth of undiluted MERM" (ibid.: 93). For Knapp, this is of primarily interpretive interest: what does it mean that these shows do not indulge in this particular fantasy? But we can borrow his concept to advance our essentially formalist discussion. When we are not in MERM, we are in some other mode, which we might term MURM (Musically Un-enhanced Reality Mode). MURM prevents characters from dancing on the ceiling. It may prevent – and this is closer to Knapp's point – the utopian imagination of sexual, racial, and gendered identities which move beyond the scripts offered by mainstream social expectations. And it also has purely musical effects. MURM reinstates the distinction between diegetic and non-diegetic music. For it is not the case that the only music in film musicals is that of the musical numbers. There is other music, sometimes a great deal of it, and during the MURM sequences, it obeys the standard Hollywood grammar of the Narratological Model.

This much is background to the fourth test case, which hinges on the qualitative difference between MERM and MURM. One might choose any musical: I have chosen Ashutosh Gowariker's *Lagaan* (2001). One might choose any two scenes in which the contrast can be recognized: my choices are the musical number "Ghanan Ghanan", and the non-musical scene in which the villainous Captain Russell is called on the carpet by his superior officers in the British army. There is a moment in "Ghanan, Ghanan" in which two characters, while dancing to the backing track of the song (which would ostensibly be non-diegetic, were we not in MERM), seize a pair of sticks adorned with jingles, which they shake and strike together, adding another layer of (ostensibly diegetic) rhythm to the music. Throughout the song, whether they are producing the music or not, they dance in time with its beat.

The scene with Captain Russell takes place in MURM, but the soundtrack is busy with non-diegetic music. Militaristic instruments are heard, most notably a trumpet and a snare drum tattoo. The music closely mirrors the cut and thrust of the conversation, and there are moments where, as characters make sharp gestures to emphasize their rhetorical points, the snare drum Mickey-Mouses their physical motions. Here, the fact that the characters are moving in time with the music strikes one as excessive, delirious, risible.

It may be that I am applying an inappropriate standard, derived from American cinematic culture, to a film shaped by Indian cinematic culture. But this tends rather to strengthen than to weaken the point that I am trying to make: there are standards for the operation of non-diegetic music which, as habitual consumers of Hollywood cinema, we apply to all music that strikes us as non-diegetic. This includes the music in the Captain Russell scene, but under no circumstance would it occur to us to apply these standards to anything that takes place in MERM. The synchronization that takes place in "Ghanan, Ghanan", although equally impossible, does not strike us as risible, or even as odd.

MERM, in short, is an exception to the Narratological Model. While MERM applies, it is usually still possible to tell which sounds have sources within the physical world of the film and which do not, but the distinction ceases to matter. We are no longer apt to feel amusement or fear when the categories become confused. That said, MERM is the exception, MURM is the rule. The fact that we can recognize MERM turning on and off demonstrates – to my mind, at least – that the Narratological Model is more than a chimera of the scholarly imagination.

I take this final example to be particularly damaging to Winters's theory, because the kind of world he describes, where music emanates from every object, and the characters could very well hear it at any time, is quite precisely Musically Enhanced Reality Mode. We could potentially use this to prove once again that Winters's category B is unusual, and that ordinary cinematic experience is solidly grounded in the categories that map onto the Narratological Model. But Winters might well respond that there *is* no difference between MERM and a 'normal' scene, that we should never be surprised if music sounds like this or if characters react to music in this way, and that if we were surprised by it, it would reveal an error in our thinking. Indeed, he does suggest that one benefit of his theory is that it would give film music the same "agency [...] which it enjoys in other fictional genres, such as opera and musical theater" (2010: 243). But note that this response, while neatly defusing the challenge posed by this pair of scenes from *Lagaan*, would essentially make Winters's account of film music into a visionary theory rather than a dogmatic one.

7   Conclusions

In each of the test cases described above, the musical effects depend on our expectations. The diegetic/non-diegetic split is not a fact of the cinematic text: it is a set of perceptual habits which shape our response to film music even when the music itself confounds the usual categories. This is very much the point that Stilwell makes in her "Fantastical Gap" article, and it resonates strongly with opinions offered by scholars such as Anahid Kassabian and David Neumeyer during the roundtable discussion in which Stilwell first coined the term (cf. Buhler, and Kassabian, Neumeyer, Stilwell 2003: 76).

But if this experiential description of the narratological model has already been entered into the scholarly record, why restate it? The answer is that Stilwell's article has not proved the last word on the subject. Later scholars have continued to advance the claim that the distinction ought to be abandoned. And who knows but that they may not some day be proven right? If the Narratological Model is to be discarded, however, the theory that replaces it will have to account for the scenes described in this essay, just as the theories that eventually replaced the Ptolemaic model of the solar system had to account for the retrograde motion of heavenly bodies. Iconoclastic theorists of film music ought therefore to test their theories on these or similar cases.

As hinted at the outset of this exercise, Winters's theory did not founder on any of the examples. It passes all four tests. But in the process, our application and interpretation of the theory has subtly changed. It is possible, even under Winters's theory, to conclude that we have a strong intuitive expectation that characters cannot hear the underscoring. (We must, because we are surprised whenever they do so.) Winters's original model did not include this premise, and if we add it, the theory looks much less distinctive and colorful. It may still be a valuable contribution to our understanding of film music, but it feels more like a pragmatic theory (i.e., an expansion on the Narratological Model rather than an alternative to it). On the other hand, the same scenes could be understood by recasting Winters's theory as visionary – and with regard to the fourth test, at least, it does seem probable that Winters would ask us to distort or outright reject our intuitive understanding of the film in order to preserve the reading that is implicit in his model.

Although Winters's model is, on the whole, a dogmatic one, there are certain passages where he advances both pragmatic and visionary lines of thought. It may be that, in order to handle the four tests described in this essay, we ended up using these pragmatic or visionary moments as a sort of intellectual escape hatch. This sort of insight, to my mind, is the real value of the four test cases, and of this entire essay. I don't expect to convince anyone to abandon their carefully constructed theories. But perhaps, in the process of addressing these problematic cases, scholars will be forced to think more carefully about the nature and scope of the claims they are trying to make.

References

Bordwell, David, Kristin Thompson (1979/2001). *Film Art: An Introduction*. 6th ed. New York, NY: McGraw-Hill.

Buhler, James, et al. (2003). "Panel Discussion on Film Sound/Film Music: Jim Buhler, Anahid Kassabian, David Neumeyer, and Robynn Stilwell". *The Velvet Light Trap* 51/1: 73–91.

Eisenstein, Sergei (1942/1975). *The Film Sense*. Trans. Jay Leyda. New York, NY: Harcourt, Brace & Co.

Gorbman, Claudia (1987). *Unheard Melodies: Narrative Film Music*. Bloomington, IN: Indiana Univ. Press.

Knapp, Raymond (2010). *The American Musical and the Performance of Personal Identity*. Princeton, NJ: Princeton Univ. Press.

Redner, Gregg (2011). *Deleuze and Film Music: Building a Methodological Bridge between Film Theory and Music*. Bristol/Chicago, IL: Intellect Books.

Stilwell, Robynn (2007). "The Fantastical Gap between Diegetic and Non-diegetic". Daniel Goldmark, Lawrence Kramer, Richard Leppert, eds. *Beyond the Soundtrack: Representing Music in Cinema*. Berkeley, CA: University of California Press. 184–202.

Winters, Ben (2008). "Corporeality, Musical Heartbeats, and Cinematic Emotion". *Music, Sound, and the Moving Image* 2/1: 3–25.

Winters, Ben (2010). "The Non-diegetic Fallacy: Film, Music, and Narrative Space". *Music and Letters* 91/2: 224–244.

Winters, Ben (2012). "Musical Wallpaper? Towards an Appreciation of Non-narrating Music in Film". *Music, Sound, and the Moving Image* 6/1: 39–54.

Winters, Ben (2014). *Music, Performance, and the Realities of Film: Shared Concert Experiences in Screen Fiction*. New York, NY: Routledge.

Winters, Ben (2015). E-mail to the author, Nov. 27, 2015.

SECTION 2

Film Music: Significant Intermedial Cases

∵

CHAPTER 5

Operatic Plurimediality in Italian Silent Cinema: Nino Oxilia and Pietro Mascagni's *Rapsodia Satanica* (1915)

Bernhard Kuhn

Abstract

During the 1910s, Italian cinema made significant aesthetic advances and became more accepted as artistic medium. Many films from the early 1910s, in particular prestigious longer productions, employ references to other media, such as literature, theater, dance, and opera, and explicitly and implicitly highlight similarities or differences between those media and film. While references to other media have been incorporated in films since the early days of cinema, in the longer films of the early 1910s, their primary cultural function was to improve cinema's cultural acceptance. In this context, *Rapsodia Satanica* (1915, by Nino Oxilia, music by Pietro Mascagni) is of particular significance, aesthetically as well as culturally. At the time, the film was compared to Wagner's musical dramas. While such a comparison might have served primarily a publicity purpose, *Rapsodia Satanica* certainly employs recognizable references to literature and music theater. Most importantly, it conveys an operatic sensation throughout the film. This operatic sensation is not created through Mascagni's music alone, but primarily through the relationship between images and music and other implicit operatic references. Furthermore, by incorporating intermedial references, *Rapsodia Satanica* responds to the film–art debate of the time period with unique artistic means. *Rapsodia Satanica* thus proves that cinema is able to create products of high artistic value appealing to a bourgeois audience.

• • •

Nino Oxilia's film *Rapsodia Satanica* and Pietro Mascagni's score were both completed in 1915 and presented to a selected audience of critics and intellectuals in March 1915. Although this preview was very well received, the first public screening was delayed until 1917 for unknown reasons (cf. Martinelli 1991: 248). Unfortunately, at that moment, the film did not receive much attention neither among the Italian audience nor the contemporary media[1] and was

---

1 The few reviews of the film in 1917 were all very positive, see Martinelli 1991.

subsequently lost, as it happened to many early films. Fortunately, Mascagni's score and an almost complete copy of the film were found and could be restored. Recently, on July 4, 2015, about 100 years after its completion, the film was screened together with Mascagni's score at the Teatro Comunale in Bologna in the context of the Festival del Cinema Ritrovato, Bologna's annual silent film festival.[2] After the spectacle, Esvan wrote:

> It was the intention of Nino Oxilia, a multi-faceted artist, to create a Gesamtkunstwerk. [...] At the end of the projection, I can say that the effect of the Gesamtkunstwerk has been reached. The audience applauded for many minutes the splendid work completed to give re-birth to such an ambitious experiment. The work has really paid off: yesterday evening 100 years felt like an instant.[3]

While it seems that the audience who attended the 2015 screening in Bologna enjoyed the audio-visual spectacle in an era where we are used to digital TV and 3-D cinema, Oxilia and Mascagni's work is even more impressive when we consider it in the context of early silent cinema.

Films were produced at least since 1895, but it took more than one decade for cinema to be established as a new medium among the other forms of entertainment and artistic expression. Crucial for the development of cinema as an art form were the 1910s when Italian cinema made significant technological and aesthetic advances and therefore became increasingly accepted as a new artistic medium. During this period, Italy created technically and aesthetically highly advanced films (cf. Carluccio 2014: 30f.).

Many films of this period, in particular prestigious longer productions of the early 1910s, such as *L'Inferno* (1911), *Cabiria* (1914), or *Rapsodia Satanica* (1915), employ easily recognizable references to literature and other media. This article reflects on the incorporation of such intermedial references in *Rapsodia Satanica* and demonstrates *how* and *why* this film makes use of them. It argues that *Rapsodia Satanica* skillfully combines cinematic characteristics with musical, pictorial, and other intermedial elements in order to elicit an

---

2 The orchestra of the Teatro Comunale performed under the direction of Timothy Brock.

3 "L'intento di Nino Oxilia, artista poliedrico, era quello di creare un'opera d'arte totale. [...] Al termine della proiezione posso dire che l'effetto di opera d'arte totale è stato raggiunto. Il pubblico ha applaudito per lunghi minuti lo splendido lavoro fatto per ridare vita a un esperimento tanto ambizioso. Il lavoro fatto è stato davvero ripagato: ieri sera cento anni sono sembrati un attimo". (Esvan 2015 online; my translation).

operatic sensation. Of particular significance in this regard is the plurimedial combination between the filmic image and Mascagni's music, which offers a unique audiovisual spectacle with a substantial narrative role of the music.

1   Intermediality in Early Italian Cinema

The incorporation of intermedial references in film is not an invention of the Italian cinema of the 1910s. From the early days of cinema, film had a relationship with literature and the stage media and many film stories were based on literary texts, operas, or plays. Literature and theater thus served film first of all on the content level by providing the story, which would be presented on film. Particularly active in this migration from page or stage to screen in Italy was the production company Film d'Arte Italiana, which, starting in 1909, produced adaptations of literary, operatic, and theatrical works. Its declared goal was to enhance the prestige of film. In addition to borrowing storylines from literature and theater, these early artistic films also adopted acting and presentation techniques from the stage media. The cast of many of these typically short adaptations included stage actors, who generally did not change their acting style in front of the camera (cf. Jandelli 2014: 65f.). The camera usually had an observing rather than narrating function and communicated visually in a fairly neutral manner. The dominant aesthetic was the tableaux style in which the camera generally presented the mise en scène from a fixed point and the viewer got the impression of watching the scene from one specific position, much like watching a play or any other stage event from a seat in the theater.[4]

Considering the audience of early Italian cinema, we know that since its beginnings, cinema had been a very popular form of entertainment in Italy, but it took several years until intellectuals and the bourgeois audience began recognizing it as a respected medium of artistic expression. At first, cinema was primarily considered a popular spectacle comparable to the circus or variety shows, and critics or intellectuals largely ignored the new medium. Around 1907, the newly founded cinema magazines as well as the daily press began writing about films and the institution of cinema. Although these magazines frequently wrote favorably about cinema,[5] many professional critics as well

---

4   Regarding stylistic aspects of early Italian cinema see Salt 1991.
5   Magazines might have promoted certain films because production companies often sponsored the magazines and used them for advertisement purposes.

as other public authorities, such as politicians or judges, expressed serious doubts about this new form of entertainment. It was not uncommon to see critics accuse films of immorality and sensationalism because of the inclusion of materials not conforming to the societal ideal of the cultural authorities (cf. Alovisio 2014: 17–19). Italy's Prime Minister Giovanni Giolitti defined cinema once as 'a real and powerful school of evil'[6] and thus de facto introduced state censorship in 1913. Analyzing the criticism against cinema, the film historian Aldo Bernardini speaks appropriately of a campaign against cinema (cf. 1981: 194). In addition to moralistic arguments against cinema, cultural critics frequently compared cinema to the highly respected art form of theater. While some critics admitted seeing future potential in the new medium, in the early 1910s, cinema was seen first of all as an industrial and commercial enterprise, generating works primarily of a reproductive nature (cf. De Berti 2014: 323). The competition between the media and the growing popularity of cinema seem the cause for the fear that cinema could undermine the cultural dominance of theater, which further increased the aversion against the newer medium (cf. Brunetta 1993: 121f.).

This generally negative attitude towards cinema slowly changed during the second decade of the twentieth century. While the adaptation of prestigious literary works, such as Dante's *Divine Comedy*, or the more serious involvement of novelists or musicians, such as Gabriele D'Annunzio or Ildebrando Pizzetti,[7] with the new medium might have helped improve cinema's reputation, the debate on whether cinema might be considered art was resolved only after the creation of films like *Cabiria* (1914) or *Rapsodia Satanica* (1915), which seem to have converted many of the most categorically critical voices against cinema. Interestingly, these high-quality films frequently include intermedial references in addition to incorporating advanced cinematic means, and specifically composed or compiled music.[8] The following analysis of *Rapsodia Satanica* will highlight the intermedial references in the film and thus underscore its intermedial and particularly operatic quality.

---

6 "[...] una vera e potente scuola del male" (qtd. Alovisio 2014: 19; my translation).
7 I am referring to the films *L'inferno* (1911) and *Cabiria* (1914). Both, Gabriele D'Annunzio and Ildebrando Pizzetti, worked for *Cabiria* (1914); see Kuhn 2012.
8 My terminology is based on theories of intermediality developed by Wolf (see 2002) and Rajewsky (see 2002). Of particular relevance for the analysis of the relationship between film and other art forms in the 1910s are "intermedial references" in film, which refer to specific different media, such as literature, painting, or opera. These references are either part of the film's story ('histoire') and thematize the other medium or are part of a medium's semiotic structure ('discours') and imitate the other medium.

2   *Rapsodia Satanica* (1915)

Rapsodia Satanica was produced in 1915 by the Roman production company Cines, which at the time was one of the largest production companies in Italy. The screenplay was written by the poet Fausto Maria Martini and Alberto Fassini, one of Cines's directors.[9] At the first screenings of *Rapsodia Satanica*, a libretto was distributed, which on the title page highlights Mascagni's name and defines the cinematographic spectacle as "poema cinema-musicale". The libretto included the poem *Rapsodia Satanica* by Fausto Maria Martini, who also wrote the intertitles for the film. Interestingly, this poem was written after the completion of the film and poetically refers to the plot of *Rapsodia Satanica*. Stylistically, Martini's poem is written in irregular eleven-syllable verse and is reminiscent of D'Annunzio's style with exaggerated metaphors or literary clichés. The film itself is part of the genre 'diva film', which was highly successful in the 1910s. According to Dalle Vacche, the diva film is typically a melodrama with a famous actress who on the one hand seems to be a strong, beautiful and dangerous femme fatale, and on the other hand is a mater dolorosa suffering because of aging, abandonment, and adultery (cf. 2005: 92f.). The main actress in *Rapsodia Satanica* is Lyda Borelli.

Rapsodia Satanica is divided into three parts: a prologue, a first part, and a second part. During the prologue, the female protagonist, an elderly countess with the expressive name of Alba d'Oltrevita, hosts a party. "Alba d'Oltrevita" means 'dawn beyond life'. The younger guests leave and she remains alone in her castle, mourning the loss of her youth and envying Faust, who is depicted in a painting next to Mephistopheles. At this moment, Mephistopheles steps out of the painting and offers Alba the chance to be young once more if she promises never to love again. She accepts. During the first part of the film, two young brothers begin courting her. One is called Tristano, the other Sergio. Alba rejects Sergio, but can't resist falling in love with Tristano. When Tristano kisses Alba, Sergio commits suicide. Tristano feels guilty about his brother's death and leaves. During the second part, Alba locks up the castle and is suffering the pain of her love for Tristano. Mephistopheles comes and tells her that every night Tristano rides over the mountains. She tells her servants to open the doors and prepare the house for the guest. She decorates the rooms with flowers. Expecting Tristano in the garden, she encounters Mephistopheles who makes her return to her old age since Alba did not keep her promise to never love again. She looks at her reflection in the pond and dies.

---

9   Fassini wrote under the pseudonym Alfa.

Already this brief summary of the plot reveals some explicit references to other media. It is obviously a story based on the Faust legend, but the main character here is not a scholar, but a woman played by Lyda Borelli, the diva of the film. Since its creation in the 16th century, the Faust story has been rendered in many different art forms, most notably perhaps in Goethe's dramas, but also in the operas by Gounod and Berlioz, which were frequently adapted by early cinema.

In connection with the Faust myth, the film also contains an explicit reference to the art of painting by showing a portrait of Mephistopheles and Faust. Since in the film Mephistopheles literally steps out of the painting, the film incorporates the other medium in a self-referential way highlighting the different possibilities of painting and filming. In contrast to the art of painting, the medium of film has the technical means to create the illusion of a person stepping out of a painting. At the same time, the depiction of a person stepping out of a painting recalls the coming to life of the portrait in E.T.A. Hoffmann's "Rat Krespel". This tale is also the textual basis of the Antonia act of Offenbach's *Les contes d'Hoffmann.*

From an intermedial point of view also noteworthy are the costumes, especially those worn by Lyda Borelli alias Alba. During the first part, she wears a costume depicting Salome. Salome represents the femme fatale myth, and it was Oscar Wilde's *Salomé* that made Borelli famous in Italy on stage in 1902 (cf. Dalle Vacche 2005: 97). But *Salome* is also the title of Strauss's famous opera. Through the Salome costume, the film thus points to the stage media of theater and opera.

From the beginning of the second part, we see Alba wearing a white dress and a long white veil. When shortly before her death the veil flutters in a dance-like fashion behind her, we may interpret this as a reference to the medium of dance and more specifically to the dancer Loïe Fuller, who was famous for dancing with flowing silk costumes (cf. ibid.: 96f.).

In addition to literature or the stage media theater, opera, and dance, the medium of architecture is evoked in the form of Alba's castle, which is portrayed from the inside as well as from the outside. Significant is also its name, "Castello delle meraviglie" ('Castle of Wonders'), which ought to be read in a self-referential way as an allegory to the movie theater, especially if we take into consideration the sudden appearances or disappearances of the devil or the rapid change of Alba's age (cf. ibid.: 98). We may even see it as an homage to Meliès's early trick films.

While these explicit intermedial references are certainly recognizable, the most culturally significant reference links the film to the medium of opera. This linkage is particularly apparent in the relationship between music and screened images.

3　　Image and Music

Regarding the role of music in plurimedial artforms, Gier notes with respect to operas that in many contemporary operas the function of music is akin to a film score since the music doesn't take an active part in the opera's narrative (cf. 2011 online). The function of music in those instances thus is rather reduced to melodramatic intensification or background sound. For music to be part of the narrative, music must be an "indispensable complement to the words" (ibid.). Music may, for example, express things that words cannot say, allude to hidden meaning in the text, or summarize long verbal explanations in a few measures. Therefore, according to Gier, in good operas, the plot leaves room for music to become a central narrative element.

While in his comparison with film music Gier probably thought primarily of today's Hollywood standards for feature films, which are certainly different from Cines and Mascagni's aesthetic expectations in 1915, what is of primary significance is his reflection on the narrative significance of music within a plurimedial work of art, in his case contemporary opera, and his claim that in opera music should have a narrative function.

Adopting Gier's argument for the plurimedial artform of cinema, I would argue that in order for film music to become a central element within the film's narrative, the other media need to leave room for the music. With respect to *Rapsodia Satanica*, it is therefore the question what significance Mascagni's score has within the cinematographic spectacle.

In early cinema, music generally played a role subordinate to the images. Its most important function was to offer a substitute for the muteness of the images. Furthermore, music typically emphasized certain filmic elements in a melodramatic fashion. Cue sheets were standard practice and only very few films had a compilation of particular pieces or a specifically composed score. Concerning Italian silent cinema, only 19 out of the 9816 Italian silent films had original scores (cf. Simeon 1991: 109). The most impressive example is arguably the score to *Rapsodia Satanica*. From Mascagni's letters we know that he attempted to connect the music with the images as precisely as possible. He also had an agreement with Oxilia and the production company Cines that the music should have priority over the other aesthetic elements (cf. Piccardi 1990: 460). Mascagni's significant role in the production of the film becomes obvious when we take in consideration that he requested a different ending from the one originally envisioned by Oxilia. The film ends referencing a Wagnerian Liebestod. Consequently, also Martini's poem makes reference to Wagner's *Tristan und Isolde* by explicitly comparing Alba to Isolde who is expecting her Tristan at the end of Wagner's opera: "Come Isaotta dal crine di sole, come

Isaotta dagli occhi di mare, offrì l'invito dei suoi cento veli lasciando che per entro vi cantasse il vento una sua rapsodia di nozze".[10]

While Mascagni's score to *Rapsodia Satanica* is a musical work which independently from the images has been evaluated as a valuable piece of music (see Huck 2004), for our 'purpose the music's relationship with the film's images and its narrative significance are most relevant. Like the film, Mascagni's score is divided into three parts, and Mascagni introduces several musical elements connecting the three parts of his score. First, he introduces leitmotifs, characterizing the main characters, as well as recurring themes defining certain moments or sentiments, such as love or the desire to be young (cf. Fabich 1993: 162–189). These themes are directly connected with the narrative of the film and thus at times convey significant narrative elements communicated neither through the images nor the intertitles.

Remarkable is further that contrary to the common practice of seeking to synchronize each film scene with corresponding musical elements, Mascagni incorporates specific musical forms, such as a Gavotte during the prologue, a Scherzo during the first part, or a dance piece "alla polacca" in the second part.[11] These pieces are predominantly formed according to their musical specifications. Their rhythm generally doesn't follow the filmic images and each piece encompasses several film sequences. Within those larger musical forms, however, musical elements clearly referring to the filmic images are included, such as motifs pointing to persons or events. The result is that a motif, which for instance is connected to a character, briefly interrupts the piece, explicitly connecting music and image in that moment. Immediately following, the music continues independently from the images. In the prologue, for example, (see Figure 5.1) when the character Mephistopheles and his theme are introduced for the first time, a Gavotte first accompanies the images from Alba's party for which it provides the couleur locale. The Gavotte is interrupted by the Mephistopheles motif, but continues immediately after the motif.

This technique to interrupt the musical forms can be observed throughout the score. Not always, however, is it musically effective since several times a musical motif is incorporated tautologically. In the second part, for example, in order to communicate Alba's longing for her lover, the camera several times shows Tristano on a horse while the orchestra plays Tristano's motif. One could say with Adorno that here the music is reduced to being a "musikalischer

---

10   Alfa/Martini 2006: 80. ('Like Isolde with her sun like hair, like Isolde with her sea like eyes, she offered the invitation of her hundred veils, allowing that when he enters the wind sings one of its marriage rhapsodies'. My translation).

11   The first part is divided into Scherzo–Trio–Scherzo, which matches the three parts of the narrative: dance scene in the garden – scene by the lake – scene in the garden. The second part also includes an Andantino pastorale and a Minuet (cf. Campana 2015: 180–182).

FIGURE 5.1 *Rapsodia Satanica,* Prologue, rehearsal no. 3, mm. 1–12
Note: For editorial reasons, this article refers to Mascagni's piano score
(see Mascagni 1917). In the orchestral score, the quoted excerpt corresponds
to Mascagni 1961: 11–13.

Kammerdiener" (a 'musical valet'; Adorno/Eisler, 1974: 38) since it communi-
cates what the images already show.

Mascagni's score also includes explicit citations from two Chopin pieces,
specifically the *Ballade I, op. 23* (Figure 5.2: *Rapsodia Satanica,* Part I, rehearsal
no. 34, mm. 1–16) and the *Valse op. 34 no. 2* (Figure 5.3: *Rapsodia Satanica,* Part
II, rehearsal no. 1, mm. 7–16).[12] In both instances, the camera shows Alba at the
piano and there seems to be an almost perfect synchrony between the images
and the music.

During the *Ballade* excerpt, the violins set in after three measures[13] and accompany the piano until the end of the passage. The shots depicting Alba at

---

12   The libretto explicitly refers to Alba playing Chopin during the first part of the film: "Non
so d'amore: solo so di languori musicali, d'aride ebbrezze dentro il pugno chiuse: or ora io
suonava [sic] un notturno di Chopin, poiché tutto silente s'era fatto il castello più grigio
del dicembre". (Alfa/Martini 2006: 78; 'I don't know about love: I only know about musical
languor, about dry thrills closed in my hands: just now I was playing one of Chopin's noc-
turnes, because the castle had become all silent, greyer than December'. My translation).

13   For the orchestral score, cf. Mascagni 1961: 112–115.

✣ Chopin - Ballata I. op. 23

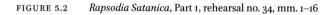

FIGURE 5.2   *Rapsodia Satanica*, Part I, rehearsal no. 34, mm. 1–16

FIGURE 5.3 *Rapsodia Satanica*, Part II, rehearsal no. 1, mm. 7–16

the piano first are intercut with images showing the two brothers in the garden. Eventually Tristano enters and interrupts Alba's play.

The sequence of the second part accompanied by the excerpts of Chopin's *Valse* exclusively shows Alba on the piano, while the orchestra sets in after seven measures of quasi-diegetic solo piano.[14]

The semantic function of these musical quotations is to underscore Alba's feelings, especially her melancholic sentiments in the second part of the film. On the meta-diegetic level, however, these intermusical references to the two Chopin pieces combined with images of Lyda Borelli playing the piano function as metareference eliciting a reflection on the aesthetic value of the audiovisual spectacle. We can assume that the bourgeois audience of the time recognized the two Chopin fragments. Furthermore, the brief simulation of diegetic solo piano music must have provoked a surprising effect, which, combined with the orchestral fade-in after several measures, has the potential to trigger a reflection on the artistic quality of *Rapsodia Satanica* and, potentially, cinema in general.[15]

Considering the over-all relationship between images and music, it is not the case that the music generally follows the images and, instead, at several moments it seems to be the other way around. Comuzio describes the relationship between music and images in *Rapsodia Satanica*, therefore, appropriately as osmosis since it seems that at times the images stop in order to enable the development of the musical discourse (cf. 2006: 22). While the score certainly includes a few instances where the music melodramatically intensifies sensations evoked by the cinematic images, in general it plays a crucial part within the plurimedial narrative. Hence, Mascagni succeeded in elevating the music to a primary role within the audiovisual narrative, far beyond merely accompanying or commenting on the images. The significance of the score within the audiovisual spectacle thus is comparable to that of the orchestra of 19th-century operas. Thus, the plurimedial combination in *Rapsodia Satanica* had a strong potential to elicit an operatic sensation among contemporary audiences.

Operatic sensation in *Rapsodia Satanica* is not only conveyed through the combination of images and music but also through several intermedial references, which strongly connect the film to the artform of opera. Amodeo developed categories to describe significant transmedial characteristics which in other media appear as opera-like. Since in our context these characteristics

---

14   For the orchestral score, cf. ibid.: 138–140.
15   Campana correctly points out that the use of Chopin itself is a wink at the bourgeois audience (cf. 2015: 185). At the same time, the incorporation of a famous, highly respected musical piece underscores the artistic quality of the audiovisual spectacle.

exclusively point to the medium of opera, they ought to be considered not as "transmedial" elements, but rather as "intermedial references" to the artform of opera.

Relevant for our purpose are the categories "craftsmanship", "spectacularity", and "natural artificiality".[16] With the term "craftsmanship", Amodeo refers primarily to elements which are part of the fictional world but are recognized by the audience as artificial. One example would be elements of the operatic stage design that might destroy the illusion by underscoring the element's artificiality, such as a blue cloth on stage representing water. E.T.A. Hoffmann's *Der vollkommene Maschinist* thematizes the spectrum between aesthetic illusion and obvious craftsmanship in opera and claims that after a good opera performance the audience knows that nothing was real except the audience's own feelings (cf. Amodeo 2007: 162–165). "Spectacularity", according to Amodeo, refers not only to the musical and scenic performance, but also to everything that fosters entertainment at the event. This may consist of unrealistic elements within the diegesis, such as the dying, but beautifully singing diva, or spectacular aspects of the theatrical event itself. Similar to the "craftsmanship" element, a successful opera performance alerts the spectator that he or she is confronted with an illusion created by artificial or unrealistic elements (ibid.: 165–173). "Natural artificiality" describes the ideal perception of the opera's audience who experiences opera's artificiality as natural. An obvious example is that the characters on stage sing to one another. Since this is part of the operatic convention, the audience not only accepts it but during the performance actually perceives this crucial but artificial operatic characteristic as natural (ibid.: 173–180).

Rapsodia Satanica includes these categories and hence strongly alludes to the medium of opera. One craftsmanship element, which also adds to spectacularity and artificiality and hence to the operatic quality of the film, is the unique coloring of the film. The film material of *Rapsodia Satanica* not only has been tinted but also been stenciled, which highlights particularities within the frames. This adds an extraordinary effect to the images, in particular during lyrical scenes with Lyda Borelli. In addition, the color assumes a referential function. Similar to a musical reminiscing motif, the stenciled color connects scenes where the same color is used. One example is the color purple of Mephistopheles's coat, which connects the purple incorporated towards the end of the second part with the character of Mephistopheles in the prologue. The

---

16   Amodeo also reflects on the operatic characteristic of 'reproducibility' underscoring that the effect of opera can be reproduced also outside the theater, for example by listening to a recording or by watching an opera at the cinema or on TV (cf. 2007: 180–183).

stenciling by hand, which was never absolutely accurate, further underscores the craftsmanship aspect of the film. This is particularly obvious in the last scene of the film where the colors flow into each other producing a blurring effect, which seems to have been intentional and adds a painterly quality to the scene (see De Kuyper 1996).

A significant spectacular element in *Rapsodia Satanica* provoking operatic sensations is Lyda Borelli's acting style and her dominance within the mise en scène, which is in congruence with the dominance of the female star of an opera. Borelli of course doesn't excel with her voice by expressing her feelings in arias, but she uses her body through gestures and facial mimics to express, for example, her love, sadness, or desperation. Comparable to an aria in an opera, at several moments in the film the actions seem to stop, and in combination with the music, we can observe Lyda Borelli slowly moving and gesturing in order to express her feelings. The film thus implicitly demonstrates that, comparable to an operatic aria, it is able to communicate thoughts and feelings, primarily however through gestures and music and without voice. On the extra-diegetic level, Lyda Borelli is the star performing in this film. Similar to a 19th-century opera diva, Lyda Borelli is the center of attention and gets the most applause and typically the honors for the performance.

The artificiality is apparent throughout the spectacle since the characters' voices are absent and the communication among them is conveyed either through gestures, intertitles or the music. Comparable to the singing in opera, the audience perceives the voicelessness of silent cinema as natural within the context of the spectacle. Additionally there are several artificial elements, such as Alba's transformations or Mephistopheles stepping out of a picture frame, which the audience accepts within the diegesis.

In addition to these operatic characteristics, even the context of the first screenings can be defined as operatic. The public opening of the film took place on July 3, 1917 at the Teatro Augusteo, which at the time was part of the Accademia di Santa Cecilia, famous primarily for its symphonic performances. Instead of defining *Rapsodia Satanica* as a cinematographic presentation, the event also was announced as "poema cinema-musicale" or as "poema sinfonico", accompanied by the images. During the first public screenings, Mascagni directed the orchestra, and for each time he chose an orchestral piece which preceded the screening and served as the quasi-overture to the audiovisual presentation. At the first public screening on July 3, 1917, he chose a symphony by Johan Svendsen; at the second screening on July 6, he chose Tschaikowsky's "Pathétique", and on July 8, the Overture from Bellini's *Norma* and the Cicaleccio from his own opera *I Rantzau* (cf. Huck 2004: 193).

On the paratextual level, the libretto with the text of Martini's poem also included a preamble, which underscored the intention to create a new work of art by conveying the sensations of all the arts. According to this preamble, the audience of *Rapsodia Satanica* would experience 'sensations of all artistic media in a new unity'. Furthermore, the theater where the screening takes place would be transformed into 'a magic melting pot of *all artistic sensations*'.[17] While we certainly need to be careful with the artistic evaluation expressed in this preamble due to its primarily promotional purpose, it unmistakably states the intention to provoke sensations associated with other media and hence create a new Gesamtkunstwerk.

Of crucial significance in the aesthetic success of the plurimedial combination in *Rapsodia Satanica* is Mascagni's music since he was able to reconcile a high-quality musical discourse with the images of the film. Considering the intermedial references within the film to literature, painting, dancing, and architecture, and the absorption of poetry, painting, and music within the audiovisual 'discours' of the spectacle, *Rapsodia Satanica* might indeed be described as a Gesamtkunstwerk, a synthesis of the arts in the Wagnerian sense, and may even come close to what Wagner envisioned as the artwork of the future. Wagner used the term Gesamtkunstwerk in his theoretical essays referring to a recreation of the ancient unity of the arts combining dance, music and poetry and thus reestablishing their original dignity. The artwork of the future would further incorporate the arts of architecture, sculpture, and painting (see Wagner 1850).

Rapsodia Satanica's plurimedial fusion is most evident in the film's last scene, which depicts Alba's Liebestod. The visual focus is almost exclusively on Alba. She first prepares herself for Tristano's arrival by dressing herself with white veils and carefully watching herself in the mirror. She leaves the house and starts dancing on the terrace. This dance scene is visually interrupted by a brief depiction of Tristano on a horse, pointing to his expected arrival. Next, Alba is shown entering the park, where she hopes to meet Tristano, but encounters Mephistopheles instead, who transforms her back to her former age. The film ends with Alba's death near a pond. In addition to the cinematic narrative, which refers to Martini's poem, this final scene explicitly points to the medium of dance. Furthermore, thanks to the seemingly imperfect stenciling technique, which softens the forms and margins of the trees in the garden,

---

17   "Una cosa di grande rilevanza rivelerà questa *Rapsodia*: La possibilità di adunare in un'opera cinematografica le sensazioni di tutte le arti; la possibilità di fare d'una sala di proiezione un magico crogiuolo di *tutte le sensazioni artistiche* in un insieme nuovissimo, mai tentato e oggi ottenuto per la prima volta". (Alfa/Martini 2006: 75; 'One fact of great significance will this *Rhapsody* reveal: the possibility to unite in a cinematographic work the sensations of all the arts; the possibility to transform the projection space into a magic melting pot of *all artistic sensations* in a new unity, never attempted before and today realized for the first time'. My translation and emphasis).

the last frames of the film gain a painterly, less naturalistic quality, which foregrounds the artistic nature of this film and underscores the craftsmanship quality, reminiscent of opera.

Most significant for the plurimedial realization of the scene, however, is the music. The music here not only adds semantic meaning with the inclusion of leitmotifs for Alba, Sergio, and Mephistopheles, but primarily connects with the images in an intimate way conveying "meaning, affect, and narrative direction" (Campana 2015: 189). The music is also responsible for letting the audience perceive the spectacularity – such as Alba's physical change or her sudden death – and artificiality of the scene as natural.[18]

4   Conclusion

Regardless of how much *Rapsodia Satanica* may have in common with Wagner's ideas, from an intermedial perspective, the film explicitly highlights other media on the level of the diegesis, for example by depicting Faust and Mephistofeles, a painting or a piano. In addition, the audiovisual spectacle implicitly imitates the medium of opera by elevating the significance of music and by employing operatic elements suggesting affinity to the medium of opera. In addition, the opening of *Rapsodia Satanica* took place in one of Rome's most famous theaters in an operatic fashion, preceded by an overture-like orchestral prelude and accompanied by a libretto.

Concerning the development of cinema, we know that cinema became an accepted form of art during the second decade of the 20th century. Cinema achieved this aesthetic success not only by adapting literary, theatrical, or operatic works, or by employing divas or divos as actresses and actors, but also – and primarily – by contrasting and skillfully combining cinematic characteristics with literary, theatrical, and operatic elements. *Rapsodia Satanica* is successful in creating a visually and musically well-balanced plurimedial work that consciously incorporates intermedial references and provokes operatic sensations. In so doing, *Rapsodia Satanica* implicitly makes a statement about the acceptance of cinema as art, a message, which finally seems to have been understood by the intellectuals and bourgeois audiences. After the preview of 1915, one critic commented:

---

18   According to Gier, "a good opera plots should include a dimension not fully accessible to logical thought and argumentation, (for instance physical reality), which leaves room for music" (2011 online).

The cinematographic projection substitutes the stage performance. Thus, we are about to see the attempt of a new cinematographic art, which has been designed with serious research. It leaves the limits of a commercial production and enters those of art.[19]

References

Adorno, Theodor W., Hanns Eisler (1974). *Komposition für den Film*. Ed. Eberhardt Klemm. Leipzig: Deutscher Verlag für Musik.

Alfa [= Alberto Fassini], Fausto Maria Martini (2006). "Rapsodia Satantica. Poema Cinema-Musicale". Aragona/Fornoni/Ravasio, eds. 75–80.

Alovisio, Silvio (2014). "Il cinema italiano dalle origini all'avvento el sonoro: un quadro introduttivo". Alovisio/Carluccio, eds. 3–29.

Alovisio, Silvio, Giulia Carluccio, eds. (2014). *Introduzione al cinema muto italiano*. Torino: UTET Università.

Amodeo, Immacolata (2007). *Das Opernhafte: Eine Studie zum "gusto melodrammatico" in Italien und Europa*. Bielefeld: Transcript.

Aragona, Livio, Federico Fornoni, Piera Ravasio, eds. (2006). *Rapsodia Satanica: poema cinema-musicale di Alberto Fassini e Fausto M. Martini. Cavalleria Rusticana: melodramma in un atto*. Bergamo: Fondazione Donizetti.

Bernardini, Aldo (1981). *Cinema muto italiano. Vol. II: Industria e organizzazione dello spettacolo 1905–1909*. Bari: Laterza.

Brunetta, Gian Piero (1993). *Storia del cinema italiano: Il cinema muto 1895–1829*. Roma: Editori Riuniti.

Campana, Alessandra (2015). *Opera and Modern Spectatorship in Late Nineteenth-Century Italy*. Cambridge: CUP.

Carluccio, Giulia (2014). "Modi di rappresentazione, messa in scena e ipotesi stilistiche nel cinema italiano degli anni Dieci: Intorno al Colossa storico, da *Quo Vadis?* a *Cabiria*". Alovisio/Carluccio, eds. 30–58.

Comuzio, Ermanno (2006). "*Rapsodia Satanica* (1915): un film-mito e la musica di Mascagni". Aragona/Fornoni/Ravasio, eds. 17–23.

Dalle Vacche, Angela (2005). "Lyda Borelli's Satanic Rhapsody: The Cinema and the Occult". *Cinémas: revue d'études cinématographiques/Cinémas: Journal of Film Studies*. 16/1: 91–115.

---

19   "La proiezione cinematografica sostituisce la recitazione: Siamo dunque dinanzi a un tentativo di una nuova arte cinematografica, concepita e condotta con intendimenti di seria ricerca. Il tentativo esce dai limiti confini della produzione commerciale ed entra in quelli confinati dell'arte". (Review in *La cinematografia italiana ed estera* 38. 31.03.1915; qtd. Martinelli 1991: 248; my translation).

De Berti, Raffaele (2014). "Le riviste cinematografiche". Alovisio/Carluccio, eds. 316–338.

De Kuyper, Eric (1996). "'Rapsodia satanica' o il fremito del colore". *Cinegrafie* 9: 53–60.

Esvan, Yann (2015 online). "Opera d'arte totale: 'Rapsodia Satanica'". *Cinefilia Ritrovata*. 5 luglio 2015. http://www.cinefiliaritrovata.it/opera-darte-totale-rapsodia-satanica/ [25/03/2019].

Fabich, Rainer (1993). *Musik für den Stummfilm: Analysierende Beschreibung orginaler Filmkompositionen*. Frankfurt am Main: Peter Lang.

Gier, Albert (2011 online). "Narrativity in Contemporary Opera – a Case Study". Opera/ Libretto Symposium Barcelona, 26–27 June 2011. http://www.obnc.cat/wp-content/ uploads/a-gier-obnc11.pdf [25/03/2019].

Huck, Oliver (2004). "Pietro Mascagni's 'Rapsodia Satanica' und die Geburt der Filmkunst aus dem Geiste der Musik". *Archiv für Musikwissenschaft*. 61/3: 190–206.

Jandelli, Cristina (2014). "'Per mondo in effigie mobile': Attori e divismo". Alovisio/ Carluccio, eds. 59–91.

Kuhn, Bernhard (2012). "The Operatics of *Cabiria* (1914): Intermediality in Early Italian Cinema". *Nineteenth Century Theatre and Film* 39/2: 1–18.

Martinelli, Vittorio (1991). "Rapsodia Satanica". Vittorio Martinelli, ed. *Il cinema muto italiano: 1917*. Roma: Centro Sperimentale della Cinematografia. 246–248.

Mascagni, Pietro (1917). *Rapsodia Satanica. Riduzione per pianoforte dell'autore*. Roma: Società Italiana Cines.

Mascagni, Pietro (1961). *Rapsodia Satanica per orchestra. Partitura*. Milano: Edizioni Curci.

Oxilia, Nino, dir. (1917 online). *Rapsodia Satanica*. Roma: Cines. https://www.youtube .com/watch?v=4XdWl4pZiFc [25/03/2019].

Piccardi, Carlo (1990). "Mascagni e l'ipotesi del 'Dramma musicale cinematografico'". *Chigiana* 42/22: 453–497.

Rajewsky, Irina O. (2002). *Intermedialität*. Tübingen: Francke.

Renzi, Renzo, ed. (1991). *Sperduto nel buio: Il cinema italiano e il suo tempo (1905–1930)*. Bologna: Cappelli.

Salt, Barry (1991). "Il cinema italiano dalla nascita alla Grande Guerra: un'analisi stilistica". Renzi, ed. 49–58.

Simeon, Ennio (1991). "L'ambiente musicale ufficiale e il cinema muto". Renzi, ed. 108–114.

Wagner, Richard (1850). *Das Kunstwerk der Zukunft*. Leipzig: Wigand.

Wolf, Werner (2002). "Intermediality Revisited: Reflections on Word and Music Relations in the Context of a General Typology of Intermediality". Suzanne M. Lodato, Suzanne Aspden, Walter Bernhart, eds. *Word and Music Studies: Essays in Honor of Steven Paul Scher and on Cultural Identity and the Musical Stage*. Word and Music Studies 4. Amsterdam/New York, NY: Rodopi. 13–34.

CHAPTER 6

Humanized Documentary, 'Light' Verse, and Music Made to Fit: G.P.O. Film Unit/Auden/Britten's *Night Mail* (1936)

Walter Bernhart

Abstract

The documentary film *Night Mail*, propagating the services of the British General Post Office in the 1930s, reflects the political ideas, typical of the period, of increased democratisation and a collective work ethic. At the same time, it reflects those advanced aesthetic ideas of the period that favoured a public function of art and saw art works as products of collaborative creative activity by artists from different media, with film taking a leading role in the coaction. The G.P.O. Film Unit was able to engage W.H. Auden and Benjamin Britten as contributors to the formation of *Night Mail*. This paper argues that their cooperative efforts turned the film into a unique case of what it calls a "collaborative *Gesamtkunstwerk*" showing a particularly close interaction of picture, words and music, and analyses the effects which the closeness of interaction has on the working of the participating media.

∙ ∙ ∙

1   The G.P.O. Film Unit

To talk about *Night Mail* means talking about an English documentary film of the 1930s which was produced by the G.P.O. Film Unit, with the purpose, above all, of promoting the General Post Office and propagating its extraordinary efficiency. It was most effective in taking mail overnight from London to Scotland so that a letter posted at Euston Station in the evening would be delivered in Glasgow, Edinburgh, or Aberdeen early next morning. It was the pressure of the rapidly developing car industry and of electricity competition which spurred the promotion of the steam-driven mail trains, whose engines accordingly play a prominent role in the film. *Night Mail* has been called the "Best Railway Film of the Century" and has become part of "British cultural nostalgia" (Anthony 2007: 83f.) as a lasting document of the spirit of its time.

© KONINKLIJKE BRILL NV, LEIDEN, 2019 | DOI:10.1163/9789004401310_007

Scott Anthony, who has written a well-researched study on the film for the British Film Institute, calls it "redolent of its era" (ibid.: 84), and it indeed mirrors in many ways some of the most significant features of the rapidly changing social and political climate of this decade in a crisis. Above all, it reflects how the 1930s steered towards increased democratisation and the activation of the labouring classes, along with tendencies towards establishing a modern welfare state. Thus, *Night Mail* vividly shows workers doing their hard, and partly dangerous, jobs. As is characteristic of the age and of the film, the emphasis is on the collaborative spirit in which the work is performed, with the subtle reminder that their work can only be successful when performed in a group. This typical 1930s collectivism, as a rallying cry of the day, and the strongly-felt urge for more social democracy asked for the introduction of mass education and general instruction, which was why the G.P.O. set up its public-sector Film Unit, an enterprise that was clearly outside the already flourishing commercial Hollywood-style film industry of its time. The Unit's mastermind was John Grierson, a significant personality in British film history, who developed a specific ethos for such public instruction and established what has been called his 'documentary school' (see Aitken 1992).[1] Film was seen as a ground-breaking and highly democratic public medium, having only fairly recently become 'talkies' with a soundtrack.[2] Grierson is reported as having regarded "cinema as a pulpit" and having used it "as a propagandist"[3] with a clearly educational purpose. Yet at the same time – and this is where it becomes interesting from an intermediality perspective – he aimed at a "creative treatment of actuality"[4] and postulated: "Let cinema attempt the dramatization of the living scene and the living theme".[5] Thus, even as far back as in 1936, it was surmised that "the documentary film may well be described as the birth of creative cinema" (Rotha 1936/1952: 71).

This introduces another reason why, with *Night Mail*, the G.P.O. Film Unit produced an exemplary document of its time and age: Grierson and his group were keen observers of the contemporary developments in the arts world and were anxious to put the recent incisive changes in aesthetics to the service of their socio-political aims. This is why Grierson hired Basil Wright as the producer of *Night Mail*, a "high-modernist" (Anthony 2007: 41), who was keenly alert to what was going on in Russia at the time and therefore found in Victor

---

1   In fact, the term 'documentary' for such films was coined by Grierson. See also Swann 1989.
2   *The Jazz Singer* of 1927 is generally considered the first sound movie.
3   Qtd. Mitchell 1981/2000: 60, and Rotha 1936/1952: 43.
4   Qtd. Mitchell 1981/2000: 61, and Hardy, ed. 1979: 11.
5   Qtd. Mitchell 1981/2000: 61, and Rotha 1936/1952: 69.

Turin's 1929 film called *Turksib* a pattern for his own *Night Mail*. This film used the Eisenstein-inspired Soviet-style montage technique, which clearly became a model for *Night Mail*.

But the liberal-minded Wright was also ambitious to gather a group of experimentally oriented artists around himself, which is why he hired Benjamin Britten for the soundtrack; the film *Coal Face* of 1935, with Britten's music (see Reed 1999), was a forerunner, a kind of "dress-rehearsal" (Anthony 2007: 50), for *Night Mail*. Britten was only 22 in 1936, he loved Hitchcock and Walt Disney (cf. ibid.: 58) and threw himself eagerly into the new task, producing no fewer than four soundtracks in 1935 and five in 1936 for the Film Unit (cf. Palmer, ed. 1984: 429). The significance of the fact that Britten, a young contemporary musician, contributed the music can be gauged by considering that only a year before, in 1934, the G.P.O. had produced a short film called *Locomotives* (obviously on a theme similar to that of *Night Mail*) that was set to music by Schubert (cf. Anthony 2007: 39). What Wright wanted instead of a background of traditional music was a flexible contemporary musical voice, and as Britten was responsible for both noises and 'proper music' for the films, he became very ingenious in collecting suitable sound sources to meet the film's demands. And although – as we shall see later – these soundtracks are by no means masterpieces, Britten could learn from them for his later creative life "discipline of writing at speed, to order, and to picture".[6]

The other 'genius' hired by the Film Unit was W.H. Auden, then 29 and already Britain's "unacknowledged legislator of the literary world" and "Court Poet of the Left" (Kildea 1999: 53). He was meant to work as an assistant director but occasionally had to fulfil minor tasks as well, yet eventually, in recognition of his extraordinary mental capacities and verbal gifts, was commissioned to write verse for *Night Mail*. This was by no means undisputed among the group of young intellectuals, mainly from the viewpoint of Harry Watt, the film director, who championed the film's story element and narrative thrust, which he feared would be jeopardized by the linguistic subtleties of poetry. Yet, as it happened, the verse was introduced into the film, but only as an "afterthought" (Anthony 2007: 42), and Auden himself can be quoted as having said: "We were experimenting to see if poetry could be used in films, I think we showed it could".[7]

The part in the film which actually uses verse is only the very final section of three and a half minutes' length, which shows the mail train crossing the border into Scotland and finally arriving at the Scottish towns already mentioned,

---

6 Anthony 2007: 57; cf. also Mitchell 1981/2000: "Preface to the New Edition" [2].
7 Qtd. Anthony 2007: 93, and Davenport-Hines 1995: 144.

where people are said to be happy receiving their mail in the early morning. In this fairly short footage we find a combination and very close interconnection of picture, music and poetry which has been highly acclaimed as a particularly successful plurimedial artistic achievement. Scott Anthony claims that "*Night Mail*'s smooth integration of sight and sound, words and music, have assured Britten's work a place in film lore", and "*Night Mail*'s greatness rests on its skilful blending of word, sound and image" (2007: 60f.; 7); "the *totality* of the integration of sight and sound [...] remains one of the film's glories"; "a combination of the arts was just what the GPO Film Unit represented and what constituted its appeal to lively creative spirits" (Mitchell 1981/2000: 83, 87; emphasis in the original).

2   'Totality of Integration'?

To which extent such a claim of 'totality of integration' of the contributing media is justified can be assessed by a closer analysis of the relevant film section (see *Night Mail* 2007 and *Night Mail* online). When the section starts, we can observe that text and music are delayed in setting in: at the beginning we get only the strong visual impression of the sprawling stark borderland hills, and eventually the soft noise of wind sets in. It is only when the train gets into focus that the speaking voice starts with the comments of Auden's poem ("Night Mail", see 1976: 113f.) on the purpose of the journey and the references in the text to the "white steam" (l. 8), the "moorland boulder" (l. 7), the "Silent miles" (l. 10), which can all be seen in the picture. What we do not see, however, are the "Birds" (l. 11), the "farm" (l. 15) and "Sheep-dogs" (l. 12) as mentioned in the text – although later in the film we in fact observe a dog running and trying to "turn her [i.e., the train's] course" (l. 13). An important narrative element of this part of the train's journey is that it is "Pulling up Beattock [i.e., the borderland hill], a steady climb" (l. 5) and that eventually "Her climb is done" (l. 17). This climb is not clearly shown in the picture, but it is the music which can typically, and very easily, mimic the intensifying strain on the engine by climbing the hill, when slow and soft rhythmical percussion sounds and quavering strings steadily increase in intensity and rise in pitch and volume. When the climb is finally done, text and music fall silent, and we see a cloudy sky, hills, and relaxed men after their hard work of firing the engine.

The text sets in again with the start of the second segment of the poem, telling that "Down towards Glasgow she descends" (l. 18), passing "cranes", "apparatus", "furnaces" (ll. 19f.), all of which we can see in the picture, and through "glens" (l. 23) visualised by the gentle wind caressing the trees. The music is equally calm, harp and string chords can be heard, into which are embedded rising and expanding melodic stretches.

This placid section comes to an abrupt stop when the virtuoso third segment starts with its literally breath-taking agitation. We are shown the now fast-running train with close-ups of track-lines, funnels, bars, and pistons, and it is here that we see the running dog and alarmed hares – not mentioned in the text – escaping from the train into the bushes. In this passage, the words of the verse famously follow the fast rhythm of the leverage in the picture with admirable precision. When this section was recorded the artists even used special tricks to suggest to the listener that the speaker never takes a breath – thus evoking literal breathlessness –, which naturally intensifies the impression of speed and energy. What the voice utters is a Gilbert & Sullivan-type patter and the jingle of excessive rhyming, and it is hardly possible to follow what is being said as the talk is so fast. The music, of course, also takes up the rapid rhythm and goes with the words in perfect synchrony; on the soundtrack we hear only percussion instruments with a constant strong beat, at times interspersed with brash trumpet flourishes.

The last segment of the film is again slow and quiet, the picture first showing glimpses of the Scottish cities, harbours and railway stations with tracks and signals, then the slow-moving train, ultimately coming to a standstill and ostensibly displaying the inscription "Royal Mail" (after all, it is a propaganda film), and finally someone calmly cleaning the engine at rest. The words we hear suggest even more quietness: "asleep" and "dreams", referring to Scottish citizens in the early morning, are notions establishing a mood of extreme calmness, which, however, distinctly changes when the text says that people "shall wake soon" (l. 51) and shall anxiously look out for their mail. The music clearly reflects this change of mood when out of the quiet brass sounds, which marked the beginning of this segment, trumpet calls of rising fifths start to emerge. They stop when also the text stops, a terminal break-off which interestingly takes place much earlier than the ultimate ending of the film. The final train passages of the film, as described before, are unaccompanied by words and, instead, the music impressively swells up, steadily developing into the grand flourish of a typical film ending, with a glamorous piano glissando worthy of any genuine Hollywood movie.

When trying to assess the level and intensity of integration of the media involved in the famous last section of the film just described, we can certainly observe that they are far more closely interlinked than in standard films: there is a high amount of mimetic illustration where, in the ideal case, the same perception is represented in all three media. This is particularly true when the perception is one of motion, as such perceptions lend themselves most directly to be represented in all three temporal media. There is also a fairly high amount of integration of two media, above all of word illustration on the screen: the landscape, the cities, the dog, for example, are mentioned in the poem and can also be seen on the screen. In such cases, however, music cannot be specific enough for readily identifiable illustration. We, furthermore, have the conflation of only words and music, without any visual support, in cases like the waking calls, where the picture could only very clumsily show, let's say, the drowsy people getting up and checking their mailboxes. It is not surprising that much of what is being said in Auden's text remains uncommented on by both picture and music, as, for instance, "a jug in the bedroom gently shak[ing]" (l. 16), or the dreams "of terrifying monsters" (l. 46), not to speak of metaphorical expressions such as furnaces "like gigantic chessmen" (l. 21). What the poem obviously offers is a richness of information that strongly attracts the listener's attention which cannot be matched by the impact of the visual input. Conversely, there are stretches of the film where the text remains completely silent – sometimes also the music –, so that attention is exclusively attracted by the picture. One gets the impression that the text acquires a dominant position once it appears, and that when the visual impact is expected to be prominent the text is better kept silent. It is interesting that music does not pose a similar problem of who should seize the mantle, it emerges far more smoothly and does not ask for dominant attention. The reason, obviously, is music's fundamental non-referential quality, while reference-oriented pictures and words battle over superiority on the cognitive level. In this film, the words give up their claim on cognitive superiority only in the third segment where their acoustic and motoric sides are emphasised and merge with the acoustic and motoric sides of music as well as the motoric side of the picture. One will necessarily admire the brilliance of Auden's rhymes and rhythms, but the ultimate triumph of his verse can emerge only when it is read at such a slow speed as allows for cognitive comprehension in addition to acoustic perception. It is not surprising that, at first, the inclusion of verse in the film was altogether rejected by the film director, and once it had been accepted, the text had to be constantly revised and adapted to fit the film. Thus, significantly, a phrase like "Uplands heaped like slaughtered horses", which Auden had included in an earlier draft, had to be cut out, on the verdict that "[n]o picture we put on the screen could be as strong at that";[8] no visual image in the film would be able to match the power of this poetic image. We can see, the old battle-horse of the 'paragone' is raising its ancient head.

---

8   Film director Harry Watt, qtd. Carpenter 1992: 183.

3   Adding a 'Human Dimension'

The reason why poetry was ultimately accepted to be included in the film lay in the fact that, as was mentioned before, Grierson and his documentary school wanted to overcome purely informational films and enrich them with the addition of a 'human dimension'. They knew that only a "dramatization of the living scene", as already quoted (see fn. 5), could achieve the desired effect of reaching the people and raising their spirit of solidarity. In this respect, Auden's text is very well able to perform the expected function by introducing the vital element of emotional identification. The train shows human features ("her shoulder", l. 8; "her blank-faced coaches", l. 12; she's "Snorting", l. 9), "All Scotland waits for her" (l. 22), and the people waiting "long" (l. 24) and "hope for" (l. 51) human contact with "a quickening of the heart" (l. 53). The last line of the poem ("For who can bear to feel himself forgotten?", l. 54) makes the strong final point that whatever the challenge and brilliance of the technical expertise of the night mail train may be, its ultimate purpose lies in an increase of the happiness of people through human communication. This also comes out in the visual side of the film, but the point is made far more strongly and directly in the poetry.

4   'Light' Verse

However, the price the poetry had to pay for becoming part of the film was, as we have seen, that it needed to sacrifice its more elaborate and complex forms of expression and choose a simpler, more popular approach. Such an approach had become attractive to Auden in the 1930s, after his earlier, high-modernist beginnings, when he developed his left-wing inclinations and new desire for an educative and public "parable-art", as he called it, in contrast to what he then began to reject as too intimate "escape-art" (1935/1977: 20; qtd. Mitchell 1981/2000: 25). The natural outcome of this attitude was Auden's new interest in 'light' verse, of which his poem "Night Mail" is a supreme example. Auden, at the time, began collecting poems for *The Oxford Book of Light Verse*, which was eventually published in 1938 and in whose "Introduction" we find a succinct statement of his spirited revolutionary views. Auden's point there is that 'light' verse should deal with general experience for a general audience, it should be the voice of the social community, its language should be "straightforward and close to ordinary speech"; it is "written for performance" and has as its subject-matter "every-day social life" (1938: viiif.). Auden stresses that there is nothing facile about 'light' verse, and that there can be – and certainly is – "serious light verse" (ibid.: xix) where no "subtleties of sensibility" are sacrificed (ibid.: xx). This approach was radically innovative insofar as, traditionally, 'light' verse had been seen in quite different terms, as reflected in the later *New Oxford Book of Light Verse* of 1978, where its editor, Kingsley Amis, in contrast to Auden, defined 'light' verse on the basis of purely formal and linguistic criteria, i.e., in terms of craftsmanship and playfulness, as a matter of technique and a light-hearted tone of voice, where the poet acts like "a juggler" and excels in intricacies of rhyme and rhythm (1978: viii). It is the greatness of Auden that his respective poetry, such as "Night Mail", answers both these contrastive definitions at the same time.

5   'Social Utility' Music

When we look at the music in the film and consider the pressures, as it were, of the other media on it in the context of *Night Mail* as a case of an 'integral' plurimedial art form, we can see that the pressures on music are even stronger than those on the poetry. The film director, Harry Watt, made it quite bluntly clear to Britten that "[t]he music has got to fit the picture, you understand, absolutely fit to a split second. Also, I want it to be rhythmic, to go with the beat of the train" (1974: 94f.; qtd. Anthony 2007: 60). As already mentioned, Britten obediently obliged, and he swiftly produced the score within two days. Yet he confided to his diary (of 9 January 1936) that this was "[n]ot very good as music – but I think that with the visuals they will be alright – one cannot write 'music' to these minute instructions when even the speed of the beat and number of bars is fixed" (qtd. Mitchell 1981/2000: 81). Britten, as this statement reflects, distinguished between what he called "'original' music" that was not "written on demand for film, radio or theatre" (ibid.: 28), and "social utility pieces", whose benefit it was, for an artist, that their techniques assisted in "augmenting the resources on which Britten could call when exercising his 'private' imagination" (ibid.: 30). Thus, the restrictions of working for the film prevented Britten from creating highly qualified music, yet they encouraged the exploration of sound sources of which he could make use in his "original", individualised works.

6   A 'Collaborative *Gesamtkunstwerk*'

By way of summary, what can be said about the film *Night Mail* as showing a claimed 'totality of integration' of the participating art forms? It is indeed a case of a high degree of integration, although with varying levels of intensity in different sections of the work. It is highest in the third section where rapid movement is the dominant idea and where all three media can equally forcefully contribute to the overall perception and effect of rhythmicised high speed. The price to pay for this totality of effect is to block out cognitive elements and reduce the perception to the experience of pure motion. When cognitive factors, such as representational elements or emotional conditions, come into play and gain prominence, pictures and words start competing for dominance of impact on the recipient, with a tendency of the words to prevail. It is significant that in the final section of *Night Mail* here discussed there are stretches without any text at all, where total absorption in the picture is guaranteed; which suggests that the words have a strong distracting power from the pictures once they set in. In all such passages of cognitive dominance, either visual or verbal, the music necessarily plays a subordinate role, though one of reinforcement and intensification of what text and picture represent. This concurs with findings of screen music studies that address music's 'wallpaper function' in films by forming a suitable backdrop for, and collaborating in the creation of, the narrative world; music is, thus, part of the narrative world, rather than a narrative voice performing a narrative function (cf. Winters 2012: 45f.).

Night Mail's attempt at a 'totality of integration' of media is part of a more universal tendency of the period to revolutionise the arts. As Edward Mendelson puts it: "All across Europe artists and technicians came together to build a new *Gesamtkunstwerk* as an instrument of social change." (1981: 281) It is particularly fascinating that a Britten diary entry (of 22 January 1936, when the Film Unit was working on *Night Mail*) tells about a discussion Britten had with Auden over lunch. What they discussed was "at great length the psychology of teaching art in combination – & possibility of an Academy of Combined art" (qtd. Mitchell 1981/2000: 87). It is fascinating to learn about this early idea by Auden and Britten of establishing an educational institution of intermediality studies. Yet they envisaged a form of *Gesamtkunstwerk* which decisively differed from the well-known Wagnerian type in at least two ways: in the envisaged new form, the work was seen as the result of the efforts not of a single person but of a collective in collaboration; and, as a clearly expressed purpose, it had to have a didactic function of precipitating social change, which again emphasised the collective perspective, as the vision of social change incorporated ideas of democracy and a collective government. As, furthermore, film was seen as the exemplary and foremost democratic artistic medium, it was only natural that film became the dominant element in the makeup of this newly-conceived *Gesamtkunstwerk* – quite in contrast, obviously, to the far more elitist Wagnerian type. In this respect, *Night Mail* can be seen as a prototypical case of what may be called a new kind of 'collaborative *Gesamt-kunstwerk*', in which the collective idea manifests itself not only in the production process, when artists from various media closely work together, but also in the subject and overall purpose of the film, which – in the end – is a song of praise of the efficiency, and the blessing, of cooperative labour in the service and for the benefit of human communication and – ultimately – human happiness in togetherness.

It is a known fact that Auden, before he joined the G.P.O. Film Unit and when he still worked at the Downs School at Colwell, had what he called a "vision of agape", a vision of brotherhood, of "what it means to love one's neighbor as oneself" (1964: 26; see Boyd 2008 and Leahy 2015). This Christianly inspired idea of universal solidarity among humans was a utopian vision which, for the young British intellectuals in the 1930s, became a leading thought, however with the typical 'socialist' political twist of the period, and for Auden, as an advocate of a "Combined art", as we have seen, a collaborative undertaking like *Night Mail* must have been just the right vehicle for letting the vision come true. Yet disillusionment soon set in and Auden left the G.P.O. in disappointment. He had realized that lofty notions were inevitably shattered by the contingencies of real life and that art would not be able to change society. "[P]oetry makes nothing happen",[9] he would famously say in 1939 before leaving for the United States. *Night Mail* thus marks a moment of precarious fulfilment of wishful thinking in which the spirit of solidarity temporarily prevailed and created an artistic product that manifested the experience of lived solidarity.

The significance of this historical moment is signalled by the fact that the year 1936 was not only of central importance in the lives of Britten and Auden,[10] it also saw the publication of two seminal art essays on the European continent, to which a *TLS* "Commentary" has recently drawn attention:[11] the second, enlarged edition of Walter Benjamin's *Das Kunstwerk im Zeitalter seiner technischen Reproduzierbarkeit* (*The Work of Art in the Age of Mechanical Reproduction*) appeared in 1936, as did the revised version, based on his Zurich and Frankfurt lectures, of Martin Heidegger's *Der Ursprung des Kunstwerkes* (*The Origin of the Artwork*). Both essays put art on a new footing: Benjamin "axed the capital A from art", as the author colourfully declares, by denying art's auratic function as "a bearer of higher truths" (Chamberlain 2014: 14); and Heidegger equally spoke against art's inwardness and demanded that "art

---

9   Auden 1976: 197 ("In Memory of W.B. Yeats", l. 36).
10   See Donald Mitchell, who highlighted this year in his important study of 1981, revised in
     2000: *Britten and Auden in the Thirties: The Year 1936*.
11   See Chamberlain 2014: "Sacrificing Beauty. 1936: The Year Art Was Set Free from the Past".

should happen" and not remain an "object hanging on the wall". Both observed an inevitable "drift towards public art" (ibid.), as also did Bertolt Brecht, who, again around 1936, for the first time announced his didactic 'theatre of alienation'. British intellectuals were strikingly sensitive to these far-reaching changes in the European aesthetic climate, and it is fascinating that they applied the new approaches and demonstrated them in art products which vividly reflect the desired public concern in new art forms of collaborative aesthetic creativity.

References

Aitken, Ian (1992). *Film and Reform: John Grierson and the Documentary Film Movement*. London/New York, NY: Routledge.

Amis, Kingsley (1978). "Introduction". Kingsley Amis, ed. *The New Oxford Book of Light Verse*. Oxford: OUP. v–xxii.

Anthony, Scott (2007). *Night Mail*. BFI Film Classics. London: British Film Institute.

Auden, W.H. (1935/1977). "Psychology and Art To-day". Edward Mendelson, ed. *The English Auden: Poems, Essays, and Dramatic Writings, 1927–1939*. New York, NY: Random House. 332–342. (Orig. publ.: Geoffrey Grigson, ed. *The Arts To-day*. London: John Lane The Bodley Head).

Auden, W.H. (1938). "Introduction". W.H. Auden, ed. *The Oxford Book of Light Verse*. Oxford: OUP. vii–xx.

Auden, W.H. (1964). "Introduction". Anne Fremantle, ed. *The Protestant Mystics*. Boston, MA: Little, Brown and Company. 12–30.

Auden, W.H. (1976). *Collected Poems*. Ed. Edward Mendelson. London: Faber and Faber.

Benjamin, Walter (1935/1989). "Das Kunstwerk im Zeitalter seiner technischen Reproduzierbarkeit". *Gesammelte Schriften*, vol. 7. Werkausgabe, vol. 1. Eds. Rolf Tiedemann, Hermann Schweppenhäuser. Frankfurt am Main: Suhrkamp. 350–384. (First ed. 1935; second enlarged ed. 1936).

Boyd, Craig A. (2008). "Introduction: Perspectives on Love and *Agapé*". Craig A. Boyd, ed. *Visions of* Agapé*: Problems and Possibilities in Human and Divine Love*. Aldershot/Burlington, VT: Ashgate. 1–14.

Carpenter, Humphrey (1992). *W.H. Auden: A Biography*. Oxford: OUP.

Chamberlain, Lesley (2014). "Commentary: Sacrificing Beauty. 1936: The Year Art Was Set Free from Its Past". *The Times Literary Supplement* (April 18): 14f.

Cooke, Mervyn, ed. (1999). *The Cambridge Companion to Benjamin Britten*. Cambridge: CUP.

Davenport-Hines, Richard (1995). *Auden*. London: Heinemann.

Hardy, Forsyth, ed. (1979). *Grierson on Documentary*. London: faber & faber.

Heidegger, Martin (1935/2012). *Der Ursprung des Kunstwerkes*. Ed. Friedrich-Wilhelm von Herrmann. Frankfurt am Main: Klostermann. (First ed. 1935; second rev. ed. 1936, in *Holzwege*).

Kildea, Paul (1999). "Britten, Auden and 'Otherness'". Cooke, ed. 36–53.

Leahy, Conor (2015). "Forests of Green: W.H. Auden and Older Scots Poetry". *The Times Literary Supplement* (July 3): 14f.

Mendelson, Edward (1981). *Early Auden*. London/Boston, MA: faber & faber.

Mitchell, Donald (1981/2000). *Britten and Auden in the Thirties: The Year 1936*. The T.S. Eliot Memorial Lectures 1979. New ed. Aldeburgh Studies in Music 5. Woodbridge/Rochester, NY: Boydell Press.

Night Mail (1936/2007). DVD Video. British Film Institute Digital Restoration. BFIVD833.

Night Mail (online). https://www.youtube.com/watch?v=FkLoDg7e_ns [28/07/2018].

Palmer, Christopher, ed. (1984). *The Britten Companion*. London/Boston, MA: faber & faber.

Reed, Philip (1999). "Britten in the Cinema: *Coal Face*". Cooke, ed. 54–77.

Rotha, Paul (1936/1952). *Documentary Film*. Third ed. London: faber & faber.

Swann, Paul (1989). *The British Documentary Film Movement, 1926–1946*. Cambridge: CUP.

Watt, Harry (1974). *Don't Look at the Cinema*. London: Elek.

Winston, Brian (1995). *Claiming the Real: The Griersonian Documentary and Its Limitations*. London: British Film Institute.

Winters, Ben (2012). "Musical Wallpaper?". *Music, Sound and the Moving Image* 6/1: 39–54.

CHAPTER 7

An Incarnation of Memory: Song as Absence in Claude Lanzmann's *Shoah*

Ruth Jacobs

Abstract

Representing the Holocaust is impossible. Its incomprehensibility is compounded by the fragmentary nature of traumatic memory. In *Shoah*, Claude Lanzmann systematically avoids constructing a linear version of the past, and in the nine and a half hours of film there is no archival footage. Lanzmann is interested instead in the way memory manifests itself in the present. *Shoah* opens with a brief written statement about Chelmno and one of its two survivors, Simon Srebnik. As a child prisoner, Srebnik would sing folk songs while rowing Nazi guards up the Narew River. Unlike most of the film, this text is not accompanied by narration, visuals, or sound. This absence emphasizes that the narrative space of the film takes place in the present. When Srebnik returns to Chelmno, Lanzmann uses song as the vehicle through which we enter the resurrected past. The song we hear contains its own narrative trajectory that is distinct from Srebnik's past. This juxtaposition serves as a tangible reminder that his memories remain inaccessible. In this paper, I explore how he merges visual, spoken, and musical narrative structures in the opening scenes of *Shoah* to undermine a cohesive vision of memory.

•••

Representing the Holocaust is impossible, as its incomprehensibility is compounded by the fragmentary nature of individual traumatic memories, and the most important testimony belongs to the dead. But this inherent inexpressibility is inextricably linked with the necessity to speak, or as survivor Elie Wiesel states, "to wrest those victims from oblivion" (1990: 21). In *Remnants of Auschwitz*, Giorgio Agamben interrogates the absence at the heart of Holocaust testimony, maintaining that one must acknowledge the impossibility of representation without consigning events to silence:

> Those who assert the unsayability of Auschwitz today should be more cautious in their statements. If they mean to say that Auschwitz was a

unique event in the face of which the witness must in some way submit his every word to the test of the impossibility of speaking, they are right. (2000: 157)

Claude Lanzmann's seminal film *Shoah* – comprised of over nine hours of testimony and filmed over a period of eleven years (1974–1985) – systematically avoids representing the past through the use of archival footage. Like Agamben, Lanzmann believes that the unsayability of Auschwitz must be breached, but he also maintains that submitting to the impossibility of speaking is dependent on the necessary refusal of what he calls the "obscenity of understanding":

> It is enough to formulate the question in simplistic terms – why have the Jews been killed? – for the question to reveal right away its obscenity. There is an absolute obscenity in the very project of understanding. Not to understand was my iron law during all the eleven years of the production of *Shoah*. I clung to this refusal of understanding as the only possible ethical and at the same time the only possible operative attitude. (1991: 204)

Lanzmann employs a multitude of techniques to undermine the implication that the film's testimony will lead to anything other than the comprehension of minute, seemingly insignificant details. As Shoshana Felman, who has written extensively about the film, notes: "It is only through the trivia, by small steps – and not by huge strides or big leaps – that the barrier of silence can be in effect displaced, and somewhat lifted" (1991: 52). If the goal of this often relentless questioning is not comprehension, then its purpose is to speak while recognising that what is said cannot account for the silence of the dead, or attempt to explain what must remain incomprehensible.

Lanzmann seeks to conjure rather than depict the past: "To condense in one word what the film is for me, I would say that the film is an *incarnation*, a *resurrection*" (1986: 48). The film does not simply remember, but points to memory that is inaccessible, as it has been obliterated by extreme trauma or is altogether absent in the minds of the living. Lanzmann uses song as a vehicle through which we experience the 'incarnation' of what is missing. The film opens with survivor Simon Srebnik's return to Chelmno where he re-enacts the past by singing a Polish folk song he used to sing to Nazi guards. The song we hear contains its own narrative trajectory that is distinct from Srebnik's experience. This juxtaposition serves as a reminder that his memories remain inaccessible, while the song creates a perceptible residue of the past. Jean-Louis Pautrot recognises musical memory's affinity with oblivion: "musical memory is generated from the inescapable vanishing of reality – from disappearance, invisibility, and silence – rather than from a mimetic representation of reality" (2001: 168). The return of Srebnik's song undermines a cohesive vision of memory by re-enacting a fragment of the incomprehensible past. In this way, the song embodies what is missing, making us painfully aware of the immense disjunction between what we are witnessing in the present and what remains inaccessible. This vision of song as absence provides a lens through which to view Lanzmann's conception of *Shoah*. This confrontation between the traumatic past and the incarnation of its residue serves as the creative locus of the film.

Before returning to Srebnik's song, I would like to explore how Lanzmann subverts linear narrative in order to negate individual stories. Although many kinds of absence permeate Holocaust memory, Lanzmann reveals that his conception of *Shoah* emerged from the lack of witnesses to death in the gas chambers:

> What was most important was missing: the gas chambers, death in the gas chambers, from which no one had returned to report. The day I realized that this was missing, I knew that the subject of the film would be death itself, death rather than survival, a radical contradiction since it attested to the impossibility of the project I was embarking on: the dead could not speak for the dead. (2013: 419)

Sitting through over nine hours of testimony, one begins to recognise the magnitude of this abyss, as survivors struggle to transmit their own fragmented memories and are constantly confronted with their inability to bear witness to something they did not actually experience. As survivor and writer Primo Levi acknowledges: "I must repeat: we, the survivors are not the true witnesses [...]. We survivors are not only an exiguous but also an anomalous minority: We are those who by their prevarications or abilities or good luck did not touch bottom" (1989: 83).

Despite the vast number of people who appear in his film, Lanzmann avoids following any individual narrative threads. Witnesses speak, disappear, and re-surface (sometimes hours later), creating the illusion of endlessly cycling testimony that brings us no closer to understanding. Lanzmann maintains that the survivors he interviewed were not interested in telling their own stories, but "naturally express themselves in the name of all, considering the question of their own survival almost as anecdotal, of little interest, since they too were fated to die – which is why I consider them as 'revenants' rather than as survivors" (2013: 424). This fragmented narrative construction not only parallels the process of remembering trauma, but also emphasises Lanzmann's desire to incarnate the voices of the dead, rather than represent stories of survival:

> From the moment I became convinced that there would be no archive footage, no individual stories, that the living would be self-effacing so that the dead might speak through them, that there would be no 'I,' however fantastical or fascinating or atypical an individual fate might be (ibid.: 423).

Lanzmann's decision to exclude archival footage emphasises that the narrative space of the film takes place in the present. He confronts the unsayability of Auschwitz by refusing to depict the past. *Shoah* is the past as it manifests itself in the present, including its fragmentation, its silence, or what Pautrot has referred to as the paradoxical presence of an absence (cf. 2001: 169).

Before we enter this world, Lanzmann presents a written text about survivor Simon Srebnik. Unlike the majority of the film, this text isn't supported by visual images or narration. While Lanzmann provides contextual information about Chelmno, he is careful to emphasise that *Shoah* takes place in the present, as the opening line reads: "The story begins in the present at Chelmno, on the Narew River, in Poland" (1985: 1). He then reveals that Chelmno was where the first Jews were exterminated by gas. With 400,000 deaths, there were only two survivors, Michaël Podchlebnik and Simon Srebnik. We read that as a child of 13, Srebnik would sing Polish folk tunes to a Nazi guard as they rowed up the Narew River. Two days before Soviet troops arrived, Srebnik was executed with the other remaining Jews in the work details. The bullet missed the vital areas of his brain; he was discovered by a Polish farmer, and later treated by a Soviet Army doctor. Lanzmann's decision to open the film with Srebnik, one of Chelmno's two survivors, re-enforces Levi's assertion that "[w]e, the survivors are not the true witnesses".

Immediately following the film's opening text, we witness Srebnik's return to Chelmno. What is most un-settling is the peacefulness of the river, a feeling that is undermined by what we have just read. *Incarnation*. Lanzmann often repeats this word when discussing not only the film, but other times he experiences the almost violent return of the past. These moments almost always result from the collision between his imagined conception of the past and the real places where events occurred. He explains that before visiting the former camps, "the terror it evoked in me whenever I dared to think about it had consigned it to a different time, almost to another world, light years away, beyond human time" (2013: 412). For a long time, Lanzmann was reluctant to visit Poland, and he sought incarnation through testimony itself, believing that "if the Holocaust existed somewhere, it was in the minds and the memories of the survivors and of the killers, and could therefore be talked about in Jerusalem, in Berlin, Paris, New York, Australia or South America" (ibid.: 424). When he reaches Poland, however, the continued presence of Treblinka forces Lanzmann to shift his perception of the Holocaust from a distant reality to the complex vision of the present we experience in *Shoah*:

> Treblinka became real, the shift from myth to reality took place in a blinking flash, the encounter between a name and a place wiped out everything I had learned, forced me to start again from scratch, to view everything that I had been working on in a radically different way. (Ibid.: 474)

It is almost as though the opening text simulates Lanzmann's perception of events before traveling to Poland. Despite his emphasis that the story takes place in the present, reading in silence places the horrific events described in a separate narrative space, one that is distinct from our immediate reality. As we enter the Chelmno of the present, however, we are confronted with a reality that is coherent with our experience of the world. These geographical sites of memory play a pivotal role in *Shoah,* as Lanzmann's decision to conduct his interviews in the physical spaces where the past occurred reveals the vast distance between the present narrative – which we are capable of perceiving – and the incomprehensibility of the past.

It is only when the knowledge that we cannot and must not understand collides with the reality of these physical spaces that traces of this past become perceptible. As Lanzmann articulates: "The persistence and the disfigurement of places coexisted, wrestled with each other, impregnated each other, chiselling perhaps even more finely, more heartrenderingly, the presence of what remained of the past" (ibid.: 475). Lanzmann provides us with a visual reality that we can relate to, while his questions constantly remind us that what occurred there cannot be articulated.

Felman notes that "[t]he film does not stop [...] at the site of its own findings, does not settle at its initial point of arrival, but rather, uses the arrival as a point of departure for another *kind* of journey, *a return trip* which, going back to the originally unperceived historical scene, takes place as a journey to another frame of reference" (1991: 59). Music has a capacity for repetition that enables a kind of resurrected past that is inaccessible to other modes of communication. The disconnect between the horror described in the silent opening text and the peaceful images of a man singing a folk tune while floating down the river creates a space where the past remains perceptible, but incomprehensible. Our capacity to experience the song further emphasises this lack of understanding. We hear the gentle melody and its text of innocent longing, as the song carries its own narrative trajectory that is distinct both from Srebnik's past and the narrative space of the film. The song expresses a nostalgic longing for a little white house, the innocence of childhood that Srebnik never experienced. When we first hear his voice, we cannot see Srebnik's face, and it is *almost* possible to forget why he is singing. As the camera zooms in, however, the pain masked by the seemingly innocent text is immediately apparent, as Lanzmann explains in the introduction to the written text of the film: "The faces of those who are speaking, their mimicry, their gestures, in other words, the image itself is the natural support of the subtitle, its incarnation" (1985: vii).

Felman maintains that the text of the song creates another layer of displacement between past and present, innocence and violence: "*Shoah* begins with the apparent innocence of singing, only to thrust us more profoundly and astonishingly into the discrepancy between the lyrics and their context, only to point us more sharply toward the ambiguity that lies behind that innocence" (1991: 72). Felman also draws a parallel between the white house that is described in the song and the whiteness of erasure. She suggests, that having viewed the rest of the film, the text takes on more meaning:

> For the viewer who has seen the film, and who has come full circle – like the film, like the song – to start again at the beginning, the 'white house' brings to mind not just the snow that, whitely covering the peaceful meadows, covers up the emptied graves from which the dead bodies were disinterred so as to be reduced to ashes, burned away, but similarly in a different sense, the later image of white houses in the Polish village of Wladowa, a village once inhabited by Jews but whose Jewish houses have been since vacated (like the graves under the snow) by their original inhabitants (obliterated in extermination camps) and are now occupied, owned and inhabited by Poles. (Ibid.: 70)

Felman acknowledges that this textual meaning is constructed by the context of the film and is not inherent in the original folk song, or even present in the first viewing of the film. Attributing this kind of meaning to the text of the song in some ways undermines Lanzmann's intention in including it. Part of *Shoah's* power comes from Lanzmann's refusal to find meaning beyond the literal, for to do so would imply that meaning can be found in incomprehensible horror. While Felman's analysis of the text provides valuable insight into her experience of the song within the context of the film, it is important to remember that this meaning is not inherent in the text itself.

Perhaps more important than the meaning of the words is the language in which they are sung. The testimony in the rest of the film is significant not only because of the meaning of the words, but also in its preservation of voice. Lanzmann was determined to preserve the voices of and languages of the people he interviews in the film. Even the subtitles are given slightly after the words are spoken in order to emphasize that, as Felman notes, the language of the film "is a language of translation, and, as such is double foreign: that the occurrence, on one hand, happens in a language foreign to the language of the film, but also, that the significance of the occurrence can only be articulated in a language foreign to the languages of the occurrence" (ibid.: 46). In bringing translation to the fore, Lanzmann emphasizes what is lost, both in the translation of languages and the impossibility of translating extreme horror into language.

The Polish folk song allows Srebnik to speak (in his own language), to embody the significance of his return to Chelmno, while simultaneously refusing to articulate his incomprehensible past. Lanzmann reveals that much of what Srebnik told him was so extreme that he chose to exclude it from the film because it inhibited any form of transmission: "I didn't understand one word of what Srebnik was telling me [...]. The degree of horror was so high that this would have destroyed my purpose. My purpose was the transmission" (1991: 93). The song allows for Srebnik's voice to inhabit the paradoxical presence of absence inherent in his return. While the act of singing can be repeated, its text is in many ways irrelevant, as it does not and cannot transmit his ungraspable experience. The words, however, are important for what they do not say and the significance of hearing them sung in his voice and in his language allows us to perceive the music as the absence of testimony. The opening text has provided us with just enough information to recognise what is missing in the song. Here, music does not have the capacity to transmit what defies representation, but it does make this absence perceptible. From the moment he heard Srebnik sing, Lanzmann knew this was the only way to bridge the gap between the extreme horror of his past and the desire to speak: "I knew for certain that this man singing would go back with me to Chelmno, that I would film him singing on the River Ner, that this would be the opening sequence of *Shoah*" (2013: 438). Srebnik's return to Chelmno was an essential part of the song's capacity to communicate. As Felman notes: "Paradoxically enough, it is from the very evidence of its enactment as an antitestimony that the song derives the testimonial power of its repetition, and the historic eloquence of its unlikely and ghostly return" (1991: 76). The immediacy enacted by the return of the song initiates the film's process of listening.

The song also brings the original act of listening to the fore, as Srebnik's song is interrupted by the testimony of Polish villagers, who recall hearing him sing as a child. While we hear them, we do not see them, as the camera remains focused on Srebnik's face. This recalls their original place of listening, as they hear him only from a distance. One of the villagers comments that hearing Srebnik again re-animates his memory, causing him to re-experience the past: "When I heard him again my heart beat faster because what happened here [...] was a murder. I really relived what happened" (Lanzmann 1985: 2). The testimonial power of the song depends not only on its return, but also on those who listen. The villager's assertion that he "relived what happened" only reveals that his role as a witness to the horror of Chelmno is fundamentally flawed. This statement only emphasises the contradiction between his experience of passive listening – which can be re-lived – and Srebnik's, which cannot even be fully recalled. Any agency that is perceived in Srebnik's singing is undermined by the German song he was forced to sing by the guards. As Felman notes, this song and its language reminds us that it (along with the Polish folk song) is "a sadistic tool by which the singing child becomes a hostage to the Germans, an instrument of torment and abuse through which young Srebnik is reduced by his adult spectators to a chained, dancing marionette transformed – playfully and cruelly – into a singing toy" (1991: 74).

The level of this disparity is only heightened when we first hear Srebnik speak. After what feels like hours of silent walking, he and Lanzmann pause. Srebnik focuses on the physical space: "It's hard to recognize, but it was here. They burned people here. Yes this is the place" (Lanzmann 1985: 3). We witness Srebnik grappling with the vast distance between his memory of extreme violence and the reality of returning to the physical landscape of Chelmno:

> No one can describe it. No one can recreate what happened here. Impossible? And no one can understand it. Even I, here, now ... I can't believe I'm here. No, I just can't believe it. It was always this peaceful here. Always. When they burned two thousand people – Jews – every day, it was just as peaceful. No one shouted. Everyone went about his work. It was silent. Peaceful. Just as it is now.
>
> LANZMANN 1985: 3

Srebnik's assertion that "[n]o one can recreate what happened here" – that even he cannot fully grasp the significance of his return – undermines any potential reading of the song's capacity to re-create the past. The resurrection of the song not only embodies absence, but also demonstrates the incomprehensibility of what remains present. Srebnik's revelation that the peaceful countryside we are viewing is the same as it was when "they burned two thousand people – Jews – every day", further unsettles our sense of place and time. The unchanged landscape simultaneously brings the past closer to our present reality and incarnates the chasm of oblivion. Even Srebnik, who experienced the Chelmno of the past, struggles to comprehend the reality of its physical spaces: "And no one can understand it. Even I, here, now ... I can't believe I'm here".

Srebnik disappears from the narrative space of the film, as we hear testimony from a number of people, including Michaël Podchlebnik, the only other survivor of Chelmno. As Lanzmann illustrates, however, "*Shoah* had to be built like a musical piece, where a theme appears at a lower level, disappears, comes back at a higher level or in full force, disappears" (qtd. Felman 1991: 76). We see the landscape first, as Srebnik's disembodied voice returns, describing the inconceivable task of grinding the bones that were too big to burn:

> There was a concrete platform some distance away, and the bones that hadn't burned, the big bones of the feet, for example, we took ... There was a chest with two handles. We carried the bones there, where others had to crush them. It was very fine, that powdered bone. Then it was put into sacks, and when there were enough sacks, we went to a bridge on the Narew River, and dumped the powder. The current carried it off. It drifted downstream.
>
> LANZMANN 1985: 10f.

We see Srebnik pick up a handful of dirt, running it through his fingers to demonstrate the consistency of the powdered bone, juxtaposing what can easily be simulated with the incomprehensibility of what it represents. His words, "[i]t drifted downstream", are heard as we view the waters of the Narew glide past the boat.

At this moment, the song returns for a second time. This time, however, we do not see Srebnik, as the melody of nostalgic longing floats down the river in place of the powdered bones, once again incarnating absence itself. Both the song and the moving image of the river remain as Lanzmann questions Auschwitz survivor Paula Biren: "You never returned to Poland since?" The residue of the song and the image of present-day Poland haunt her response: "I wanted to, many times, but what would I see?" (1985: 11). Her words undercut the landscape we are witnessing. What are we seeing? Nothing. But that is precisely what Lanzmann wants us to see. His refusal to include images from the past, his return to these original sites of memory, the attention to details: all of these methods reveal that we must create a space for absence in order "to wrest those victims from oblivion" (Wiesel 1990: 21). But underneath all of this, though barely audible, the song persists. Srebnik's voice carries the residue of the past with it, and as Victor Zuckerkandl reveals, the "melody declares to us that the past can be there without being remembered" (1956: 235).

References

Agamben, Giorgio (2000). *Remnants of Auschwitz*. Cambridge, MA: MIT Press.

Felman, Shoshana (1991). "In an Era of Testimony: Claude Lanzmann's *Shoah*". *Yale French Studies* 79: 39–81.

Lanzmann, Claude (1985). *Shoah, an Oral History of the Holocaust: The Complete Text of the Film by Claude Lanzmann*. New York, NY: Pantheon.

Lanzmann, Claude (1986). "An Evening with Claude Lanzmann". First part of Lanzmann's visit to Yale, 4 May 1986; videotaped and copyrighted by Yale University. Felman 1991: 48.

Lanzmann, Claude (1991). "Seminar on *Shoah*". *Yale French Studies* 79: 82–103.

Lanzmann, Claude (2013). *The Patagonian Hare*. New York, NY: Farrar, Straus and Giroux.

Levi, Primo (1989). *The Drowned and the Saved*. London: Abacus.

Pautrot, Jean-Louis (2001). "Music and Memory in Fiction: Listening to *Nuit et brouillard* (1955), *Lacombe Lucien* (1973), and *La ronde de nuit* (1969)". *Dalhousie French Studies* 55: 168–182.

Wiesel, Elie (1990). *From the Kingdom of Memory*. New York, NY: Summit Books.

Zuckerkandl, Victor (1956). *Sound and Symbol*. Princeton, NJ: Princeton Univ. Press.

CHAPTER 8

Accumulating Schubert: Music and Narrative in Nuri Bilge Ceylan's *Winter Sleep*

Heidi Hart

Abstract

The soundtrack for Ceylan's 2014 film *Winter Sleep* includes only five minutes of music: the opening passage of Schubert's A-major Piano Sonata no. 20, Andantino, repeated in moments suggesting the main character's *Bildung* and introspection. As the film progresses, this musical signal takes on increased narrative weight; its repetition adheres to a growing sense of the damage this character's privilege enacts on his wife and on the families who owe him rent. Drawing on Irina Rajewsky's recent work on transmedial movement, this paper argues for repetition and accumulation as narrative strategies across media, while pointing out the material associativity unique to music – in this case a Schubert passage that, in its broken-record replication, exposes the cost of traditional European bourgeois values in a Turkish household as patriarchal as it is 'western'. Here music does not intensify an emotional-narrative arc but adds a critical dimension to dialogue and visual storytelling.

•••

In his 2002 novel *Snow*, Orhan Pamuk describes his poet-protagonist Ka as the proud wearer of a German overcoat from the Galeria Kaufhof department store in Frankfurt. As Ka navigates the accumulation of snow, stories, and political intrigue in the eastern Turkish city Kars, his coat gives him what he experiences as the pleasurable weight of European male authority. Likewise, in Nuri Bilge Ceylan's 2014 film *Winter Sleep*, a 'westernized' Turkish writer and former actor seems quite attached to his Chesterfield coat; he carries privileged heft through his days, as he meets – and often brushes off – the concerns of his tenants, sister, and wife. This weight accumulates less through the often-banal conversations in the film than through the associative force of a repeated Schubert passage, the A theme of the Andantino movement in the A-major Piano Sonata no. 20. What looks and sounds at first like a familiar trope of reflective European masculinity – in scenes showing the writer Aydin walking home or entering his comfortable study – begins to take on a menacing gravity, as the same passage recurs like a broken record in a film otherwise empty of music. This lack of an ongoing musical soundtrack, as is notable in Ceylan's 2011 film *Once Upon a Time in Anatolia*, foregrounds not only the occasional musical fragment in *Winter Sleep* but also amplifies everyday sounds such as the clinking of tea glasses or the roar of a jeep's engine, making the film's physical environment almost oppressively palpable.

Ceylan's film adapts Chekhov's story "My Wife"/"The Wife", striking like the film in its use of banal dialogue and the slowly accumulating pressure of familial power. In the story, a landowner and his estranged wife reach a crisis point when her independent famine-relief project threatens his patriarchal comfort. His efforts to take over her work, with his money and condescending attention to her financial records, only cause her pain; despite both of their attempts to flee their tension-filled estate, they simply cannot. The landowner hears a voice repeatedly telling him that he is a "swine" (or, in one translation, a "reptile"), alongside his memory of the words "Virtue brings its own reward" or "How pleasant it is to be good" (Chekhov 1892/1989: 43, and 2013 online). In Ceylan's film adaptation, the landowner – and writer of railroad histories – is a hotel owner and former actor, now occupied with and endlessly frustrated by his attempt to write the history of Turkish theater. His tenants in the local village, in the famous Cappadocia mountains, live in crushing poverty amid the snow-dusted cliff ruins. Aydin is as aloof from them as he is kind to his hotel guests. His much younger wife Nihal lives quite apart from him in the hotel and begins to host community meetings to address problems of poverty and education. In the evenings, Aydin's sister lounges on the sofa behind him in his study; the siblings heckle each other mildly about each other's lack of real accomplishment. Aydin dabbles in philanthropy, in the case of a young woman whose plight seems to appeal to him more aesthetically than authentically. When he discovers his wife's further-reaching activities, he feels his authority threatened, and the story plays out similarly to Chekhov's plot. With no imaginary voice to call Aydin a "reptile", however, the film requires another form of critical commentary: music.

As Michel Chion points out in his well-known study of sound in film, 'pit' or non-diegetic music can serve several functions in relation to the images and action onscreen (cf. 2009: 410–413). Chion adds more complexity to Hanns Eisler and Theodor Adorno's distinction, in their 1947 *Composing for the Films*, between "redundant" and "contrapuntal" film sound (ibid.: 430); he notes that while film music usually works to intensify affective states played out onscreen, either through empathy or indifference that in fact reinforces the emotion "while giving it a different inflection", music can also work through "didactic counterpoint" (ibid.: 431) similar to Brecht's *Verfremdungseffekt*, or alienation effect, in the theater. This form of counterpoint works at critical as well as emotional levels, linking familiar musical tropes to "particular ideas: culture, power, social origins" (ibid.). In *Winter Sleep,* Schubert's piano music could also be heard as what Ben Winters calls "intradiegetic" music, which emanates from characters who do not hear it (2010: 231). The Andantino passage can certainly be heard as carrying associations with European cultivation or *Bildung*; because the passage is repeated only in scenes showing the male protagonist (or, increasingly, anti-hero), the music also bears associations with educated masculinity and its attendant privilege, as in Luis Bacalov's score for the film *Il postino,* with its melancholy accordion-piano "I sogni del postino". In *Winter Sleep,* the repetition of the Schubert passage makes it harder and harder to hear as mere background; as the film develops, showing more and more of Aydin's semi-conscious lording of power over his tenants and the women in his life, each return of the piano passage sounds less poignant and more sinister. The music's fragmentary aspect, a quality of the entire Schubert sonata, also heightens its reified cultural status, as a broken piece of bourgeois *Kulturgut.*

Repetition of a musical fragment in *Winter Sleep* works similarly to a re-cycled theme in a musical work or to language-echoes in a textual narrative. This similarity occurs in the field Beate Schirrmacher has called "transmedial common ground" (2015: 1f.), drawing on Lars Elleström's point that movement between media depends on "qualifying" or similar elements (2010: 24f.). Just as the repetition of a phrase can add increasing weight to one aspect of a novel (e.g., the repeated phrase "the leaden circles dissolved in the air" and other references to Big Ben accumulating association with Septimus Warren's suicide in Virginia Woolf's *Mrs. Dalloway*; 1925/1981: 4, 186), or as the buildup of repeated images (such as the stones in Jan Troell's 1971 film *The Emigrants*) can enact "a threatening exponential curve" (Bruhn 2013: 79f.) in visual storytelling, sound repetition in film can achieve a similar cumulative effect, as in Peter Lorrie's also increasingly sinister whistling of Grieg in Fritz Lang's film *M.* Irina Rajewsky has noted the ease with which rhythm can move across media borders, from poetry to music to the punctuation of images onscreen (cf. 2014), though of course its material manifestation is very different in each medial field. Similarly, repetition can move from the imagined voice in a Chekhov story ("you are a reptile") to the critical counterpoint of Schubert in *Winter Sleep,* but with a more embodied, performative quality that in turn adds more weight to the story's textual voice, if read with the film in mind.

To return to Eisler and Adorno, traditional tonal music has already been repeated so often through several centuries that it has accumulated associative weight before it even reaches the screen; repeating a single (or similar) passage nine times in a film containing only five minutes of music draws attention to its role as a cinematic trope. The music's material and affective-associative accumulation is actually essential to its critical function, just as the *Stimmung* or mood of a lyrical poem also includes a cognitive aspect that can expose socio-political costs or power structures implicit in the poetic world it calls up (cf. Pfau 2005: 12f.). This occurs in Heinrich Heine's puncturing of the very bourgeois cultural material he evokes with nightingale or lily tropes in his *Buch der Lieder* and in Paul Celan's triple-meter dance rhythms and other "metric structures inherited from Romanticism" that foreground "the problematic status of 'songful' verse after the Holocaust" (Englund 2012: 83, 85). In the case of *Winter Sleep*, a comfortably melancholy, drawing-room *Stimmung* easily associated with Schubert's late piano music (however existentially raw its moment of composition, at the end of the composer's life) can change into something more troubling – and more illuminating – if repeated at enough key moments. As Fredric Jameson has noted in his treatment of Brecht, repetition can reify aesthetic material to the point of exposing its very reification, a homeopathic form of *Verfremdung* (cf. 1999: 169). Another take on film music's critical potential is Lawrence Kramer's note that "no narrative is entirely truth" but is "vexed by the truth", an uncomfortable state of affairs that music can "underscore [...] in place of language", whose "falsifications can let truth appear" (2014). Such falseness also becomes increasingly apparent in the film's dialogue, particularly in Aydin's voice, just as it does as Chekhov's story develops. Over the course of *Winter Sleep*, Schubert sounds less and less like familiar classical background music and more and more like the Eurocentric, patriarchal cultural currency implicit in the hotel owner's speech.

How does this critical force accumulate in the film? The Schubert fragments come from either the first few bars of the Andantino A section or its slightly more complex reprise at the end of the movement. This Schubert passage tends to 'follow' the Aydin character from the snowy landscape outside into his cozy European-bourgeois study, which forms a tableau throughout the film, as it does in 'still life' descriptive moments in Chekhov's story. Sometimes it overlaps with scenes in which Aydin is not present, but in general, the 'intra-diegetic' music seems to work as a psychic attachment or extension of his character, similar to the voice in Chekhov's landowner-anti-hero's head. The tableau framing of these scenes slows down cinematic time to focus on Aydin as film cliché turning gradually inside-out to reveal his disturbing absorption of privilege. As Agnes Pethö has noted, the tableau vivant expresses nostalgia for older, bourgeois image-forms in cinematic space; rather than enacting a pause, the tableau becomes "a prototype of other repetitions and the focal point of circular movements" reaching to encompass a "big picture" (2014: 67f.). In the case of *Winter Sleep*, the bourgeois male study and its accompanying Schubert passage beg the question: what do such tableaux box *out*? Aydin's wife appears only marginally, and in musical-soundtrack silence, at the edges of the iconic male study-domain (her workspace in the Chekhov story is also described as a "corridor between drawing-room and bedroom"; 1892/1989: 37), until later in the film, when her village activism begins to take over the film's time and space. The 'enframing' of the study scene is a kind of containment and even entrapment, which the music gradually unsettles in exposing its status as cultural cliché.

In the first example, Aydin's head is gradually framed from behind by the study window; the camera makes a penetrating approach, as if embodying the inner voice that calls Chekhov's source character "a reptile". Other examples show Aydin entering or leaving the study space or the hotel lobby, until he is located mainly outdoors, often in scenes showing recently killed animals. In the final scene, which breaks from the Schubert passage to Italian film composer Luciano Michelini's "Desolation" for orchestra, a dual framing – Aydin's ostensibly humble interior monologue while re-entering the hotel, Nihal's continuing entrapment behind an upstairs window – the male figure lands at his study desk and is at last able to begin his book, while his wife remains emotionally shut down upstairs.

A look at the Schubert sonata itself sheds light on its effective use as repetition, an essential aspect of the work itself. The F-sharp minor Andantino's A section is almost obsessively repetitive, with 'sighing' seconds over dropping C-sharp octaves that seem stuck in time and place. That Schubert employs a 3/8 dance meter here creates a paradox of movement and stasis. What audiences do not hear in the film is the movement's tempestuous B section, with jagged, improvisational runs and sforzando outbursts. Composed in the last months of Schubert's life, this is one of three cyclically linked sonatas that, in their wordless drama and in formal connective tissue, mirror the bleak and subtle minor-major workings and obsessive piano ostinati of the *Winterreise* cycle. The A section's conclusion also echoes, harmonically, the chorale-like prelude of Schubert's 1817 song "Death and the Maiden", which he reworked into the famous string quartet of that name shortly before his death. The 'stuck' quality of the A section is a musical element also exploited by Chopin in his A minor Mazurka, Op. 17, no. 2, which contains a heavy-footed dance-within-a-dance that goes nowhere, until it breaks on its own broken-record pattern in an also-stuck-sounding fortissimo diminished-seventh chord before returning to the melancholic A theme. In both cases, this repetition creates cumulative tension; Schubert releases it in a crazy fantasia, but in Ceylan's film, the A-theme passage never gets that far. The only 'new' music occurs at the very end of the film when Aydin's wife appears hopelessly bound to the hotel in its remote winter landscape. An orchestra briefly rushes in with a piece titled "Desolation" and is gone.

To conclude, Nuri Bilge Ceylan's film *Winter Sleep* adapts Chekhov's story "The Wife" not only as a film set in Turkey but also as a transmedial work that applies musical repetition to similar critical effect as the inner voice that calls Chekhov's main male character a "swine" or "reptile". The associative buildup of Schubert's piano music, more or less easily associated with European interior spaces and masculine melancholy, takes on a critical effect as the film progresses. The cost of hotel-owner Aydin's power over his wife, sister, and impoverished tenants becomes more and more apparent as the Schubert passage follows him in and out of his comfortable study. By the end of the film, even his attempt at a transformative journey into the snow only leads to a restoration of the status quo for his wife, whose own attempts to help her community and to escape her oppressive household have failed. All of this said, what remains after the film's conclusion is an echo of the obsessively repeated Schubert passage, perhaps as an 'earworm' following audience members out of the movie theater or away from the screen at home, a material trace that – having served its critical function – continues to resound in a way that repetitions in literary or visual storytelling do not. Whether this echo retains or escapes its critical force is a matter of individual reception, an indication of music's slipperiness, adhering to narrative for as long as it can.

References

Bruhn, Jørgen (2013). "Dialogizing Adaptation Studies". Jørgen Bruhn, Anne Gjelsvik, Eirik Frisvold Hanssen, eds. *Adaptation Studies: New Challenges, New Directions*. London: Bloomsbury. 69–88.

Ceylan, Nuri Bilge, dir. (2014). DVD. *Winter Sleep*. Adopt Films.

Chekhov, Anton (1892/1989). "My Wife". *A Woman's Kingdom and Other Stories*. Transl. Ronald Hingley. Oxford: OUP. 22–59.

Chekhov, Anton (2013 online). "The Wife". http://www.onlineliterature.com/anton_chekhov/1261/ [08/01/2015].

Chion, Michael (2009). *Film: A Sound Art*. Transl. Claudia Gorbman. New York, NY: Columbia Univ. Press.

Eisler, Hanns, Theodor W. Adorno (1947/2007). *Composing for the Films*. London/New York, NY: Continuum.

Elleström, Lars (2010). "The Modalities of Media: A Model for Understanding Intermedial Relations". *Media Borders, Multimodality and Intermediality*. Lars Elleström, ed. New York, NY: Palgrave Macmillan. 11–48.

Englund, Axel (2012). *Still Songs: Music In and Around the Poetry of Paul Celan.* Farnham: Ashgate Publishing.

Jameson, Fredric (1999). *Brecht and Method.* London/New York, NY: Verso.

Kramer, Lawrence (2014). "Music and the Rise of Narrative". Lecture. Duke University, Department of Music. 11 September 2014 .

Pamuk, Orhan. *Snow* (2002/2004). Transl. Maureen Freely. New York, NY: Knopf.

Pethö, Agnes (2014). "The *Tableau Vivant* as a 'Figure of Return' in Contemporary East European Cinema". *Film and Media Studies* 9: 51–76.

Pfau, Thomas (2005). *Romantic Moods: Paranoia, Trauma, and Melancholy, 1790–1840.* Baltimore, MD: Johns Hopkins Univ. Press.

Rajewsky, Irina O. (2002). *Intermedialität.* UTB 2261. Tübingen/Basel: A. Francke.

Rajewsky, Irina O. (2010). "Border Talks: The Problematic Status of Media Borders in the Current Debate about Intermediality". Lars Elleström, ed. *Media Borders, Multimodality and Intermediality.* New York, NY: Palgrave Macmillan. 51–68.

Rajewsky, Irina O. (2014). "Transmediality". Seminar lecture. Linnaeus University, Växjö, Sweden, Centre for Intermedial and Multimodal Studies. 17 December 2014.

Schirrmacher, Beate (2015). Manuscript. "The Transmedial Common Ground of Intermedial References: Performativity in Elfriede Jelinek's *Die Klavierspielerin*".

Winters, Ben (2010). "The Non-diegetic Fallacy: Film, Music, and Narrative Space". *Music & Letters* 91/2: 224–244.

Woolf, Virginia (1925/1981). *Mrs. Dalloway.* New York, NY: Harcourt/Harvest Books.

CHAPTER 9

Mise en Scène, Mozart, and a Borrowed Chorale: Learned Style and Identity in Pawlikowski's *Ida*

Christopher Booth

Abstract

Pawel Pawlikowski's *Ida*, revered for its visual elements and unique cinematography, has gained considerable attention since its 2014 international release. In addition to its stunning black and white photography and academy ratio format, the film imparts multivalent layers of meaning with its score, which uses preexisting music almost exclusively. The music is largely contemporaneous with the film's 1960s setting, however two selections stand out as uniquely meaningful: Mozart's Jupiter Symphony and Busoni's transcription of Bach's "Ich ruf' zu dir, Herr Jesu Christ". In fact, inasmuch as Pawlikowski formulates his two primary characters, employing mise en scène to demonstrate psychological and emotional conditions, he deploys these two musical works as supplemental indicators of these characters' respective motivations. In this paper, I will discuss the hermeneutic representation of preexisting music as it establishes and even alters filmic narrative. Through analysis of text, texture, and form, I will describe the auteur's unique presentation of narrative nuance, both connotative and denotative.

The titular character's internal struggle, a dominant component in the narrative, is both complex and dynamic. The same could be said for the protagonist's aunt, Wanda, though the two share few similarities. Coincidentally, however, each is driven by music. The music not only acts as supplement to the dramatic presentation of each character, but as an interpreter between act and significance. For Ida, who is driven to an austere, repressed existence, Bach/Busoni's music frees her from external forces and allows her introspective identity to crystalize. For Wanda, a retired judge who is constantly driven from the very order and discipline for which she is publicly known, Mozart's symphony is an addiction that modifies her behavior.

•••

Hermeneutic analysis in film musicology hinges upon musical source, along with other considerations, and the presence of preexisting music expands such inquiry. In many films, the meaning of particular scenes can be fundamentally hifted or enhanced by the presence of preexisting music. Often such preexisting music is textual, either operatic, from an oratorio or chorale, or otherwise conceived around a specific text. Regardless, the way we read films is inextricably linked to the way we hear music, textual or not. In "The Pleasures of Ambiguity: Using Classical Music in Film", Mike Cormack asks, "[why] film-makers [should] use preexisting classical music on a film soundtrack rather than either a score written specifically for the film or recent popular music which the audience is more likely to recognize?" (2006: 19f.). He then posits that "there are some fairly obvious reasons: it is likely to be cheaper, and it can be used to marshal particular connotations of culture and class", but he adds that "the music might also be chosen because of [how it] conveys meaning when taken out of its original context and given the new context of a narrative film" (ibid.). In the case of Pawel Pawlikowski's *Ida*, Cormack's description of the capabilities of preexisting music in film is perfectly suited. Like in many films of Stanley Kubrick, Ingmar Bergman, Quentin Tarantino, and others, all music in Pawlikowski's film is preexisting. No composer was hired, as Claudia Gorbman puts it in her seminal monograph *Unheard Melodies*, to "[lull] the audience into a state of psychic regression, making spectators more suscepti-ble to confuse the fantasy figures on the screen with reality", a typical behavior of traditional film scoring (qtd. Buhler 2014: 218f.).

Ida, which won the 2015 Academy Award for best foreign language film and was nominated for achievement in cinematography, is a much debated, cel-ebrated, and at times harshly censured film (see Brody 2014 online). Visually and musically unique, the film portrays life in post-WWII Poland with an al-most austere realism, similar to the French New Wave films of Robert Bres-son. The auteur himself states that "*Ida* is a film about identity, family, faith, guilt, socialism, and music" (Pawlikowski 2014a online). He goes on, "I wanted to make a film about history that wouldn't feel like a historical film – a film that is moral, but has no lessons to offer. I wanted to tell a story in which everyone has their reasons; a story closer to poetry than plot" (ibid.).

The music in *Ida*, again exclusively preexisting, is sparse. Most scenes are extremely silent: dialogue is minimal, and sound effects are faint. With two very notable exceptions, music is diegetic and contemporaneous. Pawlikowski interpolates songs that were popular in the early 1960s in Poland, whether they were actually composed during that decade or not. Speaking of his intention in this regard, he claims that "pop songs were a key from the start. They were fatally imprinted on my childhood memory. They really color the landscape" (ibid.). The popular music he mentions is mostly bebop and specifically that of John Coltraine. The exceptions, however, are not contemporaneous, outside of a given character's opportunity to hear recordings. Several scenes in the film contain a diegetic recording of Mozart's Jupiter symphony, and one pivotal and climactic scene deploys virtually the only non-diegetic music in the film: a recording of Ferruccio Busoni's transcription of a Bach chorale, performed by Alfred Brendel.

As we know, music has a profound effect on viewer interpretation. In historical fiction film, music is most commonly intended to complement the film in an aesthetic sense, but the result could actually be inappropriate and the choice objectionable. For example, consider the climactic scene in Tom Hooper's 2010 WWII drama, *The King's Speech*, which consists of King George VI's live radio address to the nation in which he declares war with Germany. The preexisting music was seemingly chosen for aesthetic purposes, but for many viewers, the *Allegretto* from Beethoven's seventh symphony carries an unsuitable connotation, considering that the Op. 92 symphony, which premiered alongside the Op. 91, "Wellington's Victory", was seen by the Viennese public as an especially patriotic Beethoven work, celebrating a long-awaited peace for Germany and Austria after the Napoleonic occupation.

Musicologist Jonathan Godsall studied numerous sources, including blog posts, about Hooper's musical selection; many describe it as ironic, confusing, or inappropriate, while others defended it, claiming that Beethoven's music simply belongs to the whole world (cf. 2014: 106f.). Alexandre Desplat, composer of the original score for *The King's Speech*, lends credence to this view in noting that the Allegretto "worked marvelously, and it made sense, since it has such a universal quality to it [...]. It's universal beyond countries and cultures" (qtd. ibid.). Regardless of whether one accepts Desplat's comment, the choice of the Beethoven symphony engendered criticism.

Perhaps a much more suitable example of preexisting music in a WWII drama is found in Roman Polanski's 2003 *The Pianist,* which takes place in Nazi occupied Poland. The protagonist, the Jewish pianist Wladyslaw Szpilman, played by Adrien Brody, performs Chopin works throughout the film, at least when he has access to a piano. After the Nazis invade, and while Szpilman is in hiding, he hears the first movement from the so-called "Moonlight" sonata being played by a pianist whom Szpilman eventually learns to be a German Captain named Wilhelm Hosenfeld. Hosenfeld discovers Szpilman, and asks him to play something, which turns out to be the Chopin G-Minor *Ballade*. Polanski's dichotomy of two pianists each playing the music of his own nation presents a sort of Herderian musical nationalism among wartime opponents. More importantly than the appropriate nationalist perspective deployed by Polanski's musical selections, is the notion that the chosen music instantiates character identity, a concept very much appropriated by Pawlikowski in *Ida*. The latter film contains two primary characters: the titular protagonist, a novitiate who, at the onset of the film, intends to take her vows in the coming weeks, and her biological aunt, Wanda, whom Ida meets very early in the film. Like Polanski's conjunction of Beethoven to Hosenfeld and Chopin to Szpilman, Pawlikowski associates Mozart's final symphony with Wanda, and, albeit only in the final scene of the film, Bach's chorale "Ich ruf zu dir, Herr Jesu Christ" with Ida.

As important as the auteur's musical choices are the film's breathtaking visuals. David Denby, film critic at *The New Yorker*, writes, "we are so used to constant movement and compulsive cutting in American movies that the stillness of the great new Polish film [*Ida*] comes as something of a shock. I can't recall a movie that makes such expressive use of silence and portraiture; from the beginning, I was thrown into a state of awe by the movie's fervent austerity. Friends have reported similar reactions: if not awe, then at least extreme concentration and satisfaction. This compact masterpiece has the curt definition and the finality of a reckoning – a reckoning in which anger and mourning blend together" (2014 online). Set in 1961, during the Stalinist dictatorship, the film, through its characters and music, channels the past; almost every element in the story evokes the war years and their aftermath.

Anna (Agata Trzebuchowska), also named Ida, is an 18-year-old novitiate in a remote Polish abbey. In the opening scene of the film, we see her touching up the paint on a statue of Jesus, and the mother superior calls her in to give her the news that before she will be allowed to take her vows and permanently enter into monastic life, she must travel to the city to meet her only living relative, Wanda (Agata Kulesza). Anna, who was orphaned as an infant and raised by the nuns, knows nothing about her past, but within minutes of her arrival, Wanda brusquely explains to Anna that she is actually Jewish and was born Ida Lebenstein. Her parents put Ida up for adoption before they went into hiding with a Christian family during the war.

Though the Lebensteins presumably perished in the war, the whereabouts of their bodies are unknown, and Wanda uses her niece's visit as a pretext to drive to the family's old farmhouse – now occupied by the son of the man who sheltered them – and try to find out what happened to Ida's parents.

Slate film critic Dana Stevens describes the filmic narrative as "an admirably compact and elegant (if ultimately gut-wrenching) road movie that traces the developing relationship between the naïve, pious Anna and the disillusioned Wanda, a high-functioning alcoholic who works as a judge in the communist government. Now a wearily cynical bureaucrat, she was known a decade ago as 'Red Wanda' for her zeal as a prosecutor of enemies of the state [...] she can hardly repress a smile at the mention of her niece's all-merciful God" (2014 online). As the two eventually reach Anna's hometown she never knew, the viewer learns that Wanda had a son who died along with Ida's parents. As Denby eloquently describes it, "the filmmakers have confronted a birthplace never forgiven but also never abandoned" (2014 online).

Lack of forgiveness forms in many ways the crux of Wanda's characterization; the judge lauds decency and decorum in her professional life, while driven to hedonism in her private life. She is celebrated at her funeral for her resilience against the anti-communist party of Poland. Her professional stalwartness, recalcitrant against any formal forgiveness, had been a thing to be praised by her comrades. This tendency bleeds into her personal life: early in the film we learn that she is aware of her niece Ida but is unwilling to claim her or be any part of her life. She abandons her, regrets it, but ultimately never asks for the forgiveness she clearly covets. When the two are forced to interact, Wanda encourages Anna towards promiscuity, saying "you should try [it] – otherwise what sort of sacrifice are these vows of yours?".

As I said, the visual is of equal importance to the musical. Mise en scène as an overall process clearly sets *Ida* apart from nearly every post-2000 film. First and most obviously, is the format. The film is entirely shot in a black-and-white Academy ratio (1.375 : 1). This antiquated format suggests the periodization of the work, since widescreen, letterbox, and other formats did not exist until after 1961, the ostensible setting of the film. Here we see Pawlikowski's vision for storytelling; keeping verisimilitude at the forefront, we see images as his intended characters would likely have seen them themselves. This technique is not entirely new or Pawlikowski's own; other recent examples include Michael Hazanavicius's 2011 *The Artist,* Steven Soderbergh's 2006 *The Good German*, and more recently Wes Anderson's 2014 *The Grand Budapest Hotel.* Each of these deploys cinematic technology as a means of relating the viewer to the specific time period of the diegesis. Anderson's film even goes as far as changing aspect ratios alongside time period shifts (cf. Wood 2014 online). What sets Pawlikowski's film apart is the combination of antiquated aspect ratio alongside the use of still, full shots throughout much of the film. With the exception of the final scene, the camera is entirely static, maintaining an almost Hitchcockian voyeurism. Close shots are extremely close, but unmoving. Distance shots are so wide that, in combination with the limited aspect ratio, much of the screen is unused.

During their journey, we see a wide-angle shot of Ida praying at an outdoor altar next to a large tree and Wanda, who is smoking a cigarette. The result is a less-than-subtle allusion to Andrei Tarkovsky's *Nostalghia,* a film with similar themes including religion, depression, and interactions with music and other arts. Tarkovsky uses several similar shots (and even the same Volkswagen model). Pawlikowski mentions Tarkovsky in several interviews as a primary influence; the allusion here likely refers to similar subject matter among the two films, including character interaction with place, the effects of political systems on character identities, familial loss, etc. The negative space of the landscape dominates each shot, and characters and events seem to move across the fixed perspective of the camera. Perhaps more importantly, however, is Pawlikowski's extreme attention to the so-called 'rule of thirds'. Peter Ward describes the rule, as "a useful starting point for any compositional grouping [...] to place the main subject of interest on any one of the four intersections made by two equally spaced horizontal and vertical lines" (2002: 124). In the vast majority of scenes in this film, including close-ups as well as wide shots, the diegesis is strictly composed alongside these imaginary lines.

This is not to say that Pawlikowski is doing something new at all; the rule of thirds is one of the most common techniques in visual literacy, regardless of medium. What is interesting about *Ida*, however, is the number of times, and specifically the occasions in which Pawlikowski breaks this rule. In each case, Pawlikowski uses these images, along with the music, for specific hermeneutic purposes. When we first encounter music of Mozart, Wanda and Anna are looking at old family photos. The second movement of the Jupiter symphony is playing on Wanda's record player, and the scene begins just at the onset of the movement. At measure 19, after a half cadence to the dominant C Major, the mode shifts to the dominant minor. Wanda is teasing Anna about her habit, and Anna finds a photograph of a boy. Both the color in the music and the photo seem to affect Wanda, who rises and changes the record to the opening of the jubilant, C Major fourth movement. Later, we will observe Wanda's intentional use of this movement as a type of self-therapy.

Mozart's second movement returns while the two are driving on their return trip, having found the bodies of Anna's parents and Wanda's son, whom Wanda wishes to rebury in a family grave. Beginning at measure 47 in the relative minor, the diegetic music played on the car stereo carries the same mournfulness, but more intensely chromatic and characteristic of Wanda's sense of loss. It is not difficult to connect the boy's photo in the earlier scene to the agonizing experience of unearthing his remains: a connection solidified through Pawlikowski's choice of the same Mozart movement. Hemiolas add to the unsettling tone of the scene; likewise, the visual effect suggests a sort of languishing brokenness, as the scene is dominated with negative space and fading images, seemingly ending in darkness.

Negative space, along with the jarring effect of relegating characters to the lowest region within the rule of thirds, increases toward the end of the film. In one example, Anna is waiting for Wanda to take her to the hospital to see the man who sheltered but later killed her parents. Having never left the convent, she knows no one in the city, and here we see her isolated and overwhelmed.

Without Wanda, we see her alone and feeling powerless. Later, she makes a deal with the killer's son, who offers to show Anna and Wanda the bodies of their family in exchange for them leaving the matter closed. Here, Pawlikowski's use of negative space suggests Anna's ignorance of, or inexperience with, her surroundings. We see this in several scenes in which Anna interacts with men.

Perhaps all of the characters in Pawlikowski's film are victims. Throughout the film and in Wanda's final scene, we see her using music as a redemptive space, especially the Mozart symphony, but after the closure of finally knowing where her son is buried, even the stirring, blissful first movement seems inadequate to temper her melancholy. The drug of Mozart had been rendered ineffective. As if she tries to let Mozart's music save her, she turns the music up as in a desperate attempt to maximize its effect, but the sound is now rendered insipid to the point of ineffectiveness. The camera never moves, the long play vinyl record continues. No non-diegetic score sensationalizes her choice. The viewer hears one more phrase of the sonata exposition, and the subsequent cut brings silence. "Wanda, we can't help thinking, *is* Polish history, both grieved over and unredeemed [...]. Red Wanda has been twice betrayed – by the slaughter of the Jews and Polish anti-Semitism, and then by Stalinism, which she enabled" (Denby 2014 online).

One could consider the music here as a positive motivation, actually giving Wanda the courage to end her life. Pawlikowski's statement lends credence to this notion, as he acknowledges the significance of the symphony: "I had a fixation [with Mozart] once in my life and I gave my fixation to Wanda. She needs it to pep herself up and to give herself energy, and it helped me a lot in the suicide scene to make that pass smoothly, heroically" (Pawlikovski/Roberts 2014 online). Regardless of whether the music hinders or encourages her self-destruction, the "Jupiter" is doubtless a type of self-therapy. The use of this particular movement of the symphony is also noteworthy as an example of Mozartian learned style. We do not hear the fugue section in the scene, but the primary theme is already contrapuntal. The meaning here is sublime: both Mozart and Wanda seem to contemplate the past; balance exists only upon the foundation of disorder that preceded it.

Having heard of her aunt's death, Anna leaves the convent again. Her grief seemingly drives her to Wanda's house, where she drinks alcohol, smokes cigarettes, and tries on Wanda's clothes. She goes to a nightclub where she decides to go home and sleep with a musician who had been flirting with her. Her actions seem erratic up to the final moments of the film, in which the cinematographic style changes for the first time. A moving camera follows Anna, the only tracking shot in the film, and finally an unsteady handheld shot places her in the center of the screen. The non-diegetic score emerges: Busoni's transcription of Bach's chorale "Ich ruf zu dir, Herr Jesu Christ", based on Johann Agricola's sixteenth-century Lutheran hymn. Both visual and musical elements suggest Anna has finally made her own choice, having been forced into each previous situation, beginning with her Mother Superior insisting that she meet Wanda. Her statement of faith is now one of her own, and in Bach/Busoni's music we hear the unspoken voice of Anna, again Christian, saying "I call to you, Jesus".

This may not necessarily be a statement of faith or religious preference on the part of Pawlikowski, as it would have been just as easy to find a similarly themed Catholic musical source, which would make more sense for the character. But Busoni's music, like the climactic scene, is one of adaptation. The auteur replaces the verisimilitude of contemporaneous music heard throughout the film with the cinematic realist move of the handheld camera. The visual shift complements the tranquil aesthetic of the music, and the viewer is left with the image of Anna, in the center of the frame, finally in control. As Pawlikowski himself explains, the Bach/Busoni is "the only piece of music that doesn't come from the film. Usually, the music is played by the band, or it's from the radio or a record, whereas that's just from me from outside the story. That helped me. There's something very melancholy but serene about that piece. It was like a new perspective that was introduced into the film. It's like we're looking at her from outside the film, and there's a feeling of reconciliation about her" (2014a online).

Here, both protagonist and film find closure. The final moments of Pawlikowski's film provide a new innovation in music, having moved from diegetic to non-diegetic music with a poetic source; newness in characterization of the protagonist, whose choices are now her own, as well as the beauty of her choice to sacrifice personal fulfillment in order to embrace her monastic vows; the seemingly instant technological development of tracking and handheld footage that renders the film doubtlessly an exploration of Anna herself; and the seemingly unlikely use of a transcribed sixteenth-century Lutheran hymn. I do not mean to suggest that Anna herself is channeling this specific hymn text and making her faith declaration according to it; there is no reason to suspect a novitiate having grown up in a post-WWII Polish convent would have access to recordings of music, and if so, certainly not Protestant hymnody. Instead, we see and hear Pawlikowski's perspective as it regards his character and her own new innovation. A Jewish nun, an adapted self, akin to Busoni's transcription: in the last moment, both character and music are performative. The camera finally yields agency to Anna, whose movement now guides the photography, and the music, to decode her choice. Anna is Anna, but Anna is also Ida.

References

Brody, Richard (2014 online). "The Distasteful Vagueness of *Ida*". http://www.newyorker .com/culture/richard-brody/the-distasteful-vagueness-of-ida [03/09/2014].

Buhler, James (2014). "Ontological, Formal, and Critical Theories of Film Music and Sound". David Neumeyer, ed. *The Oxford Handbook of Film Music Studies*. New York, NY: OUP. 188–225.

Cormack, Mike (2006). "The Pleasures of Ambiguity: Using Classical Music in Film". Phil Powrie, Robynn Stillwell, eds. *Changing Tunes: The Use of Pre-existing Music in Film*. Aldershot: Ashgate. 19–30.

Denby, David (2014 online). "'Ida', a Film Masterpiece". *The New Yorker*. http://www .newyorker.com/culture/culture-desk/ida-a-film-masterpiece [26/10/2014].

Godsall, Jonathan (2014). *Preexisting Music in Sound Fiction Film*. Ph.D. Thesis. University of Bristol.

Gorbman, Claudia (1987). *Unheard Melodies: Narrative Film Music*. Bloomington, IN: Indiana Univ. Press.

Pawlikowski, Pawel (2014). *Ida*. Paris: Canal+ Polska.

Pawlikowski, Pawel (2014a online). *Ida* (Press Notes). http://www.musicboxfilms.com/ ida [14/10/2014].

Pawlikowski, Pawel/Sheila Roberts (2014 online). "Writer/Director Pawel Pawlikowski Talks IDA, Returning to Poland, His Visual Style, Shooting in Black in White, and More". http://collider.com/pawel-pawlikowski-ida-interview/ [14/11/2014].

Stevens, Dana (2014 online). *Ida* (Review). http://www.slate.com/articles/arts/ movies/2014/05/ida_review_pawel_pawlikowski_s_hauntingly_beautiful_road _movie_is_finally.html [03/10/2014].

Tarkovsky, Andrei, dir. (1983). *Nostalghia*. Russia/Italy.

Wood, Naaman (2014 online). "The Grand Budapest Hotel". http://www.ransom fellowship.org/articledetail.asp?AID=795&B=Naaman%20Wood&TID=2 [13/12/2014].

PART 2

Intermedial Varieties

∴

CHAPTER 10

Shadow Images Moving to Music: *La Tentation de saint Antoine* in Montmartre

Peter Dayan

Abstract

December 1887 saw the first performance, at the shadow theatre of the Chat Noir cabaret in Montmartre, of a spectacle entitled *La Tentation de saint Antoine*. The following year, the mastermind behind the spectacle, Henri Rivière, published a remarkable artist's book of the same title. The book gives images derived from the spectacle, and an indication of the music played, but not the words spoken during the performance. This essay explores the relationship between music, word, and image in Rivière's two *Tentations* (the book and the spectacle), and asks why the shadow play was received as a unique masterpiece of theatrical idealism. The answer turns out to depend on the way that each medium – words, music, moving images – occupies, quite literally, indeed physically, a separate space. Rather than collaborating (in a Wagnerian way), each maintains its distance from the others, to assist them in orienting our gaze towards an ungraspable horizon of dream, materialised by the shadow theatre's blank little cloth screen.

•••

This essay concerns three works all entitled *La Tentation de saint Antoine*, dating from the period 1874–1888. Two of them are books; the third was a performance in the shadow theatre of the Chat Noir cabaret in Montmartre, Paris. All three create strange, original, and thought-provoking relationships (real or imagined) between performance, music, and the moving image; and they similarly relate to each other in remarkable ways with profound implications for our understanding of intermedial connections in art, both at the time and more generally. I shall begin with the last of the three to be produced, which is also the least famous, the least studied, and the most unique and extraordinary in its format.

La Tentation de saint Antoine[1] by Henri Rivière is a book published in Paris in 1888. It appears at first sight to belong to the category of the 'livre d'artiste',

---

[1] The punctuation of the title is given in three different forms in Rivière's book: with and without the hyphen, with and without the capital on 'saint'. I use the form popularized by Flaubert.

which had been invented not long before, precisely in Paris: the illustrations and the physical quality of the book as an art object are clearly essential production values. It is indeed a strikingly beautiful thing.[2] The cover of the book gives no explicit clue to its genre. On the title page, however, we read:

> Féerie à grand spectacle
> en 2 actes et 40 tableaux
> par
> HENRI RIVIÈRE
> représentée pour la première fois sur le théâtre du *Chat Noir*
> *Le 28 décembre 1887*
> musique nouvelle et arrangée de
> MM ALBERT TINCHANT et GEORGES FRAGEROLLE
> RIVIÈRE 1888: 1

The 'Féerie' was a primarily theatrical, rather than literary, genre, unique, really, to 19th-century France, with no exact equivalents elsewhere or at other periods. Its principal ingredients were its spectacular stage-craft, with ingenious scene changes and startling special effects, often involving magical apparitions; its melodramatic and morally simplistic plot, always including magic, supernatural beings, a struggle between good and evil, and the victory of the former; and song and dance. It was universally perceived as a triumph of spectacle over plot, of the visual, musical, and choreographical over the verbal. Whereas other kinds of plays were routinely published and read as literary works in their own right, this made little sense for the 'féerie'; generally speaking, when 'féeries' were published, they were received, so to speak, as 'books of the play', to remind those who had seen and loved the stage versions of the spectacle they had experienced. (One startling exception to this rule is *Le Château des cœurs* by Gustave Flaubert, which was published as a text, explicitly designated as a 'féerie', and never performed. It is, of all the works he published, the least known. We will shortly come to another, more famous, text by Flaubert which seems, like *Le Château des cœurs*, to quote Mallarmé, 'non *possible au théâtre*, mais *exigeant le théâtre*' ('not *possible in the theatre*, but *requiring the theatre*') [1995: 242].) Rivière's book, in referencing the theatre at which the 'féerie' was performed, seems at first glance to conform to this tradition. Yet, when one goes beyond the title page, what one finds is certainly

---

2 Images of it can be found by googling on: 'tentation de saint Antoine' Henri Rivière.

not a traditional 'book of the play' – any more than it is a traditional 'livre d'artiste'.

To begin with: the words that the characters would speak in a 'féerie', which would transmit the plot and define the characters, are almost completely absent. There are, in fact, no words attributed to any protagonist, until page 34 of the book, which has a total of 88 pages. Indeed, there are few words of any kind. Each double page spread, in the book, consists of two elements. The right-hand page is entirely taken up by a wordless and untitled illustration, often richly coloured. The left-hand page gives a title which is plainly that of one of the forty 'tableaux' that compose the work; then, below that title, a piece of music, either taken from a pre-existing source (as was common practice in a 'féerie'), or written in a recognisable popular style. This lay-out is, to my knowledge, unique in the history of the 'livre d'artiste', certainly in that century. The norm, as established by Mallarmé and Manet a decade earlier, was to present poetry and visual art together, but to leave music as an art merely suggested. Rivière, on the contrary, presents music and visual art, and leaves the poetry to the imagination.

The story the book tells is, then, not made verbally explicit. But the illustrations show clearly enough what is going on; and in any case, it is a safe bet that the book's intended market was people who had either seen the shadow play, or knew Flaubert's *Tentation de saint Antoine*, published fourteen years earlier, and unambiguously the inspiration behind Rivière's work. Saint Antoine, presented as the dark figure of a tormented ascetic, dressed in rags, is being subjected to a series of temptations, designed to lead him astray from his Christian faith. He resists, despite great suffering. These temptations begin in the City of Light, contemporary Paris, with its bewildering array of appeals to greed, from gourmandise to high-society gambling. Then, clearly orchestrated by the Devil (a dark figure, like the saint), comes the temptation of science. After that, the saint is subjected to the temptation of sensuality, embodied by the Queen of Sheba, and by a troop of pretty ballerinas (whom we had already seen on the front cover). Finally, the saint is made to witness a procession of divinities from other religions, who try to persuade him of their superior attractions. He never ceases to resist, of course, despite his agonies, and is rewarded, in true 'féerie' style, by a spectacular final apotheosis, when he ascends, surrounded by angels, to a traditional Christian heaven. Apart from the scenes of contemporary Paris, the ballerinas, and the final apotheosis, the themes of these tableaux are taken more or less directly from Flaubert's book.

Most of the illustrations which occupy the right-hand pages depict both a temptation and the agonised saint, whose difficulty in resisting is always obvious. The temptation is often colourful and attractive; the saint is, in contrast, dark, small, and tormented. We have been informed on the title page that the 'Féerie à grand spectacle', first performed at the theatre of the Chat Noir on 28 December 1887, consisted of 40 tableaux. The book has 40 double pages illustrating temptations. The reader therefore assumes that each double page corresponds to a tableau in the performance; and equally, doubtless, that the music which occupies the left-hand page, opposite each illustration, represents what was played during the tableau in question.

How does that music relate to the images? The answer appears surprisingly simple. Most of it consists of tunes from well-known operas or other theatrical works of the time. Some of it was composed by Albert Tinchant and Georges Fragerolle, as the title page had informed us; but that, too, is quite conventional in style. And in every case, there is an obvious musical meaning. The music clearly illustrates one aspect of what is happening in the scene pictured on the facing page – but only one aspect. It always represents the temptation. More particularly, it represents what is attractive, tempting, in the temptation. It never represents the torment and anguish of the saint as he resists. Often, as when he is tempted by the food in 'Les Halles', the great Parisian market, or by the pretty ballerinas, the tune is a light-hearted one taken from a contemporary ballet or comic opera, by composers such as Lecocq or Delibes. Wagner is conscripted to provide the Ride of the Valkyries when the Norse gods appear; Offenbach's comic version of the Orpheus legend provides jaunty tunes to introduce the Greek muses and the gods of Olympus. There is a striking contrast between this stereotypically Parisian lightness, and the torment and resistance of the saint, which is, after all, the thread that holds the narrative together; as if the music were on the side of the City of Light which provides the first series of temptations, rather than of the eponymous hero. One might ask why. Indeed, that question, of which side the music is on, turns out, as we shall see, to hold the key to understanding the extraordinary success of Rivière's *Tentation*. But before returning to that question, let us ask where words come in, relative to both music and images.

The only text spoken by a character in Rivière's book also provides the first explicit reference to the book by Flaubert which was clearly the inspiration for Rivière's work. It comes approximately in the middle of the series of temptations, on a left-hand page, just above a line of music which, unusually, is not immediately identified. Here is the text in its entirety:

ANTOINE.
Ah! plus haut! plus haut! toujours!
... Les astres se multiplient, scintillent. La Voie lactée au zénith se développe comme une immense ceinture, ayant des trous par intervalles[;]

dans ces fentes de sa clarté, s'allongent des espaces de ténèbres. Il y a des pluies d'étoiles, des traînées de poussière d'or, des vapeurs lumineuses qui flottent et se dissolvent.

Quelquefois une comète passe tout à coup; – puis la tranquillité des lumières innombrables recommence....

(GUSTAVE FLAUBERT, *La Tentation de saint Antoine*[3], RIVIÈRE 1888: 34

Ah! higher! higher! always higher!

... The stars multiply, sparkle. At the zenith, the Milky Way unfolds as an immense belt, with holes at intervals; in these gaps in its clarity, spaces of darkness stretch out. There are showers of stars, trails of gold dust, luminous vapours which float and dissolve.

Sometimes, suddenly, a comet passes; – then the tranquillity of the innumerable lights returns....

GUSTAVE FLAUBERT, *The Temptation of Saint Anthony*

This text introduces a series, unique in the book, of three tableaux, three double-page spreads, all with the same title: 'Le Ciel' ('The Heavens'). On each of the three left-hand pages is a single line of music, a tune which continues across all three. This tune is eventually identified, at the end of the third left-hand page, as 'Rêverie', by Schumann. It is, indeed, a simplified version of the famous tune from Schumann's 'Träumerei', from his *Kinderszenen*, opus 15 (see Figure 10.1b). The dreaminess which it incarnates is certainly compatible with the otherworldly beauty of the heavens, as it is expressed in the quotation from Flaubert and materialised in the extraordinary illustrations, which represent planets (including, recognisably, the Earth), stars, and the Milky Way seen from space (see Figure 10.1a). But what is their relationship with the two dark figures that, in those illustrations, drift across those heavens? One, a black winged monster with hooves and tail, is the Devil; the other is the saint, dragged by the Devil and looking anguished, as usual. Neither Schumann's 'Rêverie', nor Flaubert's words, seem to take any account of this strange couple.

The mystery deepens if one compares these three tableaux in Rivière's book with the scene from Flaubert's *Tentation de saint Antoine* which obviously inspired them. As Flaubert's Devil takes the saint up into the heavens, the first thing to which the saint responds is the beauty of the universe, as shown in the quotation given by Rivière. But then he becomes increasingly distressed by the fact that the three-dimensional universe which the Devil shows him leaves no distinctive place for God's Heaven, no direction in which to seek Him. Antoine

---

3   The closing bracket after '*Antoine*' is missing in the original. All translations in this essay are mine.

FIGURES 10.1A/10.1B   Henri Rivière, *La Tentation de saint Antoine* (Rivière 1888: 34f.)

had always thought of Heaven as being above him; but in space, as the Devil says, there is no up and no down, only equivalent and ultimately homogenous space, in all directions. Where, then, is God? According to the Devil, He is at once everywhere and nowhere; he is not beyond the material universe, but rather coterminous with it, and Antoine's desire to believe in Him as a loving presence, a father, a great soul, above and beyond the visible world, is foolish nonsense. As the Devil advances this argument, Antoine's suffering steadily intensifies, to the point where he feels he is losing his consciousness of his own being, as the undifferentiated nature of the universe absorbs and destroys him.

This suffering is plainly visible in Rivière's startling illustrations, which show the Devil carrying Antoine, like an eagle might carry its prey, steadily further from his home on Earth, and out towards the edges of the solar system. The illustration I give here shows the first of the three images in this series, with Antoine and the Devil quite large, near the centre of the page and also near a clearly recognisable planet Earth. In the two subsequent images, Antoine becomes a diminishing black figure, shrinking as he moves, pulled by the Devil towards the edge of a magnificent colourful cosmos from whose meaning he is excluded. His suffering clearly increases as his stature and centrality diminish. But that suffering, that existential distress, expressed both in Flaubert's book and in Rivière's illustrations, is totally absent both from the music and from the words present in Rivière's book.

The music, then, appears to be saying something different from, or at least more limited than, what the pictures say. Perhaps one might be tempted to align the meaning of the music with the meaning of the words from Flaubert's *Tentation* that Rivière quotes; in those words, which are taken from near the beginning of Flaubert's scene, Antoine is still at the stage of being dazzled by the beauty of the cosmos. But anyone who knows Flaubert's text – and surely most of the readers of Rivière's book at the time would have known it – will be acutely aware of what happens in the latter part of that scene, of the way the Devil torments the saint. Thus Flaubert's words, though so few of them are there, seem to echo hauntingly the medial divide between right-hand and left-hand pages: the present words seem to agree with the music, but only absent words fully agree with the illustrations. There is a peculiar tangle of fault-lines between the apparent meanings of the music, of the visible text, of the occluded text, and of the illustrations. Why? That is the question at the heart of this essay. But before we can answer it, we have to take account of a second phantomatic presence behind this work. Just as Flaubert's book is evoked and cited in a way that encourages us to seek parallels with Rivière's book, parallels whose vanishing point appears to be in puzzlement as much as in enlightenment, so the 'féerie' in the Chat Noir cabaret is cited and evoked; and readers in 1888, unlike readers in the 21st century, would have been aware of that performance, as much as of Flaubert's book. What kind of intertext does it provide?

The title page of Rivière's book, as we have seen, says that the 'Féerie' had been performed in the theatre of the Chat Noir. What it does not specify, but what everyone at the time would have been aware of, was the diminutive size of the proscenium of the theatre in question. It was not much larger than a modern domestic flat-screen television. It measured about 1.40 metres by 1.12. It was a piece of canvas inserted into the back wall of a second-floor room in the cabaret's building in Montmartre.

The Chat Noir cabaret itself was a unique space in many ways. I doubt that any other four walls in the world have ever had between them, in the space of a dozen years, so many great and famous artists, including, for example, Victor Hugo, Émile Zola, Stéphane Mallarmé, Paul Verlaine, Erik Satie, Claude Debussy, Tchaikovsky, Toulouse-Lautrec, Degas, Monet, Renoir, and Rodin, not to mention the Prince of Wales, Clémenceau, Garibaldi, and several characters from Marcel Proust's *A la recherche du temps perdu*. This popularity and wide appeal among the social and artistic élite was not coincidental. The truly unique thing about the Chat Noir was the way it brought together the most absolute unshakeable belief in the high art tradition, the great Romantic belief in art and beauty with its concomitant hatred of philistines and rationalists and materialists, with a truly tremendous sense of irony and sarcasm based on the firm principle that there is a totally unbridgeable gap between the realm of true beauty, and the world we live in. But the world we live in nonetheless (and this is central to the Chat Noir aesthetic) provides the only possible material for art; so that at the heart of the Chat Noir experience is a vertiginous sense of comic distance between what we are currently doing, thinking, desiring, and working with in this world, and what really matters. Anyone who does not have that sense of comic distance, from the Chat Noir point of view, had to be either a bourgeois philistine or else a ridiculous idealistic idiot. The Chat Noir thus created a powerful ideological position which invited those who shared it mercilessly to mock outsiders. Those outsiders included, generally, capitalists and rationalists on the one hand, and believers in established religion on the other. That mockery of both the seriousness of rationalism, and the seriousness of religion, combined with an intense idealism, played beautifully into the French tradition of wit and lightness, as well as into the increasingly forceful idealism of the times; and the pleasures of belonging to a group that could see itself as a very French élite, superior by its wit, and able to laugh at the leaden-footed bourgeoisie, were clearly highly attractive to many of the leading minds of the time.

The cabaret and its house journal, also called *Le Chat Noir*, had a very long list of eminent contributors, but a much shorter list of people who really moulded its character. On that short list figures the now forgotten name of Henri Rivière, master of the shadow theatre, where the *Tentation de saint Antoine* was performed, as a shadow play, over a hundred times, in 1887 and 1888. Rivière was not only the creator of the book I have been describing; he was also the technical and artistic mastermind behind the shadow theatre that put on the 'féerie'.

Technically, that shadow theatre was an astonishing achievement. The audience sitting in the cabaret theatre, on the second floor of the Chat Noir building, looking at the small canvas screen set into the wall, saw nothing of the stupendous mechanism behind that screen. It was housed in an enormous wooden box, ten metres high, sticking out of the back of the building. At the back of the enormous box, three metres from the screen, was a powerful light source. Between the screen and the light source was a series of about seventy slots, some vertical and some horizontal, through which slides could be moved, up and down or from side to side, by pulling on strings. The back sixty slots were used for slides made of coloured glass or paper; these made the backgrounds. At the front were slides for the characters, which were made out of cut-out zinc. A few of these zinc characters have survived.[4] A character zinc near the front, just behind the cloth screen, would come out as a clear black shadow against the coloured background. A character zinc further back would come out as grey. The zincs and the background slides could all be moved independently to create a dazzlingly complex play of characters and colours. The most characteristic effect was the contrast of static colour, often likened to a stained-glass window, and black for the more mobile and more clearly defined main characters. The spectacle was divided up into a number of tableaux, but within each tableau, there could be more or less movement, particularly of the zincs.

Each tableau lasted for about one minute (so the whole forty-tableau spectacle lasted for forty minutes), and was accompanied both by words, and by music. The music was usually provided, as far as one can tell, by the piano, often played by Tinchant (one of the two musicians who arranged and composed the music for the shadow play). Rivière's book shows us what the character of that music was. But what of the words? We have no concrete trace of them. What we do know, from contemporary accounts, is that they were provided by the extraordinary voice of Rodolphe Salis, who spoke all of them, from his prominent station in front of the screen.

Rodolphe Salis was the very spirit of the Chat Noir. He founded, owned, and ran the cabaret, he kept his eye on every material, artistic, social and financial detail of its operation, and he seemed to be present everywhere, running everything and imprinting his character on everything. He welcomed arrivals (and decided who would and would not be allowed into the various rooms in the establishment). But above all, he was the cabaret's 'bonimenteur'. This is not an easy word to translate. A 'boniment' is usually defined as what a charlatan or a fairground performer would say to attract and dazzle his clientèle. It always has an element of wordy excess and hype and telling more or less than the truth. It also implies wit, verbal virtuosity, grandiloquence, bluff, and

---

4 Some pictures of them may be found by googling on: 'chat noir' Rivière zinc.

a certain mocking tone. Rodolphe Salis was universally recognised as a genius in this essentially improvisatory, comic, and ironic genre; and that is the style in which he provided all the words, as far as one can tell, for all the many hundreds of shadow theatre performances that formed the cultural heart of his cabaret. But of that torrent of words, we have no record at all. Rivière's book contains not the slightest hint of their existence. The few texts in the book are, as we have seen, by Flaubert, not by Salis. This evacuation of Salis's words is no chance omission. It is a key symptom of the intermedial relations at the root of the shadow theatre's extraordinary success as an avant-garde theatrical art form.

The general principle behind all the Parisian avant-garde art of the time was that art should work by suggesting something absent from the material of the work, something that appeared to come from somewhere else, somewhere outside what we could physically see or hear. This avant-garde art of suggestion was universally defined as an art of idealism, in opposition to naturalism, which was seen as the dominant mode of the despicable bourgeois novel and theatre. The Chat Noir shadow theatre was received from the beginning by critics and by artists as a uniquely successful example of non-naturalist, idealist, suggestive theatrical art. In this, it was truly remarkable. In poetry and painting, idealist suggestive art had had some success by 1887, in the verse of Verlaine and Mallarmé and the paintings we now call impressionist. (It is, of course, no coincidence that many of the poets, painters, and musicians who had been instrumental in creating this aesthetic were known to frequent the Chat Noir, or to contribute to its house magazine.) But in the theatre, that aesthetic had struggled to realise itself. The reason for this struggle between the theatre and the new aesthetic was being carefully theorised by Mallarmé in 1887, precisely, in a series of theatre reviews which he subsequently collected and published (in revised form) in his volume *Divagations* under the title 'Crayonné au théâtre' ('Pencilled in the Theatre') (Mallarmé 1897: 153–233). The fundamental problem is that in the theatre, all the media are physically present together. So suggestion becomes much more difficult. How can music suggest an absent poetry when there is actually poetry present? How can poetry suggest a visual scene when the visual is actually present? Rivière's stroke of genius was to separate the media in space as well as in tonality, while keeping them simultaneously present in time. His shadow theatre separated the images from the sound, so that one came from behind the screen while the other came from in front. They were juxtaposed, but they did not occupy the same space. That aesthetic of juxtaposition is brilliantly materialised in the book by the separation between the music, on the left-hand pages, and the images on the right; as if the fold in the middle represented the screen in the cabaret.

Furthermore, what the music suggests is always related to the images, but is always also very deliberately exceeded by the images. What is missing from the music is that black zinc figure of the saint, and indeed the black zinc figure of the Devil. As they silently move across the screen, they seem to accuse the music of being stuck in the world of meaning, the world in which we believe we can know what things are and what they signify. But the Chat Noir sense of comic distance always tells us at the same time that the meaning of the music, so relentlessly light-hearted, is not to be taken as a full expression of the true artistic value of the work, or of the ideals that it embodies. They go beyond what music can say.

To return to the essential question of situation: in the book, then, the images on every right-hand page go beyond what the music on the left-hand page seems to say. Similarly, in the theatre, the images on the screen would have gone beyond what the music in front of the screen would have been saying; and the physical distance between the piano in front of the screen, and the shadow theatre mechanism behind it, would have figured that intermedial separation. One might add that just as the shadow play is haunted by Flaubert's work, so the music is haunted by the composers it borrows from, from Offenbach to Haydn, Schumann and Wagner. Behind both is an idealism which is not quite expressed in the other. And what of Salis's words? In the theatre, they, like the music, would have come from in front of the screen. They would, of course, have interpreted for the audience the drama being played out on the screen. But that interpretation would always have presented itself as ironic, never as exhaustive. Salis never saw himself as a poet, as someone whose words had a literary value; he was always a facilitator of art, a 'cabaretier', never a verbal artist himself. (He had for a time been a visual artist; he soon realised his true genius lay elsewhere.) His role as 'bonimenteur' was to create, not high art in words alone, but the sense of comic distance to which I have referred. In the theatre, this comic distance could be materialised in the physical distance between himself, before the screen, and the zinc characters behind it. It would have been immediately obvious, of course, that the voice one was hearing was his, not Antoine's or the Devil's.

In a book, how could this be represented? We are so used to relating printed words directly to the character who is meant to have said them – how could the book have materialised the fact that the words were in Salis's style and voice, and not in the silent, imagined voice of the zinc characters? How could it have reproduced the distance between the place where Salis stood, and the screen? It would have been impossible. His improvised comic 'boniment', if printed, would have rooted the characters in their verbal representation, instead of maintaining their separation from it. That would have ruined the ideal suggestiveness of the work. Rivière's solution was to exclude the words totally. Or rather – that is how it appears to us. But in 1888, it is a safe bet that no one would have purchased this book, with its explicit reference to the Chat Noir theatre on the title page, without knowing full well what the Chat Noir style was, without knowing who Rodolphe Salis was, indeed without having either experienced his 'boniments', or having read his comic prose in the house magazine. Haunting Rivière's book, then, we should imagine not only Flaubert's work and the music evoked, but also those words, that 'boniment', never published but always present at every performance of the 'féerie' that Rivière's book purports to be. And to the extent that the remembered 'boniment' from the performance haunts the book from which it is absent, so, too, does another aspect of the performance which the book occludes: the movement of the images. The fame and effect of the Chat Noir shadow theatre, as constructed by Rivière, was a product of the fact that its tableaux were not static. The zinc characters moved, during the scenes; so, too, did the coloured background slides – although, as with the words, we have absolutely no contemporary accounts that tell us exactly what happened. Anyone reading the book, and having seen or heard about the 'féerie' in its original theatrical form, will therefore be drawn not to see the pictures, music, and words in the book as forming a coherent, closed, and mutually referential intermedial unit, but as the stimulus to imagining all the ghostly presences that they suggest, and which escape them. The words of Salis and of Flaubert, the musical world from which Tinchant and Fragerolle borrow, and the moving images of the shadow theatre are all there to be imagined in their absence, as is the inexpressible idealism of the saint at the heart of the work.

The Chat Noir shadow theatre was, I think, the only theatrical spectacle of those years which was received both as magnificently idealist (and hence anti-naturalist), and magnificently popularly successful. Zola, the prince of naturalism (who, of course, came to the Chat Noir), had been trying to revolutionise the theatre in the direction of naturalism; his aesthetic enemies rejoiced in the success of the shadow theatre in accomplishing a revolution heading in precisely the opposite direction.

> Pends-toi, Zola! cette révolution [...] s'est réalisée [...] loin des vulgarités de ton naturalisme, dans le domaine de la fantaisie et du rêve, par le théâtre [...] que Rivière vient d'asseoir dans sa forme définitive avec cette *Tentation de saint Antoine* [...]; conception d'artiste et de poète, théâtre idéal [...] théâtre suggestif aussi, où une ligne, un trait, ouvrent à l'imagination du spectateur les horizons insaisissables du rêve.

Zola, you may as well go and hang yourself! This revolution [...] has been accomplished [...] far from the vulgarities of your naturalism, in the realm of fantasy and dream, by the theatre [...] that Rivière has established in its definitive form with this *Temptation of Saint Anthony* [...] it is the conception of an artist and a poet, an ideal theatre [...] as well as a theatre of suggestion, where a single line can open up to the imagination the ungraspable horizons of dream.

This review by Edouard Norès, entitled '*La tentation de Saint Antoine* de Rivière au Chat Noir' and published in the magazine *Les Premières illustrées* in 1887 (qtd. Lucet 2006: 146), is a perfect example of the intermedial style of the time. To begin with, note how it uses the word 'poète': not to indicate what Rivière did with words – Rivière did nothing with words, he left those to Flaubert and Salis – but to indicate a property of a non-verbal medium, in this case a visual medium, which was opposed to naturalistic representation. A poet in this sense is exactly and precisely *not* someone who writes poetry. On the contrary, a poet is someone who uses non-verbal media to produce that effect of poetry which goes beyond words. That 'going beyond the medium' is also figured here, as it always is, through the emphasis on suggestion, on an opening out onto what cannot be grasped – the ungraspable horizons of dream. And to keep those horizons ungraspable, Norès strategically omits all reference to what really enables this theatre of suggestion to work: its music and the 'boniment' of Rodolphe Salis, which carry the work through the forty minutes of its representation and create at once the link to the familiar time of the spectator, and the ironic distance between voice and image that propels us towards 'les horizons insaisissables du rêve'. Norès does not mention the music, Salis's words, or the movement of the slides in the shadow theatre. Nor, as I have said, do any of the other descriptions of the spectacle that have come down to us; not even Rivière's own descriptions, in his wonderfully evocative posthumously published autobiography (see Rivière 2004: 46–61). This is no coincidence. What it signifies is that Rivière's contemporaries understood full well the necessity of leaving entire the space of suggestiveness around the work. Just as Rivière does in his book, so all the people who saw and appreciated his achievement knew that they had to leave the 'boniment' of Salis, the movement of the images, and the true nature of the music unspoken in print. They were an indispensable part of the spectacle's ideal force and success, but only thanks to the distances that the shadow theatre was able to maintain between them. In the pages of a book or of a journal, those distances must be replaced by silences, and much of what was physically present in the theatre has to be become ghostly.

As well as its house journal, the Chat Noir published a book which became extremely popular: *Les Gaîtés du Chat Noir*. It was largely a collection of the hilarious tales that were told in the cabaret and published in the journal. The book contained none of the words associated with the shadow plays. But in the preface to the second edition, in 1894, Jules Lemaitre, one of the leading spirits of the cabaret, paid an appropriate homage to Rivière, to his theatre, and to the idealism of which it was the Chat Noir's purest incarnation: an idealism at the heart of the cabaret, but which its printed words and static images could not capture. After describing the comic force of the cabaret, Lemaitre wrote:

> Et, en même temps, le Chat-Noir contribuait au 'réveil de l'idéalisme'. Il était mystique, avec le génial paysagiste et découpeur d'ombres Henri Rivière. L'orbe lumineux de son guignol fut un œil-de-bœuf ouvert sur l'invisible.
>
> LEMAITRE 1894: VII

> And, at the same time, the Chat Noir was contributing to the 'awakening of idealism'. It was mystical, with Henri Rivière, creator of shadow shapes and landscape painter of genius. The luminous orbit of his puppet theatre was an ox-eye window opening onto the invisible.

It was not by chance that this idealist shadow theatre flourished in the atmosphere created by the Chat Noir, and nowhere else. When Rodolphe Salis died in 1897, the shadow theatre for which he was the 'bonimenteur' died too. It could not work without him, and without the theatrical space that he created and animated. Henri Rivière himself lived until 1951, and had a successful career as an artist. But he never tried anything like the shadow theatre again. He knew that it was born of a unique moment, when the music and the words on one side of the screen knew how to entertain their audience while always keeping their respectful distance from the silent images behind them, stiffly moving on that extraordinary series of grooves receding into the distance. Nowhere else, perhaps, have popular music and entertaining banter been so perfectly married in theatrical time with the purest and most silent form of high art; and what enabled this unique moment in artistic time, to which Rivière's lovely book bears witness, was that little cloth screen between the source of the sound, in front of the screen, and the source of the images, behind it.

The relationship between words, music, and the moving image in Rivière's *Tentation de saint Antoine* is, then, to be understood in terms of distances, hauntings, absences, ungraspable horizons, and windows onto the invisible, at least as much as in terms of synergies, mutual support, and collaboration.

In this, though its genre is unique (as I have said, I know of no other book that combines visual art and music in this way), it represents perfectly intermedial relations as they have defined a certain high art tradition since the days of the Romantic revolution, two centuries ago. The arts, in their different media, have constructed themselves in relation to each other not by working together in peaceful harmony, but by keeping each other at a certain kind of distance; and it is the quality of that distance that matters. To appreciate the character and value of this distance, my strategy has been to examine how works of art which involve several media actually keep those media apart, in such a way that one cannot properly theorise the relationship between them except as a distance, a gap, a space in which something happens which escapes all media and indeed all theory, including mine. That space is where art lives. What is, to me, uniquely expressive about the Chat Noir shadow theatre is that there this space can actually be physically localised. It is that thin piece of blank cloth in the wall. Behind it are moving images. In front of it are music and words. The spectators in the theatre were actually focusing their eyes on the space between them, the space where they do not quite meet, the screen that is itself nothing but a veil; a veil that we ourselves will never see, but can imagine, as an ungraspable horizon of our dreams.

References

Flaubert, Gustave (1874). *La Tentation de saint Antoine*. Paris: Charpentier.

Lemaitre, Jules (1894). "Préface". *Les Gaîtés du Chat Noir*. Deuxième édition. Paris: Paul Ollendorff. v–xi.

Lucet, Sophie (2006). "Tentation des ombres à l'époque symboliste: l'attraction du Chat Noir". *Le Spectaculaire dans les arts de la scène du romantisme à la Belle Époque*. Études réunies sous la direction d'Isabelle Moindrot. Paris: CNRS Éditions. 138–146.

Mallarmé, Stéphane (1897). *Divagations*. Paris: Eugène Fasquelle.

Mallarmé, Stéphane (1995). *Correspondance: Lettres sur la poésie*. Ed. Bertrand Marchal. Paris: Gallimard (collection Folio classique).

Rivière, Henri (1888). *La Tentation de saint Antoine*. Paris: E. Plon, Nourrit et Cie.

Rivière, Henri (2004). *Les Détours du chemin: souvenirs, notes et croquis, 1864–1951*. Saint-Remy-de-Provence: Éditions Équinoxe.

CHAPTER 11

'The Big Turnaround in the Middle': On the Silent Movie and the Film Music Interlude in Alban Berg's Opera *Lulu*

Marion Recknagel

Abstract

In the middle of his second opera, *Lulu*, Alban Berg inserted a silent movie that is accompanied by film music. Although Berg gave precise instructions for the film scenario and its association with the music outlined in the Particell, many directors omit the film in stage performances. However, the film is essential to the opera dramaturgically because it fills the gap that Wedekind had left in between his two dramas, *Erdgeist* ('Earth Spirit') and *Die Büchse der Pandora* ('Pandora's Box'). Berg initially considered having a speaker narrate the intermediate story but decided on a silent film which depicts the events. In this article, the film and its music are analyzed to show how they together fulfill three functions: as a narration of the missing link; as a mirror axis for the opera's symmetrical design; and as the pivot of the whole opera.

• • •

In memory of Karl Olbricht

In a short article entitled "Das 'Opernproblem'" published in *Neue Musik-Zeitung* in September 1928, Alban Berg replied to the question, "What do you think about the further development of opera as suited to the times?".[1] With his first opera, *Wozzeck*, he himself had made an important contribution to modern opera and seemed to be the suitable person to give an answer. However, he evaded a precise response by splitting the question. For the "further development of opera" would crystallize when the time will have arrived, because he believed "that someday a masterpiece will be written that points so much to the future that by its very existence we will be able to talk about the 'further

---

1 Berg 2014: 216. "Wie denken Sie über die zeitgemäße Weiterentwicklung der Oper?" (Berg 1928: 285).

development of opera'".[2] To compose an up-to-date opera, in contrast, seemed easy to him because it would be enough to use contemporary means. This would not be pioneering, he explained:

> The use of means 'suited to the times' – like cinema, revue, loudspeakers, and jazz – proves only that such a work is up-to-date. But this cannot be called real progress because we are already there and cannot go further with such things alone.
>
> To say that the art form of opera has developed further – as happened, for example, with Monteverdi, Lully, Gluck, Wagner, and finally in Schoenberg's stage works – requires other means beyond the simple application of the latest acquisitions and things that are in fashion.[3]

What suits the times is not necessarily suitable for the future because it is part of the present. New means, as the named composers devised, would be necessary for opera to advance. Modest as he was, he did not rank himself among these innovators. Instead he modified the question: "But must it always 'further develop?'", he asks. "Isn't it enough, to take the opportunity to make beautiful music for good theater, or, better said, to make music so beautiful that – in spite of it – good theater will result?".[4] Thus, he came to speak about his own work and the intentions that had governed the composition of his first opera, *Wozzeck*. They were, if one chooses to believe his statement, very humble. Primarily he had the "wish to make good music". Moreover, he wanted "to fulfill musically the intellectual content of Büchner's immortal drama" (Berg 2014: 216) and "to translate his poetical language into a musical one". Beyond that, Berg had the principal aim "to give the theater what belongs to the theater, that is, to create music that *at any moment* is aware of its duty to serve the drama, – even more far-reachingly: that it creates, only from within itself, everything

2   Berg 2014: 216. "[...] daß nämlich eines Tages ein Meisterwerk geschrieben sein wird, das so sehr in die Zukunft weist, daß man auf Grund seines Daseins von einer 'Weiterentwicklung der Oper' wird reden können" (Berg 1928: 285).

3   Berg 2014: 216. "Die Verwendung 'zeitgemäßer' Mittel, wie Kino, Revueartiges, Lautsprecher, Jazzmusik, gewährleistet ja nur, daß ein solches Werk zeitgemäß ist. Aber ein wirklicher Fortschritt kann das wohl nicht genannt werden; denn ebenda sind wir ja angelangt, können also dadurch allein nicht weiterkommen. Damit man von der Kunstform der Oper wieder einmal sagen kann, sie habe sich weiterentwickelt – wie dies zum Beispiel durch Monteverdi, Lully, Gluck, Wagner und zuletzt durch Schönbergs Bühnenwerke geschehen ist –, bedarf es wohl anderer Mittel als der bloßen Heranziehung der letzten Errungenschaften und alles dessen, was gerade beliebt ist" (Berg 1928: 285).

4   Berg 2014: 216. "Aber muß denn immer 'weiterentwickelt' werden? Genügt nicht die Gelegenheit, zu gutem Theater schöne Musik zu machen, oder – besser gesagt: so schöne Musik zu machen, daß – trotzdem – gutes Theater daraus wird?" (Berg 1928: 285).

required for putting the drama on stage, thereby demanding already of the *composer* all the essential tasks of an ideal director". In spite of this devotion to the drama and to stage requirements, music should still uphold its "absolute (purely musical) right to exist; in harmony with its independent existence free from extra-musical restrictions".[5]

Thus, as an opera composer, Berg felt that he was a servant to three masters: as a musician, he served the music as an absolute art; as a director, he served the stage requirements; and as an ideal reader, he served both, the drama and its message. Already in 1927, one year before he published his article on "Das 'Opernproblem'", Berg had begun work on his second opera, *Lulu*, thus facing the challenges of a great poet for a second time. However, the problems posed by Wedekind's text were completely different from those he had encountered with Büchner's *Woyzeck*. Both of Wedekind's *Lulu* tragedies were reputed to be immoral and lewd. *Die Büchse der Pandora* was confiscated right after it had been published in 1904 and forbidden after three years of legal proceedings. This played a role in Berg's preliminary considerations, for he did not wish to compose an opera that would be rejected right away by the opera houses or could possibly be shown in private only, as he wrote to his friend Soma Morgenstern (cf. Morgenstern 1995: 195). Berg knew what he said because he had become acquainted with Wedekind's *Die Büchse der Pandora* in a private presentation, organized by Karl Kraus in Vienna in 1905. In addition to the moral concern, it turned out to be difficult to remodel Wedekind's plays as an opera libretto. Berg suspected, as he wrote to Soma Morgenstern, that their highly dialectical dialogues could not be understood when they were sung (cf. ibid.). Furthermore, the length of the two dramas forced him to delete four-fifths of the text. Berg wrote the libretto simultaneously with the composition. In a letter to Arnold Schönberg from 7 August 1930, he called this labor "a torture" (qtd. Perle 1985: 41), and this in two ways: he had had to decide which sections to retain or eliminate, and he had had to adapt Wedekind's style and diction to a musical structure without destroying its peculiarities.

---

5   My translations of Berg's text. This is the complete passage in the original text: "Abgesehen von dem Wunsch, gute Musik zu machen, den geistigen Inhalt von Büchners unsterblichen Drama auch musikalisch zu erfüllen, seine dichterische Sprache in eine musikalische umzusetzen, schwebte mir [...] nichts anderes vor, als dem Theater zu geben, was des Theaters ist, das heißt also, die Musik so zu gestalten, daß sie sich ihrer Verpflichtung, dem Drama zu dienen, *in jedem Augenblick* bewußt ist, – ja weitergehend: daß sie alles, was dieses Drama zur Umsetzung in die Wirklichkeit der Bretter bedarf, aus sich allein herausholt, damit schon vom *Komponisten* alle wesentlichen Aufgaben eines idealen Regisseurs fordernd. Und zwar all dies: unbeschadet der sonstigen absoluten (rein musikalischen) Existenzberechtigung einer solchen Musik; unbeschadet ihres durch nichts Außermusikalisches behinderten Eigenlebens" (Berg 1928, 286).

In the end, Berg succeeded in cutting Wedekind's double tragedy down to the duration of a three-act opera, which could be performed on a single evening, while maintaining the basic design of the drama and preserving the nature of the plot and its characters. This is remarkable, especially since Berg brings the subject matter into a shape of which the idea is implied in Wedekind's tragedies, although the author himself had never realized it. Berg, by contrast, cherished a distinctive preference for symmetrical structures. In *Lulu* he recognized the possibility of designing the opera like a mirror image corresponding to Lulu's rise and fall (cf. Jarman 1991: 56f.). Berg divided the opera according to content and form so that each part comprises one and a half acts. Between these two parts he provided a whole series of musical relations and of analogies of content. The most prominent indication of this is the correspondence of Lulu's three husbands with the three customers whom Lulu, as a London prostitute, takes up to her attic in the third act. The customers are played by the same singers as the husbands, and they share the same music.

The symmetrical design of the opera emphasizes its center. Alban Berg made it – in the true sense of the word – the pivot of the opera. This decision is not merely formal. On 21 March 1934, he wrote in a letter to the conductor Erich Kleiber: 'Now that I have the overview, I am all the more convinced of the opera's profound morals – *rise* and *fall* are balanced; in the middle [...] there is the big turnaround'.[6] The 'big turnaround' in the middle is the moment that balances the two parts and safeguards the morals of the opera. It is the point in time where Lulu's fate turns into tragedy. Berg isolates this turning point by deviating from customary opera designs. Between the first and second scenes of the second act the curtain falls and a silent movie is shown, which is accompanied by film music.

However, this film has seldom been shown in performances of the opera. In the premiere of the two-act version of the opera in Zurich (1937) the film was shown, but, according to Willi Reich, only in the first performance. Then it turned out that everything went much too quickly for all of the details to be precisely perceived. Hence, in the following performances, the film was omitted in favor of still pictures (cf. Reich 1963: 160). Also, the film was not included in the second premiere of the completed three-act opera more than forty years later in Paris (1979). Many directors continue to follow this example[7] but they

---

6   "Jetzt wo ich es überblicke bin ich erst recht von der tiefen Moral des Stückes überzeugt. Lulus *Auf* und *Ab*stieg hält sich die Waage; in der Mitte [...] die große Umkehr". (Steiger, ed. 2013: 118; translation mine).

7   An exception was the production at Glyndebourne Festival in 1996; see Alban Berg. *Lulu. Opera in Three Acts, Libretto by the Composer after Frank Wedekind's Plays* Erdgeist *and* Die Büchse der Pandora. Directed by Graham Vick, conducted by Andrew Davis. DVD Glyndebourne 1996.

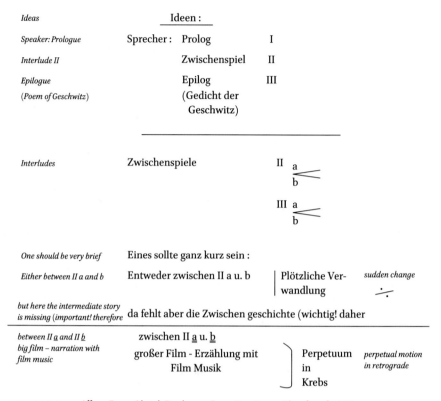

Ideas   **Ideen :**

Speaker: Prologue   Sprecher : Prolog   I

Interlude II   Zwischenspiel   II

Epilogue   Epilog   III
(Poem of Geschwitz)   (Gedicht der
                                 Geschwitz)

Interludes   Zwischenspiele   II a
                                                  b

                                              III a
                                                  b

One should be very brief   Eines sollte ganz kurz sein :

Either between II a and b   Entweder zwischen II a u. b | Plötzliche Ver-   *sudden change*
                                                              | wandlung

but here the intermediate story
is missing (important! therefore da fehlt aber die Zwischen geschichte (wichtig! daher

between II a and II b   zwischen II a u. b
big film – narration with   großer Film - Erzählung mit   Perpetuum   *perpetual motion*
film music   Film Musik   in   *in retrograde*
                                                                   Krebs

FIGURE 11.1   Alban Berg. *Sketch Book 1927*. ÖNB, F 21 Berg 28/III f.35, f.35'. Transcription: Ertelt 1993: 177 (translation mine).

do so without regarding the dramaturgical reasons that the film is essential for the opera.

The movie and its music are meant to fill a gap that Wedekind had left between the two dramas *Erdgeist* and *Die Büchse der Pandora*. *Erdgeist* ends when Lulu has fatally shot her third husband, Dr. Schön, and his son, Alwa, consigns her to the police. *Die Büchse der Pandora* begins when a year later Lulu is set free from jail by her dedicated entourage, headed by Gräfin Geschwitz. Wedekind did not indicate what may have happened in between. Berg felt uneasy about this gap. In his sketch book of 1927, where he jotted down ideas for interludes in acts two and three, he noted 'but here the intermediate story is missing (important!' (see Figure 11.1). He designed a film scenario to supply that link. A movie with a duration of barely three minutes shows Lulu's detention, the trial, her conviction and admission to prison plus the stages of her liberation so boldly planned and executed by Gräfin Geschwitz. Berg synchronizes the movie scenes with the music so that it is clearly determined, bar by bar, how the scenes of the movie and the music are interrelated.

It posed no problem for Wedekind that his tragedies followed each other loosely. Berg, however, desired the transition with the perceptible display of the particular moment where the course of the plot reverses. He, thus, connected the two parts of the opera, through a kind of mirror axis, by detaching this point in time clearly from all other stage events. He exchanged the direct and spatial display of the stage performance for an film representation of merely two dimensions. During Alban Berg's lifetime, this implied a loss of color because the age of color movies had barely begun in the nineteen-thirties. Thus, the effect of the film is evident detachment. The audience's view of the events is no longer direct but governed by the camera. The only thing that can be seen is what the camera records, and only from its perspective. In addition, Berg deprives his characters of their vocal expression, either spoken or sung. Lulu is muted. In jail, she is under the control of an anonymous power that lacks any feeling for her as a person. The anonymity of the judiciary corresponds to the anonymous and unfeeling view taken by the camera, which registers Lulu's fate just as indifferently as justice has condemned her.

Early sketches reveal that Berg considered inserting at this turning point an interlude with a speaker to give an account of events (see Figure 11.2). Perhaps

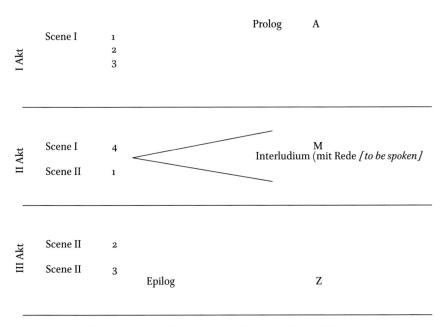

FIGURE 11.2   Alban Berg. *Sketch Book 1927*. ÖNB, F 21 Berg 28/III f.38' (transcription mine)

to satisfy his wish for symmetry, Berg contemplated providing an epilogue at the end of the third act to complement the prologue of the animal tamer and to bridge both by an interlude in the middle of the second act (cf. Ertelt 1993: 174). Following the word "Interludium" is noted in brackets "mit Rede" ('to be spoken'). Wedekind offers no text for this. Therefore, Berg had to decide how to fill this gap and write a narrative text. A few pages on, there is the sketch where Berg indicated that the linking story is missing (see Figure 11.1). Above this, under the caption "Ideen" ('ideas'), there are the notes "Prolog I" – "Zwischenspiel II" – "Epilog III" and, in front if this, "Sprecher" ('speaker'). Further down on that page there are detailed notes related to the second-act interlude. It should be 'very brief' ("ganz kurz") and should show a 'sudden change' ("Plötzliche Verwandlung"). After the cue, 'but here the intermediate story is missing (important!' – "da fehlt aber die Zwischengeschichte (wichtig!" –, the following consequence is noted: 'therefore between II a and b big film – narration with film music' ("daher zwischen II a u. b großer Film – Erzählung mit Film Musik"). On the right-hand side Berg made a note of how to design the film music, which he conceived to be a 'perpetual motion in retrograde' ("Perpetuum in Krebs"). Thus, it was important for Berg to 'narrate' the interlude story. But why did he ultimately choose to do so by way of two forms of art which – to put it mildly – possess a very limited capability to 'tell' a story?

The silent movie is wordless by its very nature: it can show images and events but its ability to portray thoughts and feelings is limited. However, this was exactly what Berg intended. He wished to present Lulu's initial hopes for acquittal, their subsiding and her resignation, as well as her re-awakening courage to face life, the gradual succeeding of the escape plan and her newly rising hopes. For presenting such developments, music is not really helpful: an old topos says that although music 'speaks', it fails to 'tell' anything. But of course, 'telling' would be indispensable if a story were to be told.

Furthermore, Berg also forced both film and music into a strictly formal strait-jacket. The concept features a two-part composition. In either half of the film, the scenes are related as if they were mirrored so that each scene of the first half corresponds to a counterpart scene of the second half. In his concept for the movie, which he wrote on a separate sheet inserted in the Particell (cf. Perle 1985: 150–152), he noted these positions side by side (see Figure 11.3). The detention corresponds to the liberation, the prison is juxtaposed with the hospital; and the trial personnel correspond to the medical advisors. Likewise, the police car corresponds to the ambulance, the judges' verdict to Gräfin Geschwitz's liberation plan, the closing of the jail door to its later opening. These analogies were intended to be applied not only to the whole scenery but also

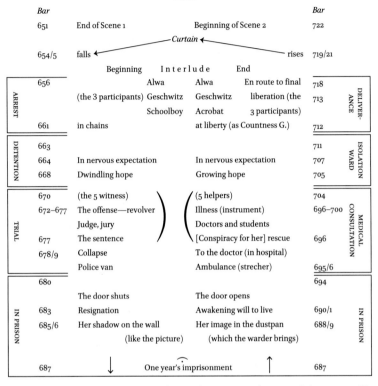

The sequence of the filmed events corresponding to the symmetrical course of the music is likewise to run in a quasi-forward and retrograde progression, wherein corresponding occurrences and associated phenomena are to be matched with one another as closely as possible. In addition to the above congruencies (placed side by side) of this sort (in the large: trial–medical consultation, detention–isolation ward, etc.), also those of a lesser and the least sort: for instance, revolver–stethoscope (hypodermic syringe), bullets–phials, generally legal–medical parallels, § and caduceus, chains–bandages, prison clothes–hospital clothes, prison corridors–hospital corridors. Likewise personal congruencies: judge and jury, medical staff and students, police–nurses.

FIGURE 11.3   Alban Berg. *Lulu Particell.* ÖNB, F21.Berg.29/11/GF Mus. Transcription and Translation: Perle 1985: 152

to all details of 'smaller and smallest kinds',[8] as Berg noted. Below the draft, he listed them: the murder weapon shown in the hearing is associated to the doctor's stethoscope; the prison uniform corresponds to the hospital clothes. The

---

8   "[...] kleinerer und kleinster Art". ÖBN, F21.Berg.29/I-III/GF Mus. Online: http://data.onb. ac.at/rec/AL00220365 [05/02/2016].

judge and jurors are juxtaposed with the body of doctors, the policemen with the nursing staff, the prison corridors with those in the hospital, etc.

In spite of the mirror-like concept of the film scenario, the movie itself runs linearly and without reversal: its direction of motion is forward along the time axis. Yet the music is different. It turns around in the middle and then flows backwards. This film music is one of the most stringent palindromes composed by Berg (cf. Morgan 1991: 124). The idea that music should express something that cannot be shown by film – such as, for instance, portraying inner processes – soon reaches its limits. For this very music lacks the freedom to adapt to the actions shown in the film since the two parts are connected by mutual bonds as basics and their reversal. Moreover, anyone is mistaken who believes that retrograde music is easily recognizable and that parallels to a basic theme can easily be heard. Besides, Berg had in mind not only retrograde music, but even a "Perpetuum", that is music in tumultuous motion. That, however, would inhibit clear musical audibility.

The two halves of the film music are each subdivided into four sections. In the first section (bars 656–662),[9] the police detain Lulu. Alwa, Gräfin Geschwitz and a high-school student are present.[10] Their twelve-tone series dominate the musical events. The film music begins with a trumpet signal (bars 656f.) that codetermines the 'alarm sound' of this first section. It comprises the tones of Alwa's series. Rising figures follow in the strings and woodwind instruments, namely the series of Alwa, the high-school student, and Gräfin Geschwitz. The section closes with the recurring trumpet signal and a one-bar transition.

It is only in the second section (bars 663–669) that Lulu-related music commences, namely the Basic Series of the opera. It represents "Lulu's universe in a general sense" and "pervad[es] the opera as a whole", to quote George Perle (1985: 153). The second section is governed by the Basic Series. Owing to the fast tempo, the fugato which defines this section is hardly heard. Rather, the approximate voice direction and its sudden reversal are realized when the Basic Series topples over into its inversion (end of bar 667). The associated second film section shows Lulu entirely on her own. It is the phase of her detention while awaiting trial and persisting hope for acquittal (bar 664), but reversely also her waning hope (bar 667) as musically indicated by the falling retrograde figure of the inversion.

---

9   For all bar references cf. Berg 1985.
10   He is called Hugenberg in Wedekind's play. In the opera he lost his name, as did several other characters, too.

The rapid semiquaver motions of the first two sections make it difficult to follow and discern the various tone series, but they offer a good background for permitting a rhythmically profiled motif to emerge in the third section (bars 670–678). The film portion is to show the trial from the entering of the witnesses up to Lulu's conviction and her collapse. Musically it is based upon two layers. On the upper layer, the woodwinds successively offer the series of all the persons who appeared in the previous scene. Some of them are now witnesses in Lulu's trial. There can be seen the Basic Series (bars 670–674, clarinet), Dr. Schön's series (bars 670–674, bassoon), the Alwa series (bars 671–674, saxophone), the series of the high-school student (bars 672–674, oboe), the Gräfin Geschwitz series (bars 673f., flute), an acrobat series (bars 673f., contrabassoon) (cf. Perle 1985: 153), and finally a series of Schigolch, the old beggar so closely allied to Lulu (bars 674–678, piano and cor anglais). Berg marked these series as 'main voices' that determine the musical events. On the lower layer another motif slowly moves forward (bars 670–678). It is heard much more distinctly than the character-related series above. This is Basic Cell I, provided by the strings and the piano, as a secondary voice at the beginning.

However, at the point when Lulu succumbs, shortly before she is convicted, the Basic Cell I appears distinctly and dominates the orchestra movement (bars 675–678, strings, brass instruments). It joins the opera's main rhythm (see Figure 11.4). The main rhythm comes forward at the fateful turning points of the opera, and, thus, here, too (cf. Perle 1985: 207f.). In addition, this motif from Basic Cell I and the main rhythm is enhanced as the sound unfolds from three voices at the beginning into seven later on. This leads to a first climax (bar 678), a fortissimo chord. The movie here presents Lulu's verdict and collapse.

FIGURE 11.4
Alban Berg. *Lulu*. Main rhythm

After this climax, there is no relaxation. A sequence of not quite two bars (bars 678f.) provides a further intensification by the sounds of the Lulu series, which represents her seductive power. It is played almost in unison by the brass instruments in relatively slow quavers. So there is good audibility. The target is the second, the real climax of the film music. It is an extended chord (bars 680 and 681) consisting of the tones of Basic Cell III. In a broken structure, Basic

Cell III also determines the semiquaver motions of piano and woodwinds. In the plot, it is the phase where the jail door closes behind Lulu. From here onwards, this fourth section is musically characterized by a distinctly slower tempo. The slowdown is achieved by both a ritardando and extended note durations. The dynamics drop from fortissimo to piano. The movie shows Lulu's resignation, coupled with the loss of her picture. She merely sees her shadow on the wall. The orchestra accompanies this by the Picture Chords in reverse order (bar 685). The target of this descent is the bottom point of it all, reached at bar 687. This is the middle of the film music. It is the center of the movie and – not in the least – of the entire opera. Musically, this center is embraced by a broken chord of piano and vibraphone. This is Basic Cell IV, which provides a formal function in the opera by sounding at the end of each act. Here it marks the end of the opera's first part and also the beginning of the second one (cf. Perle 1985: 91). Between the rise and fall of the chord there is a brief hesitation, as indicated by a fermata.

All formal events in this opera are tied inseparably to Lulu's fate. This also applies to the musical bottom point. The fermata corresponds to a time of absolute standstill, namely her year of imprisonment. But this is also the turning point. Immediately after the broken chord of Basic Cell IV has ended everything is reversed. The music runs exactly backwards from now on, and the film events occur correspondingly. Lulu sees her mirror image for the first time again in a dustpan with the Picture Chords sounding, now in the proper sequence. She regains courage to face life, and the film goes on to show the stations of her escape.

Berg succeeded in telling the intermediary story by film and music. His project has not failed by the use of insufficient means. There are several reasons for it. One is his musical concept. Berg employed the twelve-tone sets as 'leitmotifs' as defined by Richard Wagner (cf. Perle 1985: 95). From the very beginning the series are connected firmly to the respective persons so that the sets carry a definite and also recognizable meaning. In the film music the recognition of the series may be somewhat lessened by the quick semiquaver motions. However, this is different in the remaining parts of the opera where the series have catchy rhythmic profiles. So the film-music audience is supposed to be already familiar with them. Moreover, Berg also used the twelve-tone system programmatically, as he did in the first part of the film music: the Basic Series tilts into its inversion and, thus, turns its direction from rising to falling. The association to Lulu's waning hope is easy to see. In the second part of the film music, where the retrograde provides a natural turnaround, the downward direction of the inversion changes to a rising figure, parallel to which the movie shows Lulu's rising hopes.

Another reason for the success of the movie narrative can be seen in Berg's precise instructions as to the association of film and music. He outlined the movie scenario not only on a separate sheet (see Figure 11.3) but entered it also directly into the Particell, where the movie scenario is associated unambiguously with the individual bars. Consequently, he left the synchronization of movie and music not to accidental actions nor to the analytical abilities of his respective performers. Such observations reveal how Berg honored his claim that the composer should also be the ideal stage director. Evidently he was not only an able composer with a sound instinct for poetry; he also possessed a clear imagination, defining exactly how the stage performance of his works should look like. This is also obvious from his decision to show the interlude story by a movie rather than let a speaker tell it. The film is an independent element of the opera with a display mode that is distinctly different from all other stage presentations. However, Berg maintained images and pictorial language as given by a stage performance. If Berg had left it to a speaker to tell the interlude story, he might have provided an analogy to the animal tamer's prologue but at the expense of shifting the story to a completely different level of abstract language. That would have interrupted the plot. A narration would have been just as little part of the plot as the animal tamer's prologue is. Through the movie, by contrast, he maintained two opera essentials: music and pictures. The film and its music remain in the continuum of the plot.

Alban Berg did not believe that opera would further develop by the integration of modern means. However, he used whatever was at his disposal to fulfill his wish to make good theater. With the modern technique of the film, he extended his expressive means. He realized his idea of providing the missing story between the two Wedekind plays by using visual and auditory media. Interpolated at a highlighted moment at the center of the drama, the film becomes part to the opera's formal design and its story – both in such a way that the film becomes essential to the opera, equal to the stage performance and to the music.

References

Berg, Alban (1928). "Das 'Opernproblem'". *Neue Musik-Zeitung*, 49: 285–287.

Berg, Alban (1985). *Lulu: Oper nach Frank Wedekinds Tragödien* Erdgeist *und* Büchse der Pandora. Score in 2 volumes: Vol. 1, 1st and 2nd Acts. Ed. H.E. Apostel, rev. Friedrich Cerha. Vienna: Universal Edition.

Berg, Alban (2014). "The 'Problem of Opera'". Bryan R. Simms, ed. *Pro Mundo – Pro Domo: The Writings of Alban Berg*. Oxford/New York, NY: OUP. 215–217.

Ertelt, Thomas F. (1993). *Alban Bergs 'Lulu': Quellenstudien und Beiträge zur Analyse.* Alban Berg Studien 3. Vienna: Universal Edition.

Jarman, Douglas (1991). *Alban Berg: Lulu.* Cambridge Opera Handbooks. Cambridge: CUP.

Morgan, Robert P. (1991). "The Eternal Return: Retrograde and Circular Form in Berg". David Gable, Robert P. Morgan, eds. *Alban Berg: Historical and Analytical Perspectives.* Oxford: Clarendon Press. 111–149.

Morgenstern, Soma (1995). *Alban Berg und seine Idole: Erinnerungen und Briefe.* Ed. Ingolf Schulte. Lüneburg: Klampen.

Perle, George (1985). *The Operas of Alban Berg,* Vol. 2: *Lulu.* Berkeley, CA/Los Angeles, CA/London: Univ. of California Press.

Reich, Willi (1963). *Alban Berg: Leben und Werk.* Zurich: Atlantis.

Steiger, Martina, ed. (2013). *Alban Berg – Erich Kleiber: Briefe der Freundschaft.* Vienna: Seifert.

CHAPTER 12

All the Pieces Matter: On Complex TV Music

Frieder von Ammon

Abstract

This paper starts out from the thesis that the use of music in 'Quality TV' series of today differs significantly from the use of music in earlier TV series, insofar as, in accordance with other structural experiments, the potentials of music in television are explored and enlarged to an extent hitherto unknown in the respective series. In order to support this thesis a close look is taken at the use of music in three of the most critically acclaimed and influential 'Quality TV' series so far, *The Sopranos*, *The Wire*, and *Breaking Bad*.

•••

Much has been talked and written lately about the new era of television series, which is mainly, but not exclusively connected with the New York based television networks HBO and AMC. When exactly this new era of 'Quality TV' begun, whether it was in the late 1990s, or already in the 1980s, or even earlier, is – as is the term itself – a matter of dispute. What seems to be certain, though, is that the phenomenon has reached a peak in the present. With HBO and AMC original series such as *The Sopranos*, *The Wire*, *Deadwood*, *Lost*, *Mad Men*, *Breaking Bad*, *Game of Thrones*, *True Detective*, *Better call Saul*, and some others, television series – for the first time in history – in view of scope and ambition can be (and have been) regarded as equivalents to the great novels of world literature. This is mostly due to the fact that in the best of these series the potentials of serial filmic narration are explored and enlarged to an extent hitherto unknown.

If one wants to define 'Quality TV', it is a good starting point to return to the catalogue of criteria, which Robert J. Thompson offers in the preface to his seminal study *Television's Second Golden Age* first published in 1996. There has been quite a lot of debate on the accuracy and adequacy of this catalogue (as well as on other attempts at 'Defining Quality', see McCabe/Akass, eds. 2007, esp. Cardwell 2007), but nevertheless one can say that, all in all, it is still valid today, which is quite astonishing, especially if one considers the fact that it was put together twenty years ago, i.e. shortly before, with the broadcasting of *The*

Sopranos beginning in 1999, 'Television's Third Golden Age' – which, as many scholars would say, is it's true golden age – had begun. Seen from today, seven of Thompson's (originally twelve) criteria in particular seem to have stood the test of time. One: "Quality TV is best defined by what it is not. It is not 'regular' TV. [...] Quality TV breaks rules. It may do this by taking a traditional genre and transforming it [...]. Or it may defy standard generic parameters and define new narrative territory heretofore unexplored by television [...]". Two: "Quality TV tends to have a large ensemble cast. The variety of characters allows for a variety of viewpoints since multiple plots must usually be employed to accommodate all of the characters". Three – and this is a crucial point indeed: "Quality TV has a memory. Though it may or may not be serialized in continuing story lines, these shows tend to refer back to previous episodes. Characters develop and change as the series goes on. Events and details from previous episodes are often used or referred to in subsequent episodes". Four: "Quality TV creates a new genre by mixing old ones. [...] All quality shows integrate comedy and tragedy in a way Aristotle would never have approved". Five: "Quality TV tends to be literary and writer-based. The writing is usually more complex than in other types of programming". Six: "Quality TV is self-conscious. Oblique allusions are made both to high and popular culture, but mostly to TV itself". And, finally, seven: "Series which exhibit the [...] characteristics listed above are usually enthusiastically showered with awards and critical acclaim" (Thompson 1997: 13–16).

The validity of Thompson's catalogue, however, is not what is argued for, or against, in the following. Instead it is proposed to add another criterion to it. It is the following: *'Quality TV' is a highly musical genre. It makes (often uncommon) use of a wide range of music in a broad variety of ways, and in so doing, it aims at avoiding or even subverting musical clichés of any sort, and replacing them by individual musical structures which specifically fit the demands of the respective TV series.* Or, to rephrase Thompson's first and foremost criterion: *The music used in 'Quality TV' is best defined by what it is not. It is not 'regular' TV music.*

But what is 'regular' TV music? As an example one can think of *Dallas* (the original 1980s series, not its sequel broadcasted from 2012 to 2014): the score of this series (by Jerome Immel) mainly consists of a catchy, if somewhat dull title theme performed by a large orchestra, and of a certain number of unspecific and therefore interchangeable short orchestral pieces to mark the beginning or ending of an act ('Act-in', 'Act-out'), to indicate a change of sequence or setting ('bridge'), or to gap a commercial break ('bumper') (cf. Prendergast 1992: 274–287). In moments of strong emotional content or of intense suspense the composer also draws back on the traditional 'underscoring'-technique, i.e. by musical means he emphasizes what is seen on screen. This is not to say that

Immel's score for *Dallas* was a bad score, however; on the contrary: with regard to the usual requirements to TV music it is to be considered a highly effective one, and it is for this reason that it is such a good example for 'regular' TV music. In contrast to this, one of the basic features of 'Quality TV', especially since the late 1990s, is a conception and practice of film music which avoids this kind of regularity, or even undermines it. But undermining its less refined predecessors is by no means the most important function of music in 'Quality TV' series: the creators of such series have realized what great narrative effects one can achieve by using music in unusual ways, and in 'Television's Third Golden Age', in which structural experiments of any sort are no longer forbidden but in fact a necessity, they had the possibility to really explore, and enlarge the potentials of music in television – which is what they did, thoroughly and ingeniously.

In the present essay, their explorations are going to be explored, i.e. the field of what – borrowing the term from Jason Mittell's study (see 2015) – is provisionally called 'Complex TV music' here. This field is a vast field indeed, and it is an ever – and rapidly – growing field; and, what is more, research has only started to deal with it (cf. Donnelly 2005: 110–133, 134–149; see also Aslinger 2013). Therefore, it cannot be aimed for presenting a list of definitive results. What can be done, however, is to take a first look at a small selection of significant series, and to try to describe some of the forms and functions of music in it. In order to do so, three series have been chosen, all of which are unique works of art and represent different phases of 'Television's Third Golden Age': *The Sopranos* (broadcasted from 1999 to 2007), which changed – as critic Alan Sepinwall put it – "everything" (2012: 32; see also Diederichsen 2012), *The Wire* (broadcasted from 2002 to 2008), which turned out to be – to quote Sepinwall again – "the Great American Novel for television" (2012: 69; see also Eschkötter 2012), and *Breaking Bad* (broadcasted from 2008 to 2013), which pushed Complex TV to a new level (see Lang/Dreher 2013; Koch 2015). What interlinks the three, however, is (among other things) that they have a specific approach to music, and that in this respect they refer to, and even build up on, each other.

1   Musical Mobsters: *The Sopranos*

The man who created *The Sopranos* and thus changed the world of television, David Chase, has a clear conception of how music should be used in TV series, a poetics of music in television, so to speak. As it seems, the title of his series already hints at the fact that it is a highly musical show; it is rather unlikely that Chase should have chosen such a musical name as 'Soprano' for his mobster family without thinking about its musical connotations (see Neal 2006). Be that as it may: in an interview with the managing editor of the *Rolling Stone* magazine, Will Dana, Chase revealed some aspects of his conception (see Chase 2011). The crucial point for him was, so he explains, that he definitely did not want a score for his series, i.e. music which was composed specifically for it, as it used to be standard practice in 'regular' TV shows; again, one can think of *Dallas*. The reason why he did not want a score, was, he says, that he did not want to manipulate his audience in the usual manner; he did not want to tell the viewers what to think and feel through music. Instead, he decided to use pre-existing, i.e. pre-recorded music only. With regard to the scope of *The Sopranos* – which is a 90-hours show – this was quite a daring decision. As models for his decisive score-refusal Chase refers to Martin Scorsese's 1973 movie *Mean Streets* (Scorsese's first mobsters movie), in which pop songs of the day are used instead of a score, and to Stanley Kubrick, who also, and famously, used pre-existing music (almost) only. Chase could also have referred to Quentin Tarantino, but this is probably not the kind of director he wants to be compared with; other directors could be named as well (see Powrie/Stillwell, eds. 2006). The first and foremost principle of David Chase's poetics of music in television thus is: avoiding a score by any means, and replacing it by specifically chosen pre-existing music. And with this, he set a new standard for Complex TV music. With *The Sopranos*, the 'regular' score in TV series had lost its innocence, so to speak.

Consequently, no composer was hired for *The Sopranos*; instead, Chase himself, together with producer Martin Bruestle and music supervisor Kathryn Dayak, selected the music for his show. At times, Bruestle, Chase and Dayak were additionally supported by guitar player Steve van Zandt, who also plays a leading role in the series. And they did a good job, indeed: the music they selected for the show is extremely manifold, a mix of – just as the show itself – epical proportions, ranging from operatic arias of the 18th century to pop songs by Frank Sinatra or Bruce Springsteen. As a consequence, two CDs containing *Music from the HBO Original Series* The Sopranos were published – at a time, when the show was still running; not to mention several CDs which were published unofficially. This clearly indicates that the music selected for *The Sopranos* is significant even if you neglect its forms and functions in the show.

Only if you take it seriously into consideration, though, the whole significance of it becomes perceptible. Given the scope of *The Sopranos*, it is impossible to systematize the forms and functions of music in this show in one essay. But at least some systematic remarks can be made. With regard to the forms of music in *The Sopranos*, already the frame of each episode is significant, for the title sequence as well as the end credits are accompanied by music. Whereas the title sequence music – the song *Woke Up this Morning* by *Alabama 3* – stays the same throughout the entire show, the end credit music changes individually from episode to episode; twice (and each time to great effect) it is entirely omitted. To differentiate the two parts of the frame in that way was a clever decision: whereas the title song, being the signature song of the series, so to speak, guarantees its recognizability, the individual ending music leads the recipient into the open, as it were, and it does that differently each time. To what end, and how, is a matter still to be explored.

In view of the position of music on the diegetic or non-diegetic level, respectively, one can say that everything is possible in *The Sopranos*. For one, music may be placed on the non-diegetic level. In fact, Chase does that quite often; an example will be discussed below. Also, a piece of music may first be heard on the non-diegetic level and then shift to the diegetic level, or vice versa. Most typical for the show, however, is the extensive use of diegetic music or 'source music': music may be sung or played by characters themselves – in fact, main character Tony Soprano loves to sing –, songs may ring out of cars, and song texts may be quoted and even discussed by characters. This can happen rather accidentally and does not have specific implications. But the opposite can also be true: one of the crucial moments of the show is when Uncle Junior sings an old Neapolitan song at a family meeting and all the mobsters are moved to tears (see season 3, episode 13). In the interview mentioned above, Chase himself has pointed to the significance of the scene. Another (and famous) example is the final scene of the show, which begins with Tony Soprano entering a diner, where he soon starts to take a look at the play list of the juke box, and, after thinking for a while, finally chooses the song *Don't Stop Believin'* by *Journey*. This song accompanies the further course of the scene, until it is – with the word 'stop' – suddenly cut off. A black screen and absolute silence follow. The fact that the show ends with such a musical blackout, is significant: in this way, the musicality of *The Sopranos* is proven one last time, *ex negativo*, as it were.

As far as the functions of music are concerned, one can say that the indirect characterization of characters through music is of great importance for the series. An example is a sequence in the pilot, in which one sees Tony Soprano brutally beating up a guy who owes him money. The sequence is accompanied by a doo wop-song (*I Wonder Why* by *Dian and the Belmonts*), which plays on the radio of the car in which Tony chased his victim before. In this way, an aspect of Tony's mentality is revealed: for him, beating up a person is an occupation just as ordinary and innocent as a doo wop-song from the 1950s. Feelings like sympathy or guilt are – at this point – alien to him, especially when it comes to money. Also, the allusion to the 1950s could be interpreted as a reference to the time when his father used to be the head of the 'family'; the difficult relationship of Tony's to his father will turn out to be a recurring topic of the show.

Another recurring function of music in *The Sopranos* is the indirect charac terization not only of characters, but of entire social environments; an example is the music which is played in Tony Soprano's strip club Bada Bing. Over the course of the show, one gets to hear quite a number of songs in there. If you pay attention to them, you realize that was Chase and his collaborators do here (among other things) is writing a music history of the 1990s from the point of view of New Jersey mobsters (which undoubtedly is quite an interesting perspective). Thus, for music historians of the future the series might turn out to be a document of considerable value.

Yet another, and very significant, function of music in the series is the interpretation of the events shown on screen, especially through the texts of the respective songs. In the interview already mentioned, Chase commented on this technique and compared it to nothing less than the chorus in ancient Greek drama. He said, that "lyrics are just another form of dialogue" (2011). One striking example for this – as one might call it – 'chorus function' of music is the 12th episode of season 3, at the end of which one song placed on the non-diegetic level interlinks and interprets several individual sequences. The song is called *Return to Me* and was made popular by Dean Martin in the late 1950s. In *The Sopranos*, however, the song is not heard in the original version, but in a cover version by Bob Dylan. And what is more, Dylan recorded this version specifically for *The Sopranos*, although Chase had not asked him to do so. According to Chase, the opposite is true: Dylan had asked Chase whether he could make a contribution to the show. If anything, this is a proof for the significant use of music in this series; otherwise a musician like Dylan would not have wanted to participate in it. And it shows another specific potential of music in *The Sopranos* and in Complex TV music in general: due to the fact, that every large-scale series is a work in progress, the music may develop over the course of the production, and interesting interactions with the audience may take place, just as in this case: Dylan, being an admirer of *The Sopranos*, decided that his music had to be part of the show – and now it actually is.

But what did Chase do with the present Dylan had given to him? To answer this question, one first needs to take a look at the lyrics of the song: "Return to me / Oh my dear I'm so lonely / Hurry back, hurry back / Oh my love hurry back I'm yours // Return to me / For my heart wants you only / Hurry home, hurry home / Won't you please hurry home to my heart // My darling, if I hurt you I'm sorry / Forgive me and please say you are mine // Return to me / Please come back bella mia / Hurry back, hurry home to my arms / To my lips and my heart // Retorna me / Cara mia ti amo / Solo tu, solo tu, solo tu, solo tu / Mio cuore". A lover, who has betrayed his beloved, so one assumes, now tries to convince her to come back to him; and he does this by using particularly sweet language. To enhance his persuasiveness, he switches to Italian in the end; with this, unwillingly, the cheesiness of the song is enhanced, as well. On the other hand, the mixture of English and Italian made the song perfectly suitable for *The Sopranos*; and this also holds true for Dean Martin's well-known connections to the Mafia. If Bob Dylan sings the song with his croaky old voice, it's a different story, though; it entirely changes the subtext of the song: what one now hears is a song which self-ironically undermines its own cheesiness, so to speak. And what about its function in the show? If one takes a look at the scene, one realizes that the song accompanies and thereby closely ties together three sequences, in each of which a mobster, who shortly before has (in one way or another) betrayed his wife, is now returning to her. The situation of the song thus is inverted. Also, all three men are lying to their wives, showing no sign of embarrassment or regret whatsoever. They hide their emotional emptiness and cover it up by a false sentimentality, which is even worse than that displayed in the song, especially when it is heard in Bob Dylan's self-ironical rendering. In this way, the song demasks the characters as what they are: cheating, lying, emotionally disabled, in short: despicable men. This effect, however, is the result of a rather clever use of source music in a TV show. The function of *Return to Me* in *The Sopranos* thus may indeed be compared to the function of the chorus in ancient Greek drama, even if, to return to Thompson's list once again, Aristotle probably would not have approved of it.

2   Musical Verisimilitude: *The Wire*

Even if much more could (and should) be said about music in *The Sopranos*, another series is to be looked at, which, if it comes to music, is not less significant: *The Wire*. And again, already the title of the show seems to hint at its musicality: on an obvious first level of meaning, the title refers to the practice of putting a wiretap on phones. For this is what happens in the story: the police puts a wiretap on phones used by criminals and in this way listens in to what they speak to each other. On a hidden second level of meaning, though, one could interpret the title as a metaphor for listening in to the music the characters of the series listen to; for, in a way, this is exactly what the show does. How so?

In order to answer this question, one needs to step back and take a look at the musical conception of David Simon, the creator of *The Wire*. In some respect, his conception is even more radical than that of David Chase's. What Simon shares with Chase, however, is the attitude of decisive score-refusal: he, too, did not want to tell his audience what to think and feel through music, by no means; or, as producer George Pelecanos put it: he did not want "music intended to cue your emotions or instruct you how to feel" (2008: 31). For that reason, Simon, as did Chase, decided to use pre-existing music only, and therefore also did not hire a composer, but music supervisor Blake Leyh. What makes the difference between Simon and Chase, though, is Simon's radical decision to use diegetic music only. With the exception of the frame of each episode and the end of each season, in which a song on the non-diegetic level accompanies a montage sequence, the only music the recipients get to hear is music which is part of the world shown on screen. In view of the scope of *The Wire* – a 60-hours show – this is a decision even more daring than Chase's decision to use pre-existing music only. Simon wanted both: pre-existing music only, and diegetic music only. In an interview, Simon said that in *The Wire* he was aiming for "verisimilitude" (2008: 20). This also applies to his use of music: what he wanted to achieve was maximum 'musical verisimilitude', which means that all music heard in the show could indeed be heard by the characters themselves. Obviously, this differs crucially from *The Sopranos*: Tony Soprano, for example, could not have heard a song which was recorded by Bob Dylan as a reaction to the show in which he is the main character. In *The Wire*, however, the music strictly stays within the boundaries of the world it depicts. If one considers this difference, one realizes that Simon tries to emulate his predecessor by aiming for an even greater authenticity than him. As research has pointed out, 'interserial competition' of this kind is rather typical for Complex TV (cf. Jahn-Sudmann/Kelleter 2012: 207). The comparison of the musical conceptions of Chase's and Simon's makes clear that the "dynamics of serial emulation" (ibid.: 205) can also be observed on the level of music. In the light of this, one also realizes that Simon, just as Chase, though with even more ambition than him, writes the music history of the present from a specific point of view; this time, it is the Baltimore of the early 21st century. Thus, it is not – as in *The Sopranos* – just a specific segment of society the musical taste of which is documented through the show, but a whole city. If one bears that in mind, the title's hidden meaning becomes perceptible: a wiretap is not just put on the phones of criminals, but also on the city of Baltimore, Maryland, as a whole. Accordingly, for music historians of the future the series might turn out to be a document of even greater value than *The Sopranos*.

As a consequence, just as in the case of *The Sopranos*, interesting interactions between the show and its audience took place: after watching *The Wire* for a while, musicians from Baltimore told Simon that the music he had chosen so far was not 'Baltimorean' enough, and they sent him CDs with tracks they found more suitable, some of which Simon then actually used in the further course of the show (cf. Chang 2008: 44). They can be heard on the CD *Beyond Hamsterdam: Baltimore Tracks from* The Wire, which was, along with the CD '... *and all the pieces matter': Five Years of Music from* The Wire, published shortly after the end of the series in 2008.

With regard to the frames of the individual episodes, *The Wire* again builds up on *The Sopranos*: just as in this show, the title sequence is always accompanied by one song. And again, it is well chosen: the signature song of *The Wire* was written by Tom Waits and is called *Way Down in the Hole*. In turn, there's one difference to *The Sopranos*, though: in *The Wire*, the opening song stays the same, and yet it changes to some extent, for every season uses a different version of it, some of which were actually commissioned by Simon. In this way, one of the main aspects of the show is mirrored already in the opening song: that every season deals with the same problems, namely drugs, regardless which social context the narration focuses on: the projects (season 1), the harbour (season 2), city hall (season 3), the school system (season 4), or the world of media (season 5). It's always the same, only in different manifestations; and the same holds true for the song in the title sequence.

The end credit music works differently: it is not a song, but a short instrumental piece (which was composed by the music supervisor), and it stays the same throughout the show. Thus, the end frame of each episode is more defined than it was the case in *The Sopranos*; it actually closes each episode.

Even if, due to Simon's decision to use diegetic music only, the functions of music in *The Wire* are less varied than in *The Sopranos*, it is impossible to systematize them in the present essay. Crucial is, however, the indirect characterization of characters through music. As Pelecanos pointed out: "The DNA we've created for those characters determines the kind of songs – be they old school funk and slo-jam, current hip-hop, or Irish punk – they listen to" (2008: 31). According to this, all the different characters (and types of characters) have their own music: whereas the criminals usually listen to hip-hop and related styles, detective Jimmy McNulty, who is of Irish descent, prefers songs by *The Pogues*, for example, and rock music. Thus, Simon does not only write music history, in a way he also pursues a socio-musicological approach.

Finally, a look is to be taken at the only exception to Simon's strict rule of never using non-diegetic music. The sequence in question is to be found in episode 6 of season 1, and, due to its singularity, it stands out. What one sees is the appearance of Avon Barksdale, the dominant drug dealer on Baltimore's West Side, in an area of the city which is reigned by him. He is accompanied by Stringer Bell, the second-in-command of his organization, and by another member of his crew, a guy called 'Stinkum'. The appearance of these three characters is shown in slow motion and in perfect choreography – and it is accompanied by music, by a groove-driven instrumental piece, which perfectly suits the movements of the characters; in fact, even the blink of Avon Barksdale's eye is exactly on the beat. Where the music comes from, however, is not clear; it is impossible to identify its source. After several hours of listening to diegetic music only, the recipient is puzzled. But what is the function of this irritating sequence? Why did Simon ignore his own rule? As it seems, he realized that he could simply not present the druglord and his gang appropriately without using music in a way which differs from the rest. For Barksdale's power is not only based on money, and violence, it is also based on a certain attitude, on a certain style, and, last, but not least, on a certain music. Avon Barksdale and his crew are the embodiment of this music, so to speak. It is for this reason that in this case there is no source for the music: these characters *are* the music.

3   Breaking Boundaries: *Breaking Bad*

The last example to be scrutinized here is the ACM series *Breaking Bad*. With regard to music, it seems that the creator of the show, Vince Gilligan, wanted to make use of the achievements of his predecessors, but at the same time wanted to break new ground, which is in fact what he did. Thus, the 'dynamics of serial emulation' are at work here, too. To start with the common features, however: just as *The Sopranos* and *The Wire*, *Breaking Bad* employs a rather large amount of (well chosen) pre-existing music; some of it is contained in the CD *Music from the Original Television Series* Breaking Bad, which was already published in 2010, before the series came to its end three years later. The music may be placed on the diegetic as well as on the non-diegetic level. Also, the 'chorus technique' is used quite often. A striking example is a sequence in episode 2 of season 1 in which a drug dealer, after recognizing main character Walter White, who is driving by in his car, panics and runs into a tree, after which he falls down unconsciously. Meanwhile the song *You're Moving Me* by R&B singer Clyde McPhatter rings out of the car radio. In the lyrics of the song a male speaker describes his intense emotional response to a female: "You knock me out". Obviously, the contrast between an emotional response of this kind and the panicking drug dealer (who gets knocked out by a tree) is quite strong and therefore rather comical. The humour of the scene is even enhanced when Walter White drags the body of the unconscious drug dealer into his car, when he – to speak with the title of the song – is actually moving him. In short: Vince Gilligan makes brilliant use of the 'chorus technique' here, and by doing so, pays homage to his predecessor David Chase. At the same time, however, he tries to emulate him.

The same holds true, though in a different way, for another sequence (5, 3), in which Gilligan employs the technique of indirectly characterizing characters through music. The sequence in question takes place in a music store. Two small-time drug dealers, 'Badger' and 'Skinny Pete', enter the store and take a look at the instruments displayed there. While Badger picks up an amplified electric guitar and childishly starts strumming around on it, 'Skinny Pete' turns to a keyboard and starts playing a classical piano piece on it. It is a piece by Carl Philipp Emanuel Bach commonly referred to as *Solfegietto*, which is often studied by young piano players, because it requires some technical skills without being too difficult. Surprisingly, 'Skinny Pete' plays this piece fluently, although not without flaws, until he is disturbed by the noisy strumming of his friend, who obviously is – different from 'Skinny Pete' – rather tone-deaf. For a second, one can see the disappointment on Skinny Pete's face. Watching this, one realizes that Skinny Pete must have grown up in a bourgeois milieu, for he must have taken piano lessons once; also, one realizes that he has some musical talent – a talent, however, for which there is no room anymore in the world of drugs he now inhabits. Thus, in a sophisticated musical way, the tragedy of Skinny Pete (and many other kids of his generation) is revealed.

After commenting on the musical features which *Breaking Bad* shares with *The Sopranos* and *The Wire*, a special focus is now to be placed on the features unique for this show. For one, *Breaking Bad* does have a score (by composer Dave Porter). It is anything but a 'regular' score, though, for it resounds rarely, in fact its existence sometimes is almost unnoticeable, and it almost never is music in the usual sense. Porter primarily works with sounds, sounds of different kinds, electronic as well as acoustic, untouched as well as deformed, often it is difficult to keep the different layers apart. The result are idiosyncratic, irritating, and strangely beautiful soundscapes which are a perfect supplement for what can be seen on screen. A good example is the music Porter composed for the beginning of season 3: a disturbing sequence in which you see poor Mexicans crawling on their stomachs on a dirty road. Soon they are joined by two dangerous killer twins wearing expensive suits. As it later turns out, they are approaching a sanctuary of *Doña Sebastiana* or *La Santísima Muerte*, a saint widely revered in Mexico. The colours are of a dark and dirty yellow, reminding one of hellish sulfur fumes, the mood is threatening, and yet, in a bewildering way, fascinating. And so is the music: it is a dense and differentiated texture of electronic sounds and percussive elements, evoking notions of the netherworld. To describe this texture in detail, or even to transcribe it, would be a task of extreme difficulty, for it is truly unique, and as such, it perfectly suits the uniqueness of the images. Thus, Porter, in a congenial way, employs the 'mood technique' here, i.e. he finds musical equivalents for the mood evoked by the images.

Another feature unique for *Breaking Bad* needs to be mentioned: the beginning of the 7th episode of season 2, a 'cold open' (as always in *Breaking Bad*), i.e. a scene shown before the title sequence. In it, one sees three Mexican musicians wearing black clothes and hats perform a song in the style of an MTV music video. The band is called *Los Cuates de Sinaloa* and is no invention, it really exists. So does the song the band plays: it is (as the episode itself) called *Negro y Azul*. The song is a *narcocorrido*, a 'drug ballad', a genre of great popularity, especially in Mexico. Typically, narcocorridos tell stories from the drug world – real stories, referring to real events and real people. In this case, however, the narcocorrido tells the story of the main character of *Breaking Bad*: Walter White, also known as Heisenberg. In this way, his increasing fame in the drug world is suggested. As already mentioned, it is a real band, however, which plays a real narcocorrido, though on a fictional character; thereby, the ontological levels are strangely intertwined. And, moreover, the narcocorrido mentions events which have not yet been told in the series, it even seems to foreshadow the final outcome of the story (with Walter White being killed by the Mexican drug cartel). The narcocorrido is a spoiler, so to speak. As it turns out, this is a false lead, however, for in the further course of events the cartel is killed (in its entirety) and Walter White stays alive (at least for now). All in all, the sequence could be described as a *mise en abyme* (cf. Wolf 2001: 61–68): the story in which the scene is inserted is mirrored in it, although in a deformed, contorted way.

Watching this scene, a famous operatic scene comes to mind: the so-called *Nornen-Vorspiel* ('Prelude of the Norns') with which Richard Wagner's *Götterdämmerung*, the fourth part of *Der Ring des Nibelungen*, begins. In this scene, the three Norns weave the rope of destiny, and, doing so, they sing. In their song, they summarize what has happened in the story until then, and they also reveal some of what will happen in the further course of the story. Finally, though, the rope breaks and their knowledge is disrupted. The scene is part of the action, but, at the same time, it comments on it and thus is placed on a higher level; therefore, it can also be described as a *mise en abyme*.

Obviously, the sequence in *Breaking Bad* resembles this famous scene in several ways: first, being a cold open for an episode, it could also be described as a *Vorspiel*, and, moreover, just as in *Der Ring des Nibelungen*, this *Vorspiel* is not placed at the very beginning of the work, but is inserted later. Second: in the sequence, as well as in the *Nornen-Vorspiel*, one encounters three characters of the same sex, who sing throughout the entire scene. In both cases, the characters wear conspicuous costumes: whereas the three Norns wear "lange[ ], dunkle[ ] und schleierartige[ ] Faltengewänder[ ]"[1] (Wagner 2009: 325), the three Mexican musicians wear stylish black clothes and hats. And third: the sequence as well as the *Nornen-Vorspiel* are both *mises en abyme*. In the light of this, it does not seem to be too farfetched to interpret the narcocorrido-sequence in *Breaking Bad* as an intermedial actualization of the *Nornen-Vorspiel*: as opera is transferred into a television series, and Norns turned into Mexican musicians, Germanic myth is transferred into the drug world of (New) Mexico in the 21st century. If you consider Wagner's direct as well as indirect presence in cinema (see Joe/Gilman, eds. 2010), this reference does not come as a surprise. In any case: what Gilligan does here, none of his predecessors did. His idea of disguising the Norns as Mexican musicians is as fascinating as it is truly unique. Whether even this idea will be emulated one day, remains to be seen.

•••

In the course of preparing this paper for publication, HBO announced a new series: it is called *Vinyl* and its plot revolves around the music scene in New York City during the 1970s. Thus, already the setting of this new series seems to strengthen the main argument of this essay that 'Quality TV' is a highly musical genre. But that is not all yet: no less than Mick Jagger (together with Martin Scorsese) features as producer of this series. The fact that the protagonists of pop music are no longer satisfied – as was Bob Dylan in *The Sopranos* – with contributing music to a series, but even start creating a series themselves, is a further case in point.

References

Aslinger, Ben (2013). "Nip/Tuck: Popular Music". Ethan Thompson, Jason Mittell, eds. *How to Watch Television*. London/New York, NY: New York Univ. Press. 47–55.

Cardwell, Sarah (2007). "Is Quality Television Any Good?: Generic Distinctions, Evaluations and the Troubling Matter of Critical Judgement". Janet McCabe, Kim Akass, eds. *Quality TV: Contemporary American Television and Beyond*. London/New York, NY: I.B. Tauris. 19–34.

Chang, Jeff (2008). "Everything is connected". *'… and all the pieces matter': Five Years of Music from* The Wire. Booklet. 43–53.

---

1   'long, dark and veil-like pleated garments' (transl. mine).

166 AMMON

Chase, David (2011). "Die Musik von *Die Sopranos*". *The Sopranos: Staffel 6, Teil 2*. DVD 4, bonus track.

Diederichsen, Diedrich (2012). *The Sopranos*. Zurich/Berlin: diaphanes.

Donnelly, K.J. (2005). *The Spectre of Sound: Music in Film and Television*. London: British Film Institute.

Eschkötter, Daniel (2012). *The Wire*. Zurich/Berlin: diaphanes.

Jahn-Sudmann, Andreas, Frank Kelleter (2012). "Die Dynamik serieller Überbietung: Amerikanische Fernsehserien und das Konzept des Quality-TV". Frank Kelleter, ed. *Populäre Serialität: Narration – Evolution – Distinktion. Zum seriellen Erzählen seit dem 19. Jahrhundert*. Bielefeld: transcript. 205–224.

Joe, Jeongwon, Sanders L. Gilman, eds. (2010). *Wagner & Cinema*. Bloomington, IN: Indiana Univ. Press.

Koch, Gertrud (2015). *Breaking Bad*. Zurich/Berlin: diaphanes.

Lang, Christine, Christoph Dreher (2013). *Breaking Down* Breaking Bad. Munich: Wilhelm Fink.

McCabe, Janet, Kim Akass, eds. (2007). *Quality TV: Contemporary American Television and Beyond*. London/New York, NY: I.B. Tauris.

Mittell, Jason (2015). *Complex TV: The Poetics of Contemporary Television Storytelling*. New York, NY/London: New York Univ. Press.

Neal, Chris (2006). "Gangstas, Divas, and Breaking Tony's Balls: Musical Reference in *The Sopranos*". David Lavery, ed. *Reading* The Sopranos*: Hit TV from HBO*. London/New York, NY: I.B. Tauris. 121–127.

Pelecanos, George (2008). "From the Source". '*... and all the pieces matter': Five Years of Music from* The Wire. Booklet. 28–37.

Powrie, Phil, Robynn Stillwell, eds. (2006). *Changing Tunes: The Use of Pre-existing Music in Film*. Burlington, VT: Ashgate.

Prendergast, Roy M. (1992). *Film Music: A Neglected Art. A Critical Study of Music in Films*. Second Edition. New York, NY /London: W.W. Norton.

Sepinwall, Alan (2012). *The Revolution was Televised: The Cops, Crooks, Slingers, and Slayers Who Changed TV Drama Forever*. New York, NY: Touchstone.

Simon, David (2008). "Think Again". '*... and all the pieces matter': Five Years of Music from* The Wire. Booklet. 18–25.

Thompson, Robert J. (1997). *Television's Second Golden Age: From* Hill Street Blues *to* ER. Syracuse, NY: Syracuse Univ. Press.

Wagner, Richard (2009). *Der Ring des Nibelungen: Ein Bühnenfestspiel für drei Tage und einen Vorabend. Textbuch mit Varianten der Partitur*. Ed. Egon Voss. Stuttgart: Reclam.

Wolf, Werner (2001). "Formen literarischer Selbstreferenz in der Erzählkunst: Versuch einer Typologie und ein Exkurs zur *mise en cadre* und *mise en reflet/série*". Jörg Helbig, ed. *Erzählen und Erzähltheorie im 20. Jahrhundert*. Heidelberg: Winter. 49–84.

CHAPTER 13

The Music Videos of the Alternative Rock Band They Might Be Giants: Prolegomena for a Theory of Nonsense across Media

Emily Petermann

Abstract

Though the term 'nonsense' in a literary context is most often used for a narrowly defined genre with origins in the work of nineteenth-century English writers Edward Lear and Lewis Carroll, it is fruitful to consider it instead as a set of often ludic techniques for subverting the familiar common-sense order – from wordplay to inversions on the level of content to non-sequiturs, unexpected juxtapositions, and other manipulations of expectations – that may occur in a wide range of genres and media, from theater of the absurd to surrealist film, painting, and music.

In multimedial contexts, an important part of that meaning-making process is the interaction between media. The nonsense of a song characterized by "surrealistic absurdism" (Ellis 2008: 211) may lie primarily in the lyrics, in the music, in the images of the music video, or especially in contradictions between these medial components. The present paper examines nonsense in all three medial components of a music video, focusing on "Birdhouse in Your Soul" by the alternative rock band They Might Be Giants. Beginning with an analysis of nonsense strategies in the song lyrics (nonce words, incongruous situations, lack of closure), it asks to what extent parallel strategies can be found in the music (abrupt key changes, unexpected instrumentation, stylistic juxtapositions), and in the video (surrealistic imagery, disjunctive editing), as well as in their interaction.

...

1 Introduction

This is a paper that, like the surrealist material it covers, will probably raise more questions than it will answer. While focusing on techniques of nonsense and surrealism in selected music videos of the American alternative rock band They Might Be Giants (TMBG), it will specifically address the question of what constitutes nonsense or surrealism in the three main media that participate in music videos – music, lyrics, and video images – as well as in the interactions between the three.

I begin by sketching out my working definition of nonsense, which has thus far been treated as a textual genre. Then, using as a case study what is arguably TMBG's best-known and most successful song, "Birdhouse in Your Soul" from the 1990 album *Flood*, I will examine the three main medial components first individually and then in their interaction to explore the techniques used to produce nonsensical effects.

2　　　What Is Nonsense?

> "It seems very pretty" she said when she had finished it [the poem "The Jabberwocky"], "but it's *rather* hard to understand!" (You see she didn't like to confess, even to herself, that she couldn't make it out at all.) "Somehow it seems to fill my head with ideas – only I don't exactly know what they are! However, *somebody* killed *something*: that's clear, at any rate".
> CARROLL 1998: 134

Nonsense, although it should certainly not be confused with the complete absence of sense, is characterized by words and structures that resist a commonsense explanation and frequently resist closure to instead revel in ambiguity. I do not use nonsense in the narrow sense of a clearly defined sub-genre of literature[1] – but instead as a mode of writing that may appear in many different genres, as well as other media, such as visual art, film, music, and more. Though I will concentrate on the interaction between words, music, and images in music videos, work on nonsense to date has concentrated primarily on literary nonsense – with the possible exception of Susan Stewart. For Stewart, nonsense is *"any activity that produces 'not sense'"* (1978: 51), and she refuses to pin it down further than that, arguing that nonsense is always dependent upon the type of common sense it is inverting or subverting and that since common sense is also an ongoing process, neither sense nor nonsense can be

---

1　See Elizabeth Sewell 1952, Peter Köhler 1989, and Wim Tigges 1988 for examples of scholars who treat literary nonsense as a more rigidly defined genre. For another example of regarding nonsense not as a genre, but as a mode, see Kevin Shortsleeve, who defines nonsense as "a set of writerly tools – words, phrases, or texts that revel in inversion fantasies and manifest a topsy-turvyness that typically rejects authoritarian order" (2011: 191).

conclusively defined in formal terms. Though she does not restrict nonsense to a genre or even to the medium of text, Stewart does not include music at all in her analyses. Work on surrealism, too, has focused on words and images to the near exclusion of music, probably in part due to André Breton's "antagonism" towards music (1946/1978: 266f.). Anne LeBaron's (see 2002) detailed discussion of surrealist elements in postmodern music and John Richardson's work (see 2012) on neosurrealism in the popular audiovisual domain are two of the rare exceptions.[2] I return to these when discussing nonsense and surrealism in music, below.

Though my own definition of nonsense is still evolving, a few points are clear at this point. When I say I see nonsense not as a genre but as a mode, I am really referring to an open set of strategies that a text or other media product may employ in confounding recipients' usual sense-making processes (cf. Shortsleeve 2011: 191). These works do not primarily aim to 'make sense', but to challenge our everyday, common-sense ideas about language, the world, or narrative. I will tentatively propose that nonsense operates on three primary levels within a text. Nonsense may first of all be found on a linguistic level – as in Lewis Carroll's famous "Jabberwocky" ("Twas brillig, and the slithy toves / Did gyre and gimble in the wabe"; 1998: 152). Then there is a situational or semantic level – when the common-sense order of things is turned on its head in carnivalesque fashion and people walk on the ceiling instead of the floor, children or animals have power instead of the usual authority figures, or actions are carried to absurd extremes. A delightful example of such an inversion is when the child protagonist of Ogden Nash's "Isabel" encounters a fearsome bear that threatens to eat her, but:

> Isabel, Isabel, didn't worry.
> Isabel didn't scream or scurry.
> She washed her hands and she straightened her hair up,
> Then Isabel quietly ate the bear up.
> NASH 2000: 92f.

---

2 Joan Lynch discusses surrealism in music videos, but her essay is very unsatisfying for two reasons: 1) the music videos she sees as surreal are only discussed in terms of their imagery, with not a word written about their music; and 2) her use of the terms dada and surrealism is very vague, since she does not specify what features identify a video as surrealist or "pure Dada" (1984: 56). The only characteristic one can identify as surrealist here is unfortunately "Freudian imagery, the hallmark of Surrealism" (1984: 56), which she sees as fairly rare in music video.

The third level I would describe as a narrative form of nonsense; in such cases, readers' expectations of causality and closure in the narrative *as* narrative are frustrated, as texts often end inconclusively and anticlimactically. Events are portrayed as random and stories seem to lack a point. I do not propose these three types as a definitive typology of nonsense, since various other typologies have been proposed that overlap with it in places.[3] Still, I think this preliminary categorization is useful in drawing attention to the different levels of the text on which nonsense strategies may appear. When it comes to multimedial works, such as a song or a music video, we will see that the number of possible levels is further multiplied and that nonsense may take a wide range of forms. It remains to be seen whether a thorough categorization of such forms is possible or even desirable. The addition of incongruous elements in other media may add to the nonsensical effects, or may instead resolve some of the nonsensical tension of a text by underlining one interpretation over others, emphasizing coherent imagery or adding new potential meanings.

3   They Might Be Giants: Nonsense in the Lyrics

Though there are thus far no scholarly studies that I could find that discuss nonsense in music, and only very few on surrealism in music, the alternative rock group They Might Be Giants has frequently been connected with nonsense, the surreal, and the absurd in the popular press, though these terms are not generally defined and tend to be used as synonyms for 'quirky', 'whimsical', or 'idiosyncratic' rather than in their literary senses.

The most straightforward means of identifying nonsense in the works of TMBG is to look at the lyrics of their songs.[4] Since their first recordings in the 1980s they have consistently employed nonsense elements in their lyrics, so there is a vast body of material I could present here. Here is just one recent example, from the second verse of the 2015 song "Thinking Machine":

> JF: Uncle fourteen marching flame
> JL: Don't know what you said
> JF: Sleep expensive cloud enjoy

---

3   For other typologies of nonsense, cf. Tigges 1988: 37f., where he discusses various models, including Winfried Nöth's (see 1980) semiotic approach to Carroll's nonsense, which he identifies on seven levels of the text: the linguistic, sociological, physical, biological, semiotic, psychological, and philosophical/ideological.

4   See Victoria Willis's (2014) Lacanian reading of the lyrics in the early demo "Now that I Have Everything".

JL: Still not following
JF: Gurb long trom flom dim fim lim
JL: Pretty sure that's gibberish
JF: Dog dog dog dog dog dog dog
JL: Now you're just repeating the word 'dog'

What does it mean? (What does it mean?)
What does it mean? (What does it mean?)
I'll put it in my thinking machine
(2015 online)

"Thinking Machine" is perhaps the most explicit use of nonsense strategies on a textual level, or at least the most direct in its meta-reflections on nonsense. This excerpt demonstrates nonsense's challenge to the listener's natural attempt to make sense of the utterances, an attempt that is dramatized in the song's structure, in which John Flansburgh (JF) makes seemingly incoherent statements and John Linnell (JL) responds with confusion. This confusion is due not least to the absence of any context that could explain these utterances, as well as to the breaches with conventional syntax, the use of neologisms, and the foregrounding of sound over sense. Interestingly, Linnell does not simply discount the utterances as nonsensical, but also tries to find patterns in an attempt to make some kind of sense out of them, as when he labels one line with several non-words 'gibberish' and identifies the repetition of the word 'dog' in the last line of this verse. (In the first verse he objects: "That's not even a sentence" and "Some of those aren't words".) This song, however, by explicitly thematizing nonsense and the listener's attempts to make sense of it, actually becomes less nonsensical overall, as the 'gibberish' serves a clear function within a recognizable context.[5] Interpretations of the song as dramatizing communication in general, internet communication in particular, or an interpretation suggested by the video, are plausible means of explaining or giving 'sense' to these nonsense utterances.

Another example uses conventional syntax and is fairly coherent, but sets up a bizarre object as a kind of fetish, a "Shoehorn with Teeth":

He wants a shoehorn, the kind with teeth
People should get beat up for stating their beliefs

---

5 A similar use of nonsense can be seen in poems that focus on issues of faulty communication, whether via telephone, as in Laura E. Richards's "Eletelephony", or interculturally, as in the case of the aliens in Edwin Morgan's "The First Men on Mercury".

> He wants a shoehorn, the kind with teeth
> Because he knows there's no such thing
>> "Shoehorn with Teeth", 1987; released on *Lincoln*, 1988

This is actually more surreal than nonsensical, I would argue. The odd central image of the "shoehorn with teeth", of which there is "no such thing", could be fruitfully described by either term, but the use to which it is put is here psychological and reminiscent of Freudian psychoanalysis such as also intrigued the historical surrealists with their focus on dream imagery. The following verse will go on to oppose the death drive and Oedipal complexes, making the Freudian connection much more overt.[6]

The lyrics to the very popular "Birdhouse in Your Soul" (see 1989/2015 online) have been subjected to intense scrutiny by fans attempting to make sense of them. There is consensus on a few points, at least, though the more detailed interpretations tend to diverge widely as fans try to account for specific elements of the text and fit them to overarching narratives that are presumably somewhat beside the point. There is agreement however, that the song is narrated by a nightlight in the shape of a canary, "who watches over you" and urges the listener to "make a little birdhouse in your soul". On the question of whether this should be taken literally or form the basis for a more complex symbolic reading, however, opinions diverge. I am more interested in the types of nonsense strategies evident in these lyrics, on different levels of the text.

"Birdhouse in Your Soul" does not exhibit the classic nonsense device of nonce words or neologisms, although there is an interesting case of nontraditional naming: "my name is blue canary one note spelled L-I-T-E". There is first and foremost the unexpected perspective of a very specific (apparently also non-existent) kind of nightlight; it is typical of nonsense to add a wealth of detail to imaginary or impossible situations or objects, which are presented in a matter-of-fact tone. There are also other bizarre juxtapositions or seemingly random associations, such as the canary being blue rather than yellow, or the use of terms from very different semantic fields such as the "filibuster" or the "Longines Symphonette". One of the most striking examples of nonsense on a logical level is found in the contradictions of the refrain: "I'm your only friend I'm not your only friend but I'm a little glowing friend but really I'm not actually your friend but I am".[7]

---

6   Other songs, like "Purple Toupee" and "Ana Ng" (both also from the album *Lincoln*), employ historical references in a confused and confusing manner so that any straightforward message is complicated. Fans' speculations on how to interpret such songs (see *This Might Be a Wiki* [2015 online] for examples) are very illuminating in this context.

7   Again, it is important to stress that labelling something as nonsense does not mean we cannot make sense of it. Readers do exactly this all the time. We appreciate a non sequitur

4   They Might Be Giants: Nonsense in the Music

The main question here is: what musical strategies can be identified as forming a parallel to nonsense in text? If nonsense in text has to do with upset-
ting readers' expectations, setting up hurdles to their sense-making strategies,
then nonsense in music may be conceived of similarly, as using unexpected
juxtapositions, unusual instrumentation – i.e., Linnell's signature use of the
accordion as well as less familiar instruments like the rauschpfeife and sarru-
sophone used on the 2001 song "Older" (from *Mink Car*, 2001).[8]

According to Anne LeBaron, the techniques that best characterized historical surrealism were automatism and collage. She argues that the relative absence of music from the historical movement of surrealism was due in part to
a delay in the development of technologies that would support these strategies
in musical composition, such that:

> While these techniques existed in isolated examples of music before and
> after surrealism's peak, they blossomed into full-blown developments
> only with the advent of postmodernism. Technological tools used to re-
> cord and process music, along with a more open and pluralistic musical
> landscape, provided an environment for such surrealist techniques to
> flourish when placed at the disposal of composers.
>
> LEBARON 2002: 33

Though LaBaron doesn't discuss popular music in much detail, there was considerably more collage going on in this field than in art music, specifically jazz
improvisation, which she mentions only briefly. Later styles such as hiphop and
techno would then go on to make very extensive use of sampling as a technique
that is reminiscent of surrealist collage in the visual arts and of the ready-
mades of, e.g., Marcel Duchamp. The cultural borrowing and "plunderphonics"
LeBaron discusses are also evident in TMBG's oeuvre, with their eclectic mix of

---

as a non sequitur or as a source of humor; it has meaning derived from its function within
the text, and calling it nonsense refers only to a particular kind of semantic meaning that
is ostensibly lacking. Even here, something can be nonsense or not depending on the sup-
plementary information that is presumed but may be missing. Much of James Joyce's *Ulysses*
or *Finnegans Wake* can be fruitfully analyzed as nonsense, functioning more on the level of
sound than of sense, but if the appropriate references are tracked down, additional levels of
sense may be opened up as well. Nonsense must therefore always be connected to the recipient and his or her horizon of expectations, to use a term from reader-response criticism (see
Jauss/Benzinger 1970).

8   In this case, however, these instruments were apparently chosen for their archaic sound,
which means that they are somehow logical choices within the semantic if not musical
framework of the song. See interview with Terry Gross on *Fresh Air*, NPR, Nov. 26, 2003.

styles, including Edwardian musical theater, rockabilly, contra dance, and sea chantey, and that's just a partial selection from the album *Flood* alone (Reed/Sandifer 2014: xiii).[9] The best example of a kind of mixing and collage effect is "Fingertips", from the 1992 album *Apollo 18*, a collection of 21 short tracks of just 5 to 20 seconds each that take advantage of CD shuffle technology to be played in an almost infinite number of combinations (see liner notes to *Apollo 18*). The order is thus unsettled in postmodern or surrealist fashion, but even when listened to in the order they appear on the CD the abrupt transitions between diverse styles accord well with the lyrics' lack of context.[10]

In "Birdhouse in Your Soul", there are also musical quotations, particularly from The Lovin' Spoonful's 1966 "Summer in the City", both in the two-chord alternation in the verse of "Birdhouse" and the evocation of car horns blasting in the middle section (cf. Reed/Sandifer 2014: 81f.). But in this case, the musical nonsense – or surreal elements – are perhaps most evident in the frequent modulation. According to Sandifer and Reed, this song changes key a whopping 18 times in 3 minutes, 20 seconds (cf. Sandifer/Reed 2014 online), with the abrupt changes yielding a mechanical effect (cf. Reed/Sandifer 2014: 83).

Reed and Sandifer argue that the songs on the *Flood* album, including this one, exhibit what they call an "aesthetic of flooding". The music in this sense perfectly corresponds to the 'flood' of themes and images in the lyrics by reveling in a collection of styles, instruments, key changes, and other forms of "excess" (ibid.: 40). For me, though, the question remains open to what extent music participates in nonsense as well, and to what extent it merely supports

---

9   Reed and Sandifer observe that the seemingly random mix of styles that corresponds to their aesthetic of excess or flooding is actually connected by an interest in Americana: "The playful way that the duo tries on different musical styles from song to song can suggest that their investment in any particular aesthetic is pretty minimal. Zoom out and patterns emerge, though, and among the most pronounced is the apparent revelry their music takes in a specific valuation of American history – an unblinkingly austere ancestor worship that has seemed hopelessly hokey since the Nixon era" (2014: 32).

10   Linnell has been quoted as saying that "Fingertips" was an experiment in writing only the refrain to songs and omitting the verses: "The project was to write a bunch of choruses and nothing else. In other words, I had to restrain myself from writing any other parts of the songs. I wanted a collection of choruses that's something like what you see on TV late at night, like those old K-Tel commercials. I was thinking about how you know a lot of songs from these ads, but the only part you know is maybe one line, which is half the chorus. And yet they stick in your head in the way a whole song would. In a way, these tiny chips of songs seem complete, because you don't know the rest of the song". (From Bill DeMain. *In Their Own Words: Songwriters Talk About the Creative Process*; qtd. *This Might Be a Wiki* [2015 online], "Fingertips": http://tmbw.net/wiki/Fingertips). The tribute band They Might Be Gannets took these snippets as the basis for whole songs and released their album *Fingertips* online: http://www.dailyreckless.co.uk/gannets.htm.

or refrains from contradicting nonsense elements on other levels such as that of the text. Since music is not generally held to be referential in the way that language is, it is somewhat problematic to speak of 'sense' and 'nonsense' in connection with this medium. However, returning to my category of 'narrative' nonsense, or strategies that undermine readers' expectations of what a text should do, for example, by denying closure or causality, it becomes apparent that parallels can also be found in music that undermines listeners' expectations in a similar fashion. The use of incongruous juxtapositions and randomness or arbitrariness are techniques that are similarly present in music that foregrounds abrupt stylistic changes or unexpected choices in instrumentation.

5   They Might Be Giants: The Surrealism of the Video

That film can exploit surrealist strategies is much less contested than in the field of music, with surrealist filmmakers such as Buñuel or Dalí participating in the historical movement of surrealism and later filmmakers clearly influenced by such strategies, David Lynch being one prominent example. Music video, as a hybrid form with roots in narrative film, as well as television commercials and radio, has from its beginnings in the early 1980s regularly made use of strategies that in film would be considered experimental or surrealist. For example, music videos regularly break with conventions of continuity editing, such as the 180-degree rule or the 30-degree rule prohibiting jump cuts (cf. Vernallis 2004: 28, 30), showing the star in particular from angles that are perceived as jumpy and drawing attention to the cuts between shots in a way generally avoided by Hollywood film.[11] This does not, however, mean that music video is essentially avant-garde or experimental, but that it has developed a different set of conventions from those of film and that we should be cautious about transferring ideas about, say, surrealism in film directly to this rather different medial context. Carol Vernallis has studied mainstream music videos in great depth and argues – in contrast to much of the scholarship on the genre – that the majority of music videos are not primarily narrative (cf. ibid.: 3). Reasons for this non-narrativity include the cyclical or episodic structure of the popular song on which the video is based and which impedes a narrative progression; pop music's tendency to 'consider' rather than 'enact' a topic;

---

11   There's an interesting example of this at the end of the "Birdhouse in Your Soul" video, when the camera twice cuts between tracking shots, giving the impression of jumping back a short distance, or a kind of visual parallel to a record that has skipped (3:03–3:15).

and the primary goal of videos to draw attention to the music, which risks being overtaken by plot and image when the video is too strongly narrative (cf.
ibid.: 3f.). As alternatives to narrative, Vernallis identifies several other possible
structures employed by music videos: depiction of a single process, "categories,
series, or lists", extended performance settings, or "slice of life" portraits (ibid.:
20–23). Most relevant for "Birdhouse in Your Soul" is the way videos may imply
rather than actually tell or show a full-fledged story:

> Given numerous uncertainties [...] we may feel that we are simply seeing
> one tableau after another. We may connect the dots between instances,
> but what happens in the interim might be arbitrary. [...]
>
> Music videos encourage us early on to seek out a narrative, and by
> the video's close, they suggest that something crucial has transpired. But
> where, when, and how did this transformative event occur? (Ibid.: 23f.)

That is, without actually telling a story, videos use imagery to suggest certain
topics so that the viewer speculates about a story connecting them, but the dots
are not connected, the story remains fragmentary and suggestive, elusive. This
is reminiscent of what Roland Barthes said of surrealism in discussing Georges
Bataille's surrealist novel *Story of an Eye*: surrealist literature (like music videos) is poetic and metaphorical, exploiting the paradigmatic rather than the
syntagmatic axis of language (qtd. Richardson 2012: 37; see Barthes 1982). The
surrealist text chooses images from the paradigmatic axis, in Jakobson's terms,
which do not follow logically within the sequence.[12] Music videos of this type,
Vernallis seems to suggest, also use images poetically rather than referentially,
and they are juxtaposed without clear connections between them so that the
viewer is uncertain how various images relate. One way this is done is by means
of the "graphic match", which "joins two shots through shared compositional
elements such as color or shape, irrespective of content" and is used much
more frequently in music videos than in narrative film (Vernallis 2004: 30).[13]

   According to John Richardson, in his study on 'neosurrealism' in the popular audiovisual domain, music videos are a genre that is particularly open to
surrealist visual imagery:

---

12   Roman Jakobson distinguishes the paradigmatic and syntagmatic axes of language,
     which he also calls the axis of selection and the axis of combination, respectively, in his
     essay "Two Aspects of Language and Two Types of Aphasic Disturbances" (see 1956).

13   "Music video can use graphic matches so freely because the genre has reason to draw
     attention to its materials and production methods: the viewer can revel in an interesting
     edit, in a nice shape shared by two images, and in the cleverness of the director's and the
     editor's work, any of which might draw us away from the narrative of a Hollywood movie".
     (Vernallis 2004: 30).

The fact that videos are driven primarily by music makes it possible to incorporate visual imagery that is implausible, eccentric or abstruse without alienating listeners whose primary investment is, after all, in the song
and its performing star(s). This permits weird or 'arty' imagery to be more
easily accommodated in music videos than in other mainstream audiovisual forms. (2012: 50)

A very good example of this is the highly surrealist video for Peter Gabriel's
"Sledgehammer" (1986), which Richardson has analyzed in these terms (see
2010). Somewhat less extreme, as well as less direct in its quotations of classic
exponents of surrealism, is They Might Be Giants' "Birdhouse" video. Relatively
few of the images in the video stem directly from the lyrics – we do not ever
see the canary-shaped nightlight or indeed any bird imagery at all. The closest
connection is the video's strong emphasis on lighting – close-ups of light bulbs
and filaments, several lamps in the living-room-like space, patterns of neon
tube lighting along the hallway both Johns walk through in approaching the
camera at various points in the video. Ignoring the lyrics in this way, or picking
up on only a partial image suggested by the lyrics rather than following their
main thrust might seem like a particularly nonsensical strategy, but is in fact
typical of music videos, as Vernallis argues, where lyrics are seen as just "one
source of inspiration among many" along with the music, the band's image,
other paratextual information, and so forth (2004: 145).

The music is, as is typical for music videos that aim to promote the song,
more directly connected to the images of the video, primarily through rhythmic matching. Though the dancers' movements are strangely mechanical or
perhaps zombielike in a way that is completely unexplained within the context
of the video, they do indeed move to the beat of the song.[14] The way the song's
rhythm dictates the images is of course also visible in the way John Linnell's
lip-syncing matches up with the audio track of the video, and how the vast
majority of shots of the two Johns show them singing or playing the guitar in a
way that corresponds to the current point in the song – typical of music videos
that are structured around a performance of the song. Where the surrealist

---

14   One instance of a one-to-one correspondence between sound and image can be found
      when the saxophone – itself imitating a car horn – corresponds to John Flansburgh driv-
      ing some kind of industrial vehicle in a warehouse and making an exaggerated honking
      gesture at roughly 1:25. Reed and Sandifer mention this as "an ultra-rare instance in the
      band's videography of one-to-one sound-to-image correlation, again foregrounding me-
      chanical thingness: a syncopated saxophone blast is visually staged as a forklift's honk-
      ing horn, with John Flansburgh behind the wheel, outfitted as a warehouse truck driver"
      (2014: 83f.).

or nonsensical elements come in is where the performance becomes embedded in a bizarre situation or the performance is abandoned altogether. Along with the Johns' own odd movements, there are the strange dancers in red plaid shirts, who do not seem to celebrate the song as would typical music video dancers, but rather seem hypnotized or otherwise repressed. Their mechanical movements in unison, particularly tied to the warehouse imagery of parts of the video, suggest underpaid and oppressed factory workers, while their motions are also reminiscent of zombies and are thus somehow threatening. The black and white photographs of eyes,[15] copied askew, that they wear as masks also serve to dehumanize them, something that has no recognizable basis in the song's cheerful major key or in the lyrics. At one point, they begin protesting: "Stop Rock Video", though this hardly seems the type of song that would elicit such a protest, and again the motivation is extremely unclear. To top it off, the arm gestures of the protesters are reminiscent of the Nazi salute, raising interesting questions about power and danger within this context. Are the Johns and their music dangerous and deserving of protest or are the protesters themselves rather fascists, attempting to censor a liberal musical group? On the other hand, perhaps it is a mistake to see them as opposed at all, since several other shots show the Johns as part of the group, despite being set apart from it by their clothing and more individualized behavior, for example when they join the bicyclists circling the living-room space or performing mechanical dance movements similar to those of the red-plaid-shirted extras.

How do these different medial components contribute to a nonsensical or surrealist impression? What conclusions can listeners or viewers draw? The examination of the lyrics in isolation was, here, an academic exercise, as virtually no one would encounter this particular medium in isolation, and indeed John Linnell has frequently commented in interviews on the fact that, for him, the music comes first and the lyrics must be made to fit the rhythm.[16] Similarly, the music is never presented without the lyrics and the video images never without sound. It is, however, possible to compare listeners' impressions of the song

---

15   These eyes are taken from a photograph of William Allen White, a publicist and leader of the progressive movement. His image recurs frequently in TMBG's early videos, stage performances, and other materials.

16   John Linnell, discussing the lyrics to "Don't Let's Start" in an interview with Terry Gross: "The problem I've often had, is I write songs starting with the music and the melody and then I have this job of trying to fill in the words to a melody that's already written, so I end up having to sort of cram words in because the syllables fit. And that I think accounts for a lot of the lyrics in this one, which seem – they're not exactly on point all the time". (Gross 2003 online).

with those of viewers of the video. For example, I did not encounter the video when it first aired on MTV, but only many years later on YouTube, after having listened to the CD for years. Other listeners, however, might have viewed the video first and then been inspired to buy the CD based on their experience of the video. While the video contains somewhat threatening elements that are absent from the song, both the song and the video create primarily an impression of quirkiness, playful exuberance, and nonconformity or a celebration of 'uncoolness'.[17] Certainly Reed and Sandifer are correct in seeing the band's "aesthetic of flooding", of "creative excess" (2014: 40) on all the levels, and the nonsense strategies play an important role in supporting this sense of excess: the lyrics exhibit a wide range of associations such as the Congressional procedure of the filibuster, the maker of a line of watches (Longines), references to ancient Greek mythology (Jason and the Argonauts); the music explores a number of keys, exploits electronic technology (i.e., drum machine, synthesizer) to include diverse effects and display its own materiality; the video imagery adds images not suggested by lyrics or music such as the bicycles, mechanical dancers, forklift, and protesters to trigger viewers' own attempts to make sense of and correlate these disparate parts. Are there such connections and can they be explained? Certainly audiences do attempt to explain the ambiguities of nonsense, to seek a deeper psychological significance for the surrealist images, but their power often lies in their very inexplicability, which may be puzzling or humorous, or both. As Reed and Sandifer observe, "the joy of flooding isn't just the seemingly random juxtapositions of its uncovered objects, but also the hint of their infinitude. This is one reason why *Flood* fixates on posing questions and ambiguities, then leaving them unresolved" (2014: 42f.). This is one way of making sense of these ambiguities – the nonresolution of the seemingly random associations and juxtapositions, the unexpectedness and unexplainedness on all levels of "Birdhouse" support a playful desire for infinity, for ever more.[18] Randomness is placed in the service of excess, itself a favored technique in the repertoire of nonsense.

---

17   This is in keeping with TMBG's reputation as icons of 'geek rock'. Indeed, they have often been credited with helping geek rock find a place in the mainstream and making what was thoroughly uncool a badge of pride.

18   Wim Tigges (see 1988), building upon Susan Stewart's analysis of nonsense strategies, identifies infinity as a technique in the nonsense repertoire. Stewart refers to this as "play with infinity" (1978: 116–143), while Tigges clarifies that such play establishes a "series without cause and effect" (1988: 58), the simultaneity ("the strongest semiotic device of nonsense literature"; ibid.: 59) of incongruous objects strung together in a list that lacks motivation or causality.

References

Barthes, Roland (1982). "The Metaphor of the Eye". Trans. J.A. Underwood. Georges Bataille. *Story of the Eye.* By Lord Auch (pseudonym). London/New York, NY: Penguin. 119–127.

Breton, André (1946/1978). "Silence is Golden". *What Is Surrealism?: Selected Writings.* Ed. Franklin Rosemont. New York, NY, et al.: Pathfinder. 265–269. (Orig. publ.: *Modern Music* 23).

Carroll, Lewis (1998). *Alice's Adventures in Wonderland and Through the Looking Glass.* Ed. Hugh Haughton. London et al.: Penguin.

Ellis, Iain (2008). *Rebels Wit Attitude: Subversive Rock Humorists.* Berkeley, CA: Soft Skull.

Gross, Terry (2003 online). "They Might Be Giants". Interview. *Fresh Air.* NPR. Nov. 26. https://www.npr.org/templates/story/story.php?storyId=1523055 [13/11/2015].

Jakobson, Roman (1956). "Two Aspects of Language and Two Types of Aphasic Disturbances". Roman Jakobson, Morris Halle. *Fundamentals of Language.* 's-Gravenhage: Mouton. 55–82.

Jauss, Hans Robert, Elizabeth Benzinger (1970). "Literary History as a Challenge to Literary Theory". *New Literary History* 2/1: 7–37.

Köhler, Peter (1989). *Nonsens: Theorie und Geschichte der literarischen Gattung.* Heidelberg: Winter.

LeBaron, Anne (2002). "Reflections of Surrealism in Postmodern Musics". Judy Lochhead, Joseph Auner, eds. *Postmodern Music: Postmodern Thought.* New York, NY/ London: Routledge. 27–73.

Lynch, Joan (1984). "Music Videos: From Performance to Dada – Surrealism". *Journal of Popular Culture* 18/1: 53–57.

Nash, Ogden (2000). *Candy Is Dandy: The Best of Ogden Nash.* Eds. Linell Smith, Isabel Eberstadt. London: Andre Deutsch.

Nöth, Winfried (1980). *Literatursemiotische Analysen zu Lewis Carrolls Alice-Büchern.* Tübingen: Narr.

Reed, S. Alexander, Philip Sandifer (2014). *Flood.* 33 1/3. New York, NY, et al.: Bloomsbury.

Richardson, John (2010). "Plasticine Music: Surrealism in Peter Gabriel's 'Sledgehammer'". Michael Drewett, Sarah Hill, Kimi Kärki, eds. *Games without Frontiers: Peter Gabriel from Genesis to Growing Up.* Farnham/Burlington, VT: Ashgate. 195–210.

Richardson, John (2012). *An Eye for Music: Popular Music and the Audiovisual Surreal.* Oxford et al.: OUP.

Sandifer, Philip, S. Alexander Reed (2014 online). "Say I'm the Only Bee in Your Bonnet: 'Birdhouse in Your Soul' and the Revolution It Signified" http://www.slate.com/ articles/arts/culturebox/2014/02/a_history_of_the_they_might_be_giants_song _birdhouse_in_your_soul.html. *Slate* [02/08/2015].

Sewell, Elizabeth (1952). *The Field of Nonsense*. London: Chatto & Windus.

Shortsleeve, Kevin (2011). "The Cat in the Hippie: Dr. Seuss, Nonsense, the Carnivalesque, and the Sixties Rebel". Julia L. Mickenberg, Lynne Vallone, eds. *The Oxford Handbook of Children's Literature*. Oxford: OUP. 189–209.

Stewart, Susan (1978). *Nonsense: Aspects of Intertextuality in Folklore and Literature*. Baltimore, MD /London: Johns Hopkins Univ. Press.

They Might Be Gannets (online). *Fingertips*. http://www.dailyreckless.co.uk/gannets .htm.

They Might Be Giants (1988). *Lincoln*. CD. Bar/None.

They Might Be Giants (1989/2015 online). "Birdhouse in Your Soul". Dir. Bernstein, Adam. YouTube. https://www.youtube.com/watch?v=2Am-BF7ObCI [13/11/2015].

They Might Be Giants (1990). *Flood*. CD. Elektra.

They Might Be Giants (1992). *Apollo 18*. CD. Elektra.

They Might Be Giants (2001). *Mink Car*. CD. Restless.

They Might Be Giants (2015 online). "Thinking Machine" http://www.dialasong.com/ songs/thinking-machine. *Dial-a-Song* [13/11/2015].

This Might Be A Wiki: The They Might Be Giants Knowledge Base (2015 online). http:// tmbw.net/wiki [02/08/2015].

Tigges, Wim (1988). *An Anatomy of Literary Nonsense*. Amsterdam: Rodopi.

Vernallis, Carol (2004). *Experiencing Music Video: Aesthetics and Cultural Context*. New York, NY: Columbia Univ. Press.

Willis, Victoria (2014). "They Might Be Lacanian: They Might Be Giants, Jacques Lacan, and the Rhetoric of Geek Rock". Alex DiBlasi, Victoria Willis, eds. *Geek Rock: An Exploration of Music and Subculture*. Lanham, MD, et al.: Rowman & Littlefield. 69–78.

PART 3

Remediations

∴

CHAPTER 14

Thrilling Opera: Conflicts of the Mind and the Media in Kasper Holten's *Juan*

Axel Englund

Abstract

The present paper takes a look at the relation between opera and film through the lens of Danish director Kasper Holten's movie debut *Juan* (2010), a 90-minute screen adaptation of *Don Giovanni*. Trimming about half of Mozart and Da Ponte's opera and presenting the libretto in an irreverently contemporary English translation, the film makes full use of the visual language and fast pace of the movie thriller. Yet at the same time, by having all the singers perform live on the set, it aspires to the condition of filmed live opera. Whether intentionally or not, however, it seems less to effect a smooth fusion of these two sets of media conventions than to underscore their incompatibility. The resulting conflict, I will argue, is mirrored by the film's take on the protagonist, who fails miserably at living up to the Kierkegaardian ideal of unreflective vitality: instead, the media-specific techniques of cinematic narrative intervene, turning him into an introspective, self-conscious and deeply conflicted hero.

• • •

Ever since its conception, *Don Giovanni* has been the site of loudly clashing conventions. If we are to believe an often-repeated anecdote, Mozart and Da Ponte themselves were at odds, the composer being determined to compose a serious opera, while the librettist aimed for comedy throughout.[1] Whether we buy this legend or not, the result does contain plenty of *opera seria* elements within its general *buffa* framework. In musical terms, some roles (like Donna Anna and Ottavio) belong predominantly to the sphere of *seria*, while others (like Leporello and Zerlina) are purely *buffa*. The opera undeniably harbours enough darkness and drama to explain its afterlife in the nineteenth century,

---

1 Julian Rushton has questioned whether we really ought to put much faith in this narrative of the opera's birth (cf. Rushton 1981: 6f.).

where the serious elements by far overshadowed the humorous ones.[2] In the last decades of the twentieth century, the growing predominance of more-or-less iconoclastic *mise-en-scène*, in particular on European stages, made Mozart's opera a favourite target for creative deconstruction. Notorious examples include Peter Sellars' version set in south Bronx, which was staged in 1987 for the Pepsico Festival, and Calixto Bieito's smutty booze-and-drugs version, which was premiered by the English National Opera at the London Coliseum in 2001. These productions add a different kind of clash to the aforementioned ones, where the eighteenth-century words and music chafe against late-twentieth-century avant-garde staging (which, despite its claims to innovation, is of course anything but exempt from conventionality).

From this school of *Regietheater* staging emerged Danish director Kasper Holten, whose 2010 film version of *Don Giovanni* I will address in the present paper. The film, which emphasizes its distance from Mozart and Da Ponte's work through its title *Juan* (although the DVD version is marketed under the original title of the opera), is entirely based on Mozart's music, but combines it with a mercilessly contemporary adaptation of the libretto and the story. Holten's film is arguably the most consistent attempt yet to apply the conventions of modern cinema to an opera. I will argue, however, that what appears as an attempt at a smooth fusion ends up emphasizing – and, ultimately, profiting from – the incompatibility of its own constituent parts.

Of course, one could say something similar about screen adaptations of opera in general. In her 2000 book *Opera on Screen*, Marcia Citron remarks about the object of her study: "Like many hybrids it [screen opera] bears the tensions of its components, some of which may not reconcile themselves easily with the others". (2000: 6)[3] The difference between the clashes thus ascribed to the genre as a whole and their manifestation in *Juan*, however, is that Holten's film takes these incompatibilities as a central thematic concern, foregrounding them at every opportunity, and turning them into the driving force of the narrative. I will soon trace some of the ways in which this is achieved, but let me mention at this point at least one of the film's central *mise-en-abyme* strategies. In Holten's interpretation, Juan himself is a conceptual artist of sorts, and

---

2   On the cultural legacy of *Don Giovanni* in the nineteenth century, see Goehr/Herwitz, eds. 2008.

3   The various relations between opera and film have become a wide field of research in its own right. Before Citron's book, Jeremy Tambling's *Opera, Ideology and Film* (1987) and the edited collection *A Night in at the Opera* (1994) were important foundational works, and later works of significance include the collection *Between Opera and Cinema* (2002), edited by Jeonwong Joe and Rose Theresa, and Bernhard Kuhn's *Die Oper im italienischen Film* (2005), as well as Citron's own follow-up, *When Opera Meets Film* (2010).

the material of his magnum opus, with the working title "The Woman Project", consists of the digital documentation of his sexual conquests. All his affairs are recorded and organized by Leporello – or Lep, as he is called in the film – whose laptop is chock-full of movie clips and photographs, all arranged in folders according to the nationalities and hair colour of the women.[4] The Don's insatiable sexual frenzy, which has been construed as emblematic of the art of opera at least since Søren Kierkegaard's famous essay "The Immediate Erotic Stages or the Musical-Erotic" in *Either/Or* (1843/1987: 45–135), is thus explicitly framed in Holten's film as a question of media and mediation.

Holten's *Juan* puts its finger squarely on one of the sore spots of opera studies in recent years: the dichotomization of live experience and mediation through moving images, which inevitably carries Benjaminian echoes of auratic art and technological reproduction, and which is often, at least by the sceptics, conceived as a conflict between physical presence and the distance of mediation.[5] Given the recurrent conceptualization of the experience of live opera performance in terms of corporeal eroticism, this duality also resonates with the idea of mediated opera as a kind of pornography, which, in the present case, is picked up by Juan's porn-art project.[6] In the present paper, I will try to shed some light on the film's take on these issues by attending to its portrayal of two kinds of internal conflicts. The first, as I have already suggested, is located between the media conventions of filmed live opera and action thriller, and the second within the character of Juan himself.

1 Conflicts of the Media

The first shots of the film, interspersed with the opening credits, are of a vehicle swerving at high speed along a dark highway, chased by police cars with sirens wailing. Next, we see conductor Lars Ulrik Mortensen giving the preparatory

---

4 Neither the preoccupation with mediation in general nor the notion of Leporello as a pornographer is a stage novelty anymore. For instance, the 2006 production by Sergio Morabito and and Jossi Wieler for the Netherlands Opera has Leporello document the Don's conquests with a home-movie camera, the results of which form a catalogue in the guise of Kodak boxes. In the Morabito/Wieler production, it is the medium of television – in particular 1960s-style soap opera – that is merging with opera (see Will 2011).

5 For an exchange that exemplifies the arguments that typically circulate in this debate, see Treadwell 1998 and Levin 1998. Persuasive arguments in favour of studying live opera videos and DVD recordings from a media-specific perspective can be found in Levin 2007, Senici 2010.

6 For different takes on the connection between operatic performance and eroticism, see Abel 1997, Koestenbaum 1993/2001, and Risi 2006.

beat for the *Don Giovanni* overture. As the first D minor chord strikes, the film's title appears, lit by a moving searchlight, and at the ensuing A major, we see a cellist playing an intense forte. The alternation of tonic and dominant, then, is overlaid with an alternation between unmistakeable clichés of the action thriller and the live opera broadcast, and the elements of *Juan's* hybrid mediality are thus established in succession. At the exact moment when the tension between the tonic and the dominant inaugurates the drama of tonality, an analogous tension between action thriller and live opera sets off the drama of mediality. Their uneasy co-existence sets the tone for the whole film, and the friction is about to be taken up another notch.

Juan himself – played by Christopher Maltman – is in the audience, attending a performance of *Don Giovanni*. In the thirteenth bar of the overture, as the second violins start their anxious 16th-note figurations, something striking happens: having first been presented in succession, the operatic and cinematic conventions now appear simultaneously, superimposed on each other. While the music of the opera film, non-diegetic, as it were, carries on with the overture in its entirety, the diegetic music in the opera house skips ahead to the moment of the Commendatore's murder, shown on stage in traditional boots-and-doublet staging, in accordance with cinematic conventions.[7] What happens, then, is that opera time and thriller time part ways.

The distance opened up here between the two participating media serves a number of purposes. For one thing, it carries connotations of class. When opera appears in film, one of its most frequent functions is to mark the possession of capital, cultural as well as actual. Whether the object of mockery or fetishization, the idea of opera as a stereotype of high-brow culture is typically brought to the fore whenever it is filtered through the silver screen (cf. Tambling 1987: 3–7). Holten plays on this stereotype when he lets the class difference in *Don Giovanni* be represented by the institution of the opera house itself, which is where the upper-class characters – Don Giovanni, Don Ottavio, Donna Anna and her father, who is the city's chief of police in the film – first convene.

The most fundamental function of the medial rift, however, is a question of time. Again, as Citron points out, this is a conflict that marks any screen adaptation of opera: opera "tends to unfold more slowly than cinema or television", which "depend much more on movement and action, and thrive on a faster

---

7   I am using the terms 'diegetic' and 'non-diegetic' in the sense that they are employed by
    Claudia Gorbman in *Unheard Melodies* (1987). For discussions of the many possible ways
    of refining and challenging this basic distinction, see the essays by Stokes and Wolf in this
    volume.

pace" (2000: 6f.). The spectators of a thriller, then, have no patience to listen to a whole opera; the action needs to be fast-paced. There is nothing really remarkable about this medial difference, and Citron is right to mention it as her first example of the tensions that adhere to screen opera. What is interesting in Holten's opening scene, however, is that it consciously foregrounds this rift, rather than looking for a way of hiding it. During the six minutes of the overture, unfolding in the slow pace of opera time, the story of the movie has already fast-forwarded not only through the whole first act, but also through the intermission (during which Anna and Juan are introduced to each other by Ottavio); the second act (including the Stone Guest dragging Giovanni down into hell); Anna and Juan's rendezvous at a café after the performance; and, finally, their moving on to her fancy apartment, secretly followed by Lep, who is documenting the whole thing with a digital camera. The film is thus presenting us with two parallel narrative strands, moving at very different speeds. Each strand even has its own simultaneously audible sound track: while the diegetic opera is being performed on stage, watched by the characters, we can hear snippets of that performance – the Commendatore's dying words, Giovanni seducing Zerlina, his scream as he slides into the pit – superimposed on the music of the overture to the opera film. Driving a wedge between these two instantiations of *Don Giovanni* in the opening moments of his film, Holten thus deliberately directs our attention to the difference of pace – perhaps already signalled by the contrast between the speeding car and the reliably steady conductor – as the most conspicuous incompatibility between opera and cinema.

This incompatibility is amply confirmed during the rest of the film. Most obviously, the conventions of cinematic time force Holten to cuts that go way beyond what would be accepted on the opera stage: Mozart's three-hour opera is reduced to 90 minutes, most of the second act disappearing in the process. (Ottavio fares the worst, losing both of his arias.) In some instances, the cinema conventions are put to productive use: the extended time of certain instrumental passages allows Holten to add a number of elements to the story by strictly visual means. For instance, Anna and Ottavio's collaboration with the police force, who are putting Juan under surveillance, is presented in rapid sequences, while the story is not making progress in the score and libretto. As a result, the recitatives are no longer the prime locus of rapid development, but rather a point where the action slows down to the pace of a real-time dialogue. When the conventions of cinema's visual narrative are granted full access to opera, the drama can fast-forward at any point in the score: during a bar or two of an instrumental interlude, or even while the emotional reflection of an aria is going on. Also, the contrapuntal asides in duets and ensembles are neatly emphasized and clarified by interspersed close-ups of individual characters (which is of course nothing unique to Holten's project, but standard fare in opera films).

Another site of obvious clashes of convention in the film is found in the differing levels of tolerance vis-à-vis verisimilitude displayed by opera and cinema. While the plot of the run-of-the-mill crime drama may not always be a paragon of plausibility, it cannot compete with opera when it comes to the amount of willingness that needs to be mustered in order to suspend disbelief. In Holten's film, this causes a number of moments verging on the embarrassing. For example: in one scene, Anna calls Juan on Ottavio's phone, subsequently trying to divert her boyfriend's suspicions by claiming that it was Juan who placed the call. In other words, we are supposed to believe that it would not occur to her that Ottavio might check his incoming calls to verify her story (which, of course, he does). While there are numerous plot elements in *Don Giovanni* that are just as improbable, the fact that this one is *not* in the original plot, but belongs specifically to the elements *added* by the contemporary thriller, makes it stick out as utterly improbable. The same goes for a second murder committed by Juan, rather gratuitously inserted to propel the action forward and push Juan across the edge: when a teenage cashier at a gas station recognizes Juan as the wanted cop killer seen on the news, he decides to grab a baseball bat and climb over the desk to perform an act of heroism, unsurprisingly getting himself shot in the process.

But the most obvious improbability of opera is, of course, even more fundamental: the fact that everyone is singing all the time. The language of the adapted English libretto, as it were, restores fresh improbability to this the most basic condition of opera. With its ample use of twenty-first-century colloquialisms, profanities, bad grammar and broken English – all of which works towards a cinematic version of realism – it places the operatic singing within a framework where it comes across as emphatically estranged. The strangeness and improbability that are part and parcel of the art of opera sit quite uncomfortably with the level of realism expected of a contemporary thriller movie, thus creating another conspicuous gap between the conventions attached to the respective genres and media, which is the source of much of the film's comedy.

By contrast, the most successful (and original) amalgamation of conventions is to be found not in the temporal, but in the spatial aspects of the opera: with the exception of the lines sung as an interior monologue, all of the singing in Holten's film is done on site. Technically, this was accomplished by letting the singers hear the orchestral accompaniments through a minute in-ear monitor. For the recitatives, a piano was used on the set, to be replaced by harpsichord in post-production editing.

To my mind, this actually remedies the most annoying problem of opera films, amply showcased by the arias in Joseph Losey's famous adaptation of *Don Giovanni* (1979) . In her chapter on this film, which she reads in tandem with Francesco Rosi's *Bizet's Carmen* (1983) while focusing on the implications of outdoors settings in those two films, Citron notes that the recitatives, which are "shot live, sound vital and convincing, but full-blown music is sometimes unfocused. The break between the two is noticeable. Synchronization often suffers in the post-dubbed numbers (Masetto's aria in Act I is a particularly bad example)". (2000: 203) Although I fully agree with these assessments, I would add that the problem is not just that the lip-synching is not good enough, or that the transitions from the live recitatives are not smooth enough. More importantly, the fact that whether an aria takes place outdoors in a graveyard or inside a small bed chamber, the singer's voices always resound from a studio, with post-production reverberation, inevitably results in those voices being thoroughly and disturbingly divorced from their bodily presence at the set. In Holten's film, by contrast, the voice is consistently situated in an audible space. While this is obviously nothing new to film, it is new to opera film, which is brought significantly closer to the virtual liveness of a recording from the opera house, while employing the conventions and techniques of realism that have been developed during a century of cinema. João Pedro Cachopo, commenting on the often-repeated description of opera as the art form where "a guy gets stabbed in the back and, instead of bleeding, he sings", emphasises the novelty of Holten's project: "[...] as never before in an opera film (at least to my knowledge) the actor/singer playing the Commendatore – as all the other actors/singers in this production – actually sings while acting". (2014: 322) In Cachopo's words, Holten's film "gives new life to what might be said to be [...] a stillborn hybrid genre". (2014: 322).

At the same time, of course, the on-set singing does not eradicate the gap between the visual action and the audible music, but rather relocates it. In *Juan*, the gap is placed not between the visible and the audible sound track, but between the instrumental parts and the voices: the orchestra and continuo, as it were, still constitute an extra-diegetic sound track, the sound of which is clearly emerging from a different space than that of the voices. More importantly, however, the on-set-singing does not change the impression of an absolute incompatibility between the movie thriller and the opera. On the contrary, the strangeness between contemporary mainstream culture and eighteenth-century opera is more effectively foregrounded in Holten's film than in any modernized version of *Don Giovanni* that I have seen on stage. Paradoxically, the welding-together of the two media makes the gap between them yawn wider than ever. The effectiveness of Holten's film relies to a great extent on the idealism and metaphysics traditionally associated with opera – nowhere expressed with greater virtuosity than in Kierkegaard's reading of *Don Gio-vanni* – and their collision with the conventions of the contemporary thriller. Consequently, I am inclined to say that rather than subverting or unsettling traditional conceptions of opera – the direction in which Cachopo's analysis is ultimately leaning – it fortifies them, so as to make their clash with the cin-ematic medium all the more spectacular.

2   Conflicts of the Mind

It is often pointed out that Giovanni is a character with little propensity for self-reflection. The conspicuous absence of an aria where his inner life could be given voice is typically read as the lack of any such interiority, which, in the end, is what prevents him from regretting, let alone repenting, any of his sins (cf. Rushton 1981: 82, 109). The most famous reading of Giovanni as unreflective is Kierkegaard's aforementioned essay from *Either/Or*. According to Kierkeg-aard's fictional essayist, *Don Giovanni* is the opera of all operas because the relation between the topic of Don Juan and the medium of operatic music is absolute. Giovanni is not to be understood as an individual character, but as the perfect embodiment of an ideal: that of the musical-erotic. On this view, it is vital that Giovanni never stops to take a look at himself. He is the embodi-ment of a single, immense force, which is always victorious, and which always propels him in one direction only: towards the next erotic conquest. Indeed, Don Giovanni's singularity of purpose clearly contrasts him to those who sur-round him. Ottavio and Anna are wavering between hundreds of emotions ("tra cento affetti e cento / vammi ondeggiando il cor"), Zerlina wants and does not want to give in to Giovanni's seduction ("vorrei e non vorrei"), and Elvira is torn between hating and loving him ("Che contrasto d'affetti in sen ti nasce!"). Even Leporello voices an inner conflict about whether to remain with his master or not; only Giovanni never stops to attend to or question his own desires.

Holten's reading of the character, however, seems to resist the idea of Gio-vanni as an unreflecting and essentially undivided force of nature. A hint of this resistance is given as early as the overture: when we first see Juan, he is seated in the opera house. Just as the irreconcilable difference between op-era and cinema marks *Juan* from the very first seconds, so a division within Juan is suggested from the moment he sits down to watch an opera about him-self. He demonstrates his refusal to see in the story of the punished dissolute any lesson relevant to himself: during the overture, he smiles and shakes his head at Mozart's opera, and while talking to Anna in the intermission, he says

something that, although barely audible, sounds a lot like "one of the most bor-
ing art forms in the universe". Back in his seat, however, he closes his eyes, and
in an ensuing shot we see him sitting by himself in the dark salon, still watching the stage, as if its events were playing for him and him alone, inside his
head. From the very start, then, this temporary movement from outer to inner
vision shows us a Juan who is struggling hard to repress his un-Giovanni-like
inclination towards introspection.

Outwardly, of course, he keeps asserting his traditional lack of reflection
and remorse, with present-day variations on Da Ponte's libretto. When Lep
urges him to come clean – "With all shit you've done, which was, boss, work
of asshole – there is only one thing to do. You make ... Confession!" – Juan
lashes out at him in fury, insisting that his sidekick "learn some patience. We
hold our nerve, and the whole thing will vanish". His "art project", moreover, is
the product of a male gaze so incessantly locked onto the female object that
it never for a moment turns inward. However, when Juan's false promises have
lured Elvira away so he can seduce another girl (who is normally her chamber
maid, but here seems to be a random girl smoking a cigarette in the street),
we witness the destruction of his work: a blow-up of Elvira's face is consumed
by flames. Of course, this underscores the demise of Elvira (who, in Holten's
interpretation, actually kills herself shortly after), but it is also the collapse of
his "woman project".

Indeed, the "woman project" continues its road to perdition immediately
after this shot. Even so, Juan appears incapable of maintaining his focus on
the external object of seduction. In the canzonetta ("Deh' vieni a la finestra" /
"I gaze at you and wonder"), Holten has Juan spectacularly botch the task of
seduction – and not, as is usually the case, because Masetto shows up with his
vigilante gang, but simply because he forgets about the object of his seduction.
In close-up shots we see how he steps up to the smoking girl from behind, and
sings the serenade softly right into her ear, without her turning around. During
the second stanza, Juan suddenly starts crying, and as he finishes the serenade
and she turns around to obtain the promised kisses, he looks right through
her, his eyes brimming with tears. He does not even notice her as she frowns
and walks away in disappointment. Why this sudden sentimentality, so powerful that it makes him indifferent to his conquest? The answer is simple: he is
profoundly moved by the sound of his own voice. Perhaps the power of song
causes him to feel compassion for Elvira, the image of whom flashes by in the
middle of the serenade. Or perhaps – and to me, this is the more plausible and
interesting reading – the part of himself that he has fought so hard to repress
has suddenly returned to occupy the position of the verbally worshipped 'you'
in the serenade. The English translation reads thus:

To gaze at you and wonder
that simple pleasure
to see one smile returned
is all I'll ever need
If you deny my soul –
such humble treasure –
before your lovely eyes
my lonely heart will bleed

Your honeyed lips beguile me
eyes enrapture
your skin's heavenly touch
my kiss must discover
don't turn your eyes away
my heart is captured.
Open your arms to me
your wounded lover.

Whereas the wound is a stock image of emasculation and castration angst, Juan is perhaps not so much feminized by this inward turn as he is womanized: it is as if he becomes the object of his own seduction. As his gaze turns inward, away from the female object he is supposedly wooing, his eyes are suddenly riveted to a part of himself that has hitherto been lost inside. The parody is hilariously effective: it is as if the mumbo-jumbo metaphysics of musical authenticity, which is precisely what that Don Giovanni has always relied upon for his seductions, had finally blown up in his face. The voice of music cannot lie – not even to the singer himself.

The film's focus on Juan's inner conflict is also heightened by the fact that the other characters disappear from the story one by one: Elvira, in a thoroughly unconvincing combination of music and images, drowns herself in a slow and ceremonial fashion while singing "Mi tradì quell'alma ingrata" ('His ungrateful heart deceived me'); unconvinced by Zerlina's excuses, Masetto breaks off the engagement in (what is usually) the finale of Act I and the couple disappear from the action; Anna, meanwhile, accepts her doubts about her relationship and breaks up with Ottavio. Leporello is the last one to leave, but even he throws himself out of Juan's speeding car before it is too late. Ultimately, there is no one left to confront Giovanni in the final scene – except, we would assume, the Commendatore. As it turns out, however, the conventions of cinematic crime drama do not allow for spectral apparitions, and he remains stone dead rather than stone guest.

At certain a number of moments throughout the film – immediately after the murder, then again when Juan is about to get into a taxi with Zerlina to sing "La ci darem" ('Give me your hand'), during the party at the end of Act I, and once more when he mocks the Commendatore's image in the graveyard scene – a dark, hooded figure appears in the distance. We surmise that his eyes are directed at Juan, who is visibly disturbed by his presence. In the last of these sequences, Juan hears in his head the Commendatore's voice (sung by Eric Halvfarsson), and sees him in repeated flashback shots – yet it is not Anna's father, but the hooded figure, who eventually comes to haunt him.

In the final scene, Juan's conflicted psyche takes physical form: on the one hand, we see him speeding along in a stolen Mercedes, on the other hand, we see his interior, represented by the darkness of the warehouse where he was working on his art project. The artist's studio, then, becomes the arena for the return of the repressed, which enters in the guise of the mysterious hooded man. Already at the first line ("Don Giovanni a cenar teco m'invitasti, e son venuto" / 'As I promised, we are together. You invite me – and I accept it'.) the apparition's identity is given away. Although he tries his best to sound like a menacing bass, there's never any real doubt that its Maltman's own baritone that calls out to Juan. Nevertheless, Juan is shocked when he suddenly finds himself staring into his own face. Vehemently he continues to claim his un-reflective, internal emptiness: "You can't be me", he shouts to himself, "you're nothing". If, in the canzonetta, we witnessed Juan getting seduced by his own voice, in the finale seduction moves towards violation: as the apparition urges him to repent, it goes on to embrace him, locking him in his arms by force. As Maltman answers his own powerful "Yes" with a desperate "No", the overtones of what can only be labelled an autoerotic assault are clearly audible.[8]

The impression from the canzonetta, that Juan seemed to be struck by the power of his own singing, is now literally and explicitly confirmed. At this point, his inner division splits the core of the operatic subject and its erotic appeal: the voice. However obvious the point may be, it must be stressed that this incision is effected by the media-specific possibilities of film: by perform-ing the simple trick of forcing Juan into a violent encounter with his own body

---

8   In Holten's version, any idea of Juan being a rapist is otherwise absent, which is quite prob-lematic. The film consistently presents the allegations of sexual assault as fictional inven-tions by the purported victims. Not only Anna's testimony of Juan's assault on her is turned into a lie – and this has been the standard choice in contemporary productions for some time now – but also Zerlina's screams in the first-act finale: in Holten's version, she calculatingly calls for help without Juan having touched her, as a part of her strategy to win back Masetto's sympathies.

and voice, the moving image ruptures not only the psyche of the opera's protagonist, but the very art of opera itself.

3   The Conflicts Converge

In terms of media and genre, as well as in terms of character interiority, Kasper
Holten is showing us a deeply self-conscious entity, and one that does not hold
together. To point to the mutual mirroring of these two planes is not tanta-
mount to suggesting a hidden unity in Holten's film: in so far as they reflect
each other, which I hope I have been able to make plausible, the mirrors remain cracked. My point, then, is not simply that Holten turns Don Giovanni into a conscious and reflective character, thus belying the reading of his
nineteenth-century compatriot – which is hardly a rare occurrence in recent
productions of this opera – but that this reflectivity is forced upon him, as
it were, by the precarious co-existence of film and opera. In Holten's version,
Juan's self-consciousness comes across as a direct effect of the attempted amalgamation of incompatible media conventions. Maltman's Juan *wants* to be a
Kierkegaardian force of nature, an unreflective and absolutely victorious ideal
of the musical-erotic, but the media-specific characteristics and conventions
of film keep intervening: the flashback shots of his victims tear him from the
present moment; the close-ups of his facial expressions consistently pull him
back from the ideal to the individual; and the trickery of rapid cuts, finally,
splits him in two as he stands face-to-face (and voice-to-voice) with himself.
    Another way of describing the rift between the media is to align them with
their sensory channels: what we hear is the audible aspect of an opera, albeit
with a strangely contemporary libretto, and what we see is the visible aspect
of a movie thriller. In so far as we adhere to the cliché of hearing being the
more interior sense, and vision the more exterior, we might also play with the
thought that the film's operatic score is all in the protagonist's mind. From
this perspective, he is as much Don Quixote as he is Don Juan, and the film is
the aural hallucination of a megalomaniac conceptual artist and womanizer,
who, after having attended a performance of *Don Giovanni*, believes himself to
be the Don. As hopelessly out of tune with his time as the knight of La Mancha with his, Juan then perceives all the dramatic events of the ensuing days
through a distorting filter – not that of chivalric romance, but of eighteenth-
century opera. Mozart's music is running like a psycho-diegetic soundtrack
in his head, while Leporello performs Sancho Panza's role of a down-to-earth
sidekick to his master's lunatic behaviour. As viewers of the opera film, we have
the privilege of perceiving both worlds at once: the external world in all its

realistic detail through what we see, and the psychotic, internal through what we hear.

Finally, if we regard Juan's pornographic project as a *mise-en-abyme*, which I think we should, then any judgment the film passes on Juan and his art could also, by extension, apply to the film itself. On this view, the film is putting its own authenticity into question, by asking whether its cinematic mediation of opera is not analogous to the digital simulacra of pornography. Holten's version of *Don Giovanni*, I would suggest, does not really present itself as opera's way forward into the twenty-first century, but rather as a head-on collision between two media that stubbornly hold their ground. "Hear his wild flight; he speeds past himself, ever faster, never pausing", writes Kierkegaard in an image that resonates in the car chase that opens and closes the film (1843/1987: 103). When Juan, in the film's final shot, hurtles the stolen car full-speed into a concrete barricade because he is unable to come to terms with his own inner voice, we are watching the art of opera crash and burn, fuelled by the irresolvable conflict between those elements that Holten's film has tried so hard to weld together. In the end, however, the resulting explosion is as entertaining and thought-provoking as any triumph, and opera is likely to emerge from the wreckage unscathed.

References

Abel, Samuel D. (1997). *Opera in the Flesh: Sexuality in Operatic Performance*. Boulder: Westview Press.

Cachopo, João Pedro (2014). "Opera's Screen Metamorphosis: The Survival of a Genre or a Matter of Translation?". *The Opera Quarterly* 30/4: 315–329.

Citron, Marcia J. (2000). *Opera on Screen*. New Haven, CT/London: Yale UP.

Citron, Marcia J. (2010). *When Opera Meets Film*. Cambridge: CUP.

Goehr, Lydia, Daniel Herwitz, eds. (2008). *The Don Giovanni Moments: Essays on the Legacy of an Opera*. New York, NY: Columbia UP.

Gorbman, Claudia (1987). *Unheard Melodies: Narrative Film Music*. Bloomington, IN: Indiana UP.

Joe, Jeonwong, Rose Theresa, eds. (2002). *Between Opera and Cinema*. New York, NY: Routledge.

Kierkegaard, Søren (1843/1987). *Either/Or: Part I*. Ed. and trans. Howard V. Hong, Edna H. Hong. Princeton, NJ: Princeton UP.

Koestenbaum, Wayne (1993/2001). *The Queen's Throat: Opera, Homosexuality and the Mystery of Desire*. 2nd ed. New York, NY: Da Capo Press.

Kuhn, Bernhard (2005). *Die Oper im italienischen Film*. Essen: Die Blaue Eule.

Levin, David J. (1998). "Response to James Treadwell". *Cambridge Opera Journal* 10/3: 307–311.

Levin, David J. (2007). *Unsettling Opera: Staging Mozart, Verdi, Wagner, and Zemlinsky.* Chicago, IL: University of Chicago Press.

Risi, Clemens (2006). "Hören und Gehört werden [sic] als körperlicher Akt: Zur feed-back-Schleife in der Oper und der Erotik der Sängerstimme". Erika Fischer-Lichte et al., eds. *Wege der Wahrnehmung: Authentizität, Reflexivität und Aufmerksamkeit im zeitgenössischen Theater.* Berlin: Theater der Zeit. 98–113.

Rushton, Julian (1981). *W. A. Mozart: Don Giovanni.* Cambridge: CUP.

Senici, Emanuele (2010). "Porn Style? Space and Time in Live Opera Videos". *The Opera Quarterly* 26/1: 63–80.

Tambling, Jeremy (1987). *Opera, Ideology and Film.* Manchester: Manchester UP.

Tambling, Jeremy, ed. (1994). *A Night in at the Opera: Media Representations of Opera.* Bloomington, IN: Indiana UP.

Treadwell, James (1998). "Reading and Staging Again". *Cambridge Opera Journal* 10/2: 205–220.

Will, Richard (2011). "Zooming In, Gazing Back: *Don Giovanni* on Television". *The Opera Quarterly* 27/1: 32–65.

CHAPTER 15

Novel, Woodcuts, Film, Music ...: Pondering over the Title of Gara Garayev's *Symphony Engravings 'Don Quixote'*

Alla Bayramova

Abstract

The analysis of Gara Garayev's music for the film *Don Quixote* (1957) and his later work, *Symphony Engravings 'Don Quixote'* (1960), based on the film music, had always been undertaken only by the means of musicology, without any attempt to apply an interdisciplinary approach. However, the comparative method applied to the study of the Cervantes's book, and its illustrations, mostly woodcuts, on the one hand, and Garayev's music, originally created to illuminate the novel's images in motion (in Grigory Kozintsev's film), on the other, can be fruitful for discovering some of their essential peculiarities. Music reflects the moving images seen on the screen but can also assist in creating these images in the minds of readers (and thus enriching the narrative), or can visualize them, when they are invisible, when they should be performed but cannot be seen by spectators, e.g., the races of insects on the stage in a scene of Mikhail Bulgakov's play *The Run* with music by G. Garayev. The article conveys the idea of the necessity to study words, music, visual and performed arts altogether, because of the phenomenon of their inter-reflection and mutual illumination.

∙∙∙

> Senora, where there's music there can't be mischief.
>
> MIGUEL DE CERVANTES, *Don Quixote,* part 2, chapter 34

∙∙
∙

2015 was the year of the 400th anniversary of the publication of the second and final part of the novel *The Ingenious Gentleman Don Quixote of La Mancha* by Miguel de Cervantes Saavedra, and the year of the 410th anniversary of the publication of the first part of this masterpiece.

© KONINKLIJKE BRILL NV, LEIDEN, 2019 | DOI:10.1163/9789004401310_016

Besides these commemorations, there is one more, a smaller anniversary related to *Don Quixote*: 55 years ago, Soviet Azerbaijani composer Gara Garayev (or Kara Karayev, 1918–1982) created a symphony of the same title. It was based on one of his earlier works, the music for a film. In 1957, the film *Don Quixote* by Grigory Kozintsev, a Soviet film maker, appeared on the screens. This was the first live-action version of the novel in widescreen and colour. The *New York Times Movie Review* classified it as "the most handsome and impressive film yet made from Miguel de Cervantes's 'Don Quixote'".[1] The film's success was determined by all its components, including the film music by Gara Garayev.

Many years later, the film maker Grigory Kozintsev wrote in a letter to Garayev: "Yesterday there was *Don Quixote* on TV. I do not like to watch my films this way and do not like to watch my old films on the whole. But this time I did not leave the room till the end of the film mostly because of your music. I always liked it, but now, after many years, it seemed to me even much better. There is so great grief over everything and the feeling of deep sadness of this call[2] ... The novel's very essence, in its wonderful power and preciseness, is there in your music. Nothing better could have been composed. Perhaps, this coincided with something personal in you, otherwise it could not have been composed" (qtd. Abasova/Karagicheva, eds. 1988: 80; my transl.). Indeed, Don Quixote, as a novel and as character, meant a lot to Gara Garayev. This was his favourite book which he always had on his bedside table, as witnessed by his son Faraj (the composer Faraj Garayev, b. 1943). Also Don Quixote was his favourite literary character. Gara Garayev had the reproduction of Pablo Picasso's famous drawing depicting Don Quixote and Sancho Panza on the wall of his study room.

In 1960, three years after the film, Garayev, created a new symphonic work entitled *Symphony Engravings 'Don Quixote'*, based on the film music. As he wrote himself, this was, compared to the film, "reworked, rethought of, reorchestrated music" (Karagicheva 1994: 80; my transl.). It consists of eight parts: 1) Wanderings; 2) Sancho the Governor; 3) Wanderings; 4) Aldonsa; 5) Wanderings; 6) Cavalcade; 7) Pavane; 8) Death of Don Quixote.

Why did Garayev call his work "Engravings" – neither suite (as, e.g., the suite from his ballet *The Path of Thunder*), nor pictures (as, e.g., Mussorgsky's *Pictures at an Exhibition*), nor sketches, drawings, or anything else? Although some scholars tend to consider that, by choosing this title, Garayev intended to define genre specifics of his music, the origin of the title seems to be rooted in Garayev's early acquaintance with Cervantes's novel through the publication

---

1 Full quotation: "It is truly odd and ironic that the most handsome and impressive film yet made from Miguel de Cervantes's 'Don Quixote' is the brilliant Russian spectacle" (Crowther 1961 online).

2 I.e., the leitmotif associated with the 'chivalry call', the call that forces the protagonist to struggle against injustice and help those who need his protection.

of Russian translations of the work. It is not clear which editions of *Don Quixote* acquainted him with Cervantes's work, as several publications in Russian were available in Garayev's youth. Almost all of them were illustrated with plenty of woodcuts by such artists as Gustave Doré, Ricardo Balaca y Orejas-Canseco (1907), Leon Brunin (1924), Gennady Yepifanov (1934), and others.

An eager reader from early in his life, Garayev was closely attached to literature also in his professional activities. Some biographical facts can explain this attachment. Gara Garayev was born in Baku to a family from the intelligentsia. As at the time Azerbaijan was a part of the Russian Empire, his grandfather was educated in Saint Petersburg, from where he brought home fine books in Russian. Gara Garayev's father, also educated in Russia, was a doctor and the founder of pediatrics in Azerbaijan. His mother studied at the first school for Muslim girls in Azerbaijan. Garayev's parents were bilingual. They spoke to each other in Azerbaijani, but usually in Russian with their sons. Gara Garayev also was educated in the Russian language, and although he was Azerbaijani and knew the Azerbaijani language, his main language was Russian. It should be noted that this gave him easy access to world literature as there were plenty of Russian translations available in his childhood and later, much more than in Azerbaijani. From his early age on, Karik, as he was called by his parents, relatives and friends, liked to spend much time in his grandfather's library reading (cf. Karagicheva 1994: 14f.).

This may account for the fact that a lot of his music – much more than the works by other Azerbaijani composers – was inspired by literature, beginning with his earliest works based on poetry by Alexander Pushkin and Nizami Ganjavi, an Azerbaijani poet writing in Farsi. From then on many of Garayev's works had a narrative tendency, becoming "a form of intermedial transposition" and presenting "intermedial reference through thematization and imitation of other media" (Wolf 2008 online).

Garayev started his work on *Don Quixote* when the film was completed. Thus he was able to view the scenes and create music for them. Some incidents of the novel can be found in the film as well, but there are also scenes in the film which are not from the novel or are only briefly mentioned in the text in a few words.

For example, there are repeated stretches of wanderings between the protagonist's adventures both in the film and in the symphonic work, of which Cervantes describes more or less in detail only the first of Don Quixote's excursions: "[...] all the while he rode so slowly and the sun mounted so rapidly and with such fervour that it was enough to melt his brains if he had any. Nearly all day he travelled without anything remarkable happening to him, at which he was in despair, for he was anxious to encounter some one at once upon whom to try the might of his strong arm [...]. He was on the road all day, and towards nightfall his hack and he found themselves dead tired and hungry" (Cervantes online: Part 1, Chapter 2, 53). The other excursions find much shorter reflection: "[...] they sallied forth unseen by anybody from the village one night, and made such good way in the course of it that by daylight they held themselves safe from discovery [...]" (ibid.: Part 1, Chapter 7, 75).

The music of the 'Wanderings' is the link between the fragments in the film and especially in the *Symphony Engravings*, similar to the music of the 'Promenade' in Mussorgsky's *Pictures at an Exhibition* (1874). Ten movements of Mussorgsky's suite, composed for the piano, are linked together by a recurring and varied 'Promenade'. The music of Garayev's 'Wanderings' gives the feeling of commitment and tension, the feeling of dangers threatening the travelers on their way. In Garayev's opening to *Don Quixote*, preceding the music of the 'Wanderings', there is a tune, as a kind of a short introduction, to be taken as a 'chivalry call', or 'chivalry challenge', as Garayev 'converted' into music the idea which prevents Don Quixote from staying at home and forces him to start wandering: "[...] he did not care to put off any longer the execution of his design, urged on to it by the thought of all the world was losing by his delay, seeing what wrongs he intended to right, grievances to redress, injustices to repair, abuses to remove, and duties to discharge" (ibid.: Part 1, Chapter 2, 52):

FIGURE 15.1   The 'chivalric call' (Garayev 1964: 5).

The 'chivalry call' tune sounds at the very beginning of the work, and at other places is incorporated into the musical text of the *Engravings*.

An analysis of the novel's text shows that, on the whole, Cervantes rarely describes movements, while there are frequent examples of other kinds of descriptions: descriptions of clothes, armour, horse harnesses, books, etc. And of course, the novel is full of brilliant monologues, sparkling with wit and full of thought, humourous dialogues and conversations which occupy the greater portion of Cervantes's masterpiece. But how his characters move remains in the shadow. The narrative describing the notorious fight with the windmills – the most famous act of the Indigenous Gentleman Don Quixote de La Mancha – takes the author only two sentences: "Commending himself with all his heart to his lady Dulcinea, imploring her to support him in such a peril, with lance in rest and covered by his buckler, he charged at Rocinante's fullest gallop and fell upon the first mill that stood in front of him; but as he drove his lance-point into the sail the wind whirled it round with such force that it shivered the lance to pieces, sweeping with it horse and rider, who went rolling over on the plain, in a sorry condition. Sancho hastened to his assistance as fast as his ass could go, and when he came up found him unable to move, with such a shock had Rocinante fallen with him" (ibid.: Part 1, Chapter 8, 77). The remaining part of this chapter is dedicated to the conversations between the night-errant and his squire.

Another example of scarceness of description is the cavalcade. Cervantes wrote nothing that would describe the ride of the nobility: "[...] they placed the duchess in the middle and set out for the castle" (ibid.: Part 2, Chapter 30, 536), or: "The history informs us, then, that before they reached the country house or castle, the duke went on in advance and instructed all his servants how they were to treat Don Quixote" (ibid.: Part 2, Chapter 31, 538). However, Garayev illustrated the movement of the riding nobility in his music. Following the film maker Grigory Kozintsev, who introduced a scene of the cavalcade into his movie, Gara Garayev wrote fine music describing the picturesque horsemen in motion.

It could be assumed that the creation of such descriptive music was inspired by the moving images of the riders as the composer watched them on the screen. But other examples can show that Garayev's music did not need visible images (moving or non-moving) for inspiration. Rather his imagination crucially depended on literature and on images – moving or not – as created by verbal texts, even if they were not clearly described there, but could be vividly imagined by Gara Garayev as a talented and creative reader.

At the age of nineteen he wrote his first musical piece. This was piano music called *The Tsarskoye Selo Statue* (*The Statue at the Tsar Village*, 1937), referring to a massive royal estate modeled on Versailles outside of Saint Petersburg. At that time Garayev did not visit it, and it is not clear whether he had seen its picture or not. So the music was not the result of an inspiration by a statue fountain. Garayev was inspired by a poem of the same title by Alexander Pushkin (1799–1837), who in his youth studied at the Tsarskoye Selo Lyceum and reflected on the girl-with-a-pitcher fountain in a poem written in 1830. The poem describes a bronze fountain in the park of Tsarskoye Selo. The statue by P. Sokolov depicts a milk maid from a fable by Jean de la Fontaine. This is Pushkin's quatrain and its English translation by Stephanie Sandler:

Урну с водой уронив, об утёс её дева разбила.
Дева печально сидит, праздный держа черепок.
Чудо! Не сякнет вода, изливаясь из урны разбитой.
Дева, над вечной струёй, вечно печальна сидит.

PUSHKIN 1959: 333

Having dropped the urn filled with water, the maiden broke it against the
cliff.
The maiden sits sadly, holding the useless bit of pottery.
It is a miracle! The water does not dry up, pouring from the broken urn;
The maiden sits eternally sad over the eternal stream.

SANDLER 2004: 189

Garayev's early work, inspired by this poem, is marked by vivid depiction of the
movement of flowing water.

Another example: dances in the country castle take place neither in the novel nor in the movie. But Garayev gives the title 'Pavan' to the music of the scene
of Don Quixote and Sancho Panza's reception at the duke's country castle. The
pavan is known as a slow processional dance common in Europe during the
16th century. The word 'pavan' derives from the Spanish 'pavón', meaning 'pea-
cock' (cf. Sachs 1937: 356). (In modern Spanish 'pavo' means 'turkey'.) Garayev's
music is featured by the characteristic marks of the pavan in metre (slow duple
metre) and form. But nobody dances in this scene: they just pretend to play the
knight-errant welcoming joke. The reason for choosing a pavan as the musical
accompaniment for this scene lies in the way Garayev imagined the Spanish
aristocracy to move – slowly, magnificent, with dignity and without unnecessary movements, as if pretending to dance the pavan.

Cervantes was also not interested in the description of buildings. Don Quixote's house or the duke's castle are described neither from the outside, nor inside. No detailed setting of the duke's castle is presented in Part 2, Chapter 31
of the novel. Yet many illustrations are available related to this chapter. Some
of them give an idea of big space, characteristic of a nobleman's possessions,
but others do not do that. The music of the 'Pavan' also suggests the size and
grandeur of the castle hall where Don Quixote and Sancho are received by the
duke, the duchess and their court, because this kind of processional dance is
not expected to be performed in a small room.

Examples of a narrative attitude and of picturesque interpretations of literature can be found in other works by Garayev as well, for instance, in his music
for the play *The Run* (1958). This play (1927) by Mikhail Bulgakov (1891–1940),
Russian writer and playwright, tells about the dramatic period of Russia's history when after the socialist revolution of 1917 and following civil war many
people were forced to emigrate to other countries where their fortunes were
often miserable. Many of them lost their property and had to learn how to
survive. Bulgakov's characters find themselves in Istanbul in very difficult cir-
cumstances, without any money. One of the scenes in the play takes place at an
Istanbul market at the cockroaches race where people try to earn some money

by betting on the cockroaches, especially on one called Yanychar (Janissary), considered the most promising. But contrary to the gamblers' expectations, Janissary fails, which makes the disappointed gamblers think that he had purposely been intoxicated by the race owner, called Arthur, who had made him drunk with the aim of appropriating the bets. Angry people, who have lost their money, begin the scuffle. The objective point of view, as characteristic of drama, does not allow for the detailed description of actions, only the words of the play's characters give the essential information. No words in the play tell us whether the Janissary behaved inadequately and differently from the other participating cockroaches. It is impossible to show the race table with the competing insects in the realistic theatre of the first half of the 20th century. Therefore, and as the author gives no description of the cockroaches' run, the spectators can only imagine the race through the emotional response of the characters of this scene, their excited cries. The narration is provided only by the music.

Garayev's music describes the fast, 'motivated' run of the arthropod creatures so visually that it is easy to imagine the very special motions of the cockroaches. A second tune presents another type of movement: the spinning round on the spot with no progress, as if the cockroach were drunk, instead of running forward moving back and forth, right and left. This, as we can assume, is the only known portrait of a drunken cockroach in music and, perhaps, in all the arts. Thus, the narration and the picturesqueness lie obviously in Garayev's music, which not only follows and illuminates the literary text but also complements it with visual vividness by musical means.

Many years later, in 1970, the film *The Run* was produced in Russia with music by another composer, Nikolay Karetnikov. Cinema surpasses theatre in its ability to show very small objects and how they move, so in this film the scene of the cockroach race is shown in great details. If we replace the film music written for this scene by Karetnikov with the theatre music written by Garayev, we can see how it well coincides with the screen action and fits with the moving images of the cockroaches' run.

Next to the cockroach race in the movie is the musical fragment of *The Scuffle*. Garayev's music describes the fight of furious losers so naturally that we can 'hear' a series of blows which are followed by the rolling of the fighters on the ground.

In total, the works of no less than thirty-two writers, poets, playwrights and screen authors have found their musical interpretation in Garayev's legacy. These are:

- Azerbaijani authors: Nizami Ganjavi, Jalil Mammadgulizade, Mir Jalal, Samad Vurgun, Imran Kasumov, Mammad Raghim, Rasul Rza, and others;

- Russian authors: Alexander Pushkin, Mikhail Lermontov, Mikhail Bulgakov, Vsevolod Vishnevsky, and others;
- Afro-American poet Langston Hughes;
- English playwright and poet William Shakespeare;
- French authors: Prosper Mérimée, Edmond Rostand, Henri Barbusse, and others;
- German-Jewish writer Lion Feuchtwanger;
- Turkish poet and playwright Nazim Hikmet;
- Persian poet Omar Khayyam;
- South-African writer Peter Henry Abrahams;
- Greek author Alexis Parnis;
- Spanish authors: Lope de Vega, Miguel de Cervantes Saavedra.

Conclusion

1. The term 'engravings' does not mean that Garayev created a new genre or a new musical structure. He called his work *Symphony Engravings* because he provided musical illustrations to the book which usually was illustrated with engravings.

2. The talented illustrators of various works of world literature, be it artists of Islamic manuscript miniatures, who, e.g., worked on the poems by Nizami, or the artists who illustrated *Don Quixote*, often introduced the characters and details absent in the text and could see something that was not mentioned by the writer or poet but considered necessary by the artists in the visual presentation of a literary work. Gara Garayev, being acquainting with *Don Quixote* since his childhood, saw the illustrations to this novel and could note the creativeness and certain artistic freedom of the illustrators. He followed the way paved by the authors of those woodcuts (xylography): he created, for example, the sounding idea of chivalry (chivalry call), and repeated *Wanderings*. Although Cervantes paid much more attention to Don Quixote's deeds, adventures and discourse than to what was taking place between the events while traveling from one place to another, Garayev filled this gap.

3. Literature for Garayev was a great source of inspiration which stimulated him to create music that featured a high degree of picturesqueness.

4. While the term 'image' is generally related to iconography, to describe moving images and to reflect the peculiarities of movement is easier and better done by means of music. Garayev's film music is featured by a precise correspondence and brilliant correlation with moving images, as we

can see in G. Kozintsev's film *Don Quixote*. Garayev also created 'moving images' even in their visual absence on the stage through the means of his theatre music, when some movement cannot be shown and seen on the stage but needs to be imagined by the spectators, for example, during the performance of M. Bulgakov's play *The Run,* but also in other works.

5. What has been said confirms the idea of the mutual illumination of the arts. Music, rivaling with paintings, drawings, woodcuts and other art forms, can serve as a fine means for illustrating literature and making it almost visual.

References

Cervantes, Miguel [Saavedra] de (online). *Don Quixote.* Project Gutenberg. Etext 996. Trans. John Ormsby. http://www.gutenberg.org/ebooks/996 [29/02/2016].

Crowter, Bosley (1961 online). "*Don Quixote* (1957). Screen: 'Don Quixote': Russian Film Opens at Two Theatres". *New York Times Review* (January 21). http://www.nytimes.com/movie/review?res=9C03E3DF133FE13ABC4951DFB766838A679EDE [29/02/2016].

Garayev, Gara (1964). Караев, Кара. Дон Кихот. Симфонические гравюры. Переложение для фортепиано Фараджа Караева. Баку, Азгосиздательство.

Karagicheva, Ludmila (1994). Карагичева, Людмила. Личность. Суждения об искусстве. Москва, изд. «Композитор».

Pushkin, Alexander (1959). Пушкин А.С. Собрание сочинений в 10 томах. Москва, ГИХЛ. Том 2.

Sachs, Curt (1937). *World History of the Dance.* Trans. Bessie Schönberg. New York, NY: W. W. Norton.

Sandler, Stephanie (2004). *Commemorating Pushkin: Russia's Myth of a National Poet.* Stanford, CA: Stanford Univ. Press.

Abasova, Elmira, Ludmila Karagicheva, eds. (1988). Слово о Кара Караеве [*Word on Gara Garayev*]. Baku: Yazichi.

Wolf, Werner (2008 online). "Relations between Literature and Music in the Context of a General Typology of Intermediality". Lisa Block de Behar et al., eds. *Comparative Literature: Sharing Knowledge for Preserving Cultural Diversity. Encyclopedia of Life Support Systems (EOLSS).* Oxford: Eolss Publishers. http://www.eolss.net [29/02/2016].

CHAPTER 16

Film *as* Opera: Three Perspectives on *Still Life* and *Brief Encounter*

Michael Halliwell

Abstract

Opera and film is an area of scholarly endeavour that has engaged a wide variety of methodologies in recent years. The usual areas of investigation include opera on film; opera as film; opera in film, and film in opera. However, film *as* opera is a relatively new phenomenon. André Previn drew on David Lean's 1945 film, *Brief Encounter*, based on Noël Coward's 1936 play, *Still Life*, for an opera premiered in 2009. The Kneehigh Theatre Company also used the film as the basis for its 2008 production, *Brief Encounter*. This paper investigates how these three adaptations of the Coward play draw on different elements of the source work, each finding a distinctive musical response to the play.

•••

> One of the bequests of film to opera is its demonstration that song is soliloquy, not overt statement: that the voice is consciousness – or the yearning subconscious – overheard.
>
> CONRAD 1996: 273

1 Opera, the Novel and Film

The nineteenth century saw the highpoint of the depiction of opera in the novel; during the course of the century novelists increasingly incorporated operatic scenes as a means of contrasting the quotidian world of the novel with that of opera which seemed to present a heightened emotional reality outside that of the everyday.[1] Herbert Lindenberger suggests that scenes from operas

---

1 Herbert Lindenberger notes: "Opera, through the particular means at its disposal, can achieve intense and extreme effects that words on the page can approximate only with strain, if at all" (1984: 145f.). Lindenberger traces the link between passion and opera, and argues that thinkers such as Kierkegaard and Adorno "chose opera to exemplify a form of consciousness characterized by passion and an absence of reflection" (ibid.: 149).

in novels "become a reminder – for author, character, and reader alike – of the gap separating the world of operatic passion from that of ordinary life. Its very consciousness of this gap has allowed the novel throughout its history to meditate on its own sufficiency as a genre" (1984: 152). In effect, these operatic scenes "comment upon the narratives in which they are embedded" (ibid.: 153). Flaubert's use of the opera *Lucia di Lammermoor* in *Madame Bovary* might be seen as paradigmatic for other writers such as George Eliot, Henry James and Edith Wharton amongst many others.[2] Opera's intimate relationship with the novel has continued to the present, but the balance has shifted to contemporary opera increasingly drawing on films as sources.[3]

The twentieth century saw the film emerge as the dominant artistic medium, surpassing the novel in popular culture. Opera's engagement with film is virtually as old as film itself, and there is a fascinating relationship between silent film and opera – in itself this seems completely contradictory.[4] Much of the early impetus occurred in Italian culture and leads Peter Franklin to assert that *Tosca* is a "prototypical mass entertainment movie in all but medium" (1994: 84).

Opera has also used film within its own performance with an early example being Alban Berg's *Lulu*. Opera has also aspired to the nature of film – Richard Strauss, in 1923, described his *Zeitoper, Intermezzo*, with its short and rapidly-changing scenes, as "fast nur Kinobilder" (qtd. Gilliam 1992: 266). Hugo von Hofmannsthal wrote to Strauss urging a film version of *Der Rosenkavalier* in 1925 on the grounds that it would be positive for the opera, asking Strauss to

> look at my sketch for the film scenario [...] the whole thing is treated in the manner of a novel: it introduces the characters or, for those who know

---

2 Cormac Newark notes: "If the rendering of operatic storyline, décor, costume and gesture provided great writers with plenty of material to manipulate in the service of novelistic plot, dialogue, characterisation and so on, it also seemed to compel them to make genuine attempts to communicate their understanding of the mysteriously unpredictable affect of dramatic music" (2011: 11).

3 Lindenberger observes that it is significant that "the classic age of the novel, from the mid-eighteenth century through the early twentieth century, is also the period that produced those operas most securely entrenched within the repertory [...] the fusion of words and music that constitutes opera allowed the verbal medium [...] to find loftier forms of expression through music, which cultivated a high style during the very period in which literature felt forced to retreat from this style as well as from the subject matter with which it was traditionally associated" (1984: 166f.).

4 Peter Franklin argues that "operatic scenes or scenarios based on well-known operas featured as the subject-matter of a significant minority of silent films between 1903 and 1926", and the "frequently literary basis of these opera-films points to a network of issues concerning the links between late nineteenth-century opera composition and literary culture which film would inherit and extend" (1994: 80).

them, tells something new of their old acquaintances. Nowhere are the events of the opera exactly repeated – *not in a single scene*. If the film appeals, it cannot but arouse great eagerness to see the now familiar characters in the *original* action on the stage alive, speaking, singing [...] it can only whet the appetite for the opera. In this way, too, the project seems to imply value as an advertisement rather than the danger of competition.

> STRAUSS 1974: 397

A symbiotic relationship between film and opera might be seen to be embodied in the person of Erich Korngold, who found early fame primarily as an opera composer, but after his emigration to the USA his music had an important influence on the development of film music. But film was also seen by some as a direct threat to opera, and Arnold Schoenberg in 1927 resisted the ubiquity of film:

The erosion of the theatre began as the emotions of the people acting on stage came to absorb more and more of the audience's interest [...] the characters represented necessarily became even more ordinary, their emotion even more comprehensible to all. The result is that nowadays one sees on the stage almost exclusively the kind of philistines one also meets in life, whether they are supposed to represent heroes, artists or men-in-the-street. The opera is in a comparable situation. It has less to offer the eye than film has – and colour-film will soon be here too. Add music, and the general public will hardly need to hear an opera sung and acted any more.

> Qtd. FRANKLIN 1994: 89f.

Much more prevalent today, however, is the use of opera in film – there is an extensive sub-genre of films that employ opera scenes or excerpts for a variety of narrative and emotional strategies.[5] One might argue that recent film in particular has used opera in an analogous way to that in the fiction of the nineteenth century. Not only is operatic music used as part of the soundtrack, but many of these films include a visit to the opera as well – here the analogy with fiction is even more direct as the spaces in and around the theatre, and particularly the opera box, are distinctive tropes in the nineteenth-century

---

5   Opera and film has become an important area of interdisciplinary study in recent times. Studies include: Joe (2013); Joe/Rose, eds. (2002); Schroeder (2002); Citron (2000); Citron (2010); Fryer, ed. (2005).

novel where the cultural meaning of the opera house in addition to opera as performance, is crucial. Indeed, there is a fleeting glimpse of Laura and Alec in the film *Brief Encounter*, in an opera box, when Laura fantasizes about various glamorous places that they might visit if they were together as a couple: "I saw us in Paris, in a box at the opera. The orchestra was tuning up" (Coward 1984: 58). This image conveys a sense of glamour as well as unattainability for her.

Mark Weiner argues that opera is used in recent films not only for atmospheric accompaniment, "but functions as an interpretive key, and sometimes even as the central, culminating moment in so-called blockbusters, productions that are financially dependent on success with a wide and diversified audience" (2002: 75). Lindenberger sees the opera scene in the novel as a form of ekphrasis, where "operatic scenes enact a possible higher narrative against which the central line of narrative can take stock of itself" (1984: 168). This might equally validly be said of opera scenes in film. Strikingly, it is usually nineteenth- or early twentieth-century opera that is used, and mainly Italian opera at that.[6]

Using film as the sole direct source for musical adaptation has been occurring with some frequency in musical theatre, with works such as *The Lion King*, *Beauty and the Beast*, *Dirty Dancing*, *The Full Monty*, *Billy Elliot*, and *Matilda* being some recent and prominent examples. Operas that are solely based on films are much less common. William Bolcom's *The Wedding* (2004) has as its source the celebrated Robert Altman film, while Howard Shore's opera *The Fly* (2008) is based on a less celebrated B-movie. Kevin Put's version of the film *Joyeux Noël* (2005), *Silent Night* (2012), was very well received and won the Pulitzer Prize in 2012. However, one must distinguish between operas that have a work of fiction or drama as an original source, which has later been turned into an even more significant film – one thinks of recent operas such as Previn's *A Streetcar Named Desire*, for example. Many more people have seen the film than the play. One might argue that several operas that are preceded by a film based on an original work of fiction or drama have been influenced considerably more by the film – Nicholas Maw openly acknowledged that it was the film of *Sophie's Choice* that attracted him to the story for his opera, not the William Styron novel (cf. Halliwell 2012: 227).[7]

---

6 Weiner notes: "the passionate, emphatic nature of the nineteenth-century opera serves as a foil to the cynicism of the modern film, and thus also not only as an emblem of the universal and the timeless, but also as a historically specific, nostalgic escape" (2002: 80).

7 Frederic Döhl notes that the "earlier movie adaptation is not just another adaptation, but as much a point of reference for the opera as the original play or novel – and sometimes it is the main point of reference" (2016: 137).

The reason for opera turning to these varied sources is apparent. Lawrence Kramer lists a range of American operas of recent years which have the work of prominent novelists and playwrights as sources: Fitzgerald, Williams, Miller, Norris, Alcott, James, Poe, Hawthorne, Dreiser, Steinbeck, and Morrison among others. Kramer notes: "The ambition of these works depends in no small part on the specifically national illustriousness" of these names; "at this moment in its history, American opera is often the village storyteller writ large" (2007a: 67). Many of these operas

> compete with classic films as well as classic texts. As movies do, opera in America today often stakes its artistic claims on the reproduction of an older literary work. With opera in particular, the work comes more often than not from the national canon. The opera tells the story of America by retelling one of America's stories; tragic stories for the most part, but with a particular form that [...] supports a national mythology that the operas repeat and heighten – opera heightens tragic myth like nothing else can – without exactly admitting it, or even knowing it. (Ibid.)

Iconic literary works and films can be problematic in adaptation – as Kramer suggests of the *Streetcar* opera: it "is less of a setting of the play than of the play's cultural image" (ibid.: 69). The danger in operatic adaptation is that if the source work, or a film of it, is too intimidating, it is often approached with too much reverence which inhibits true creative engagement.

2   Play to Film

It is virtually forgotten today that David Lean's iconic film, *Brief Encounter* (1945), had as its source a Noël Coward play, *Still Life*, of 1936. This was one of a group of ten one-act plays that made up a cycle, *Tonight at 8.30*, written to be performed on three evenings. In the introduction to a published edition of the plays, Coward wrote: "A short play, having a great advantage over a long one in that it can sustain a mood without technical creaking or over padding, deserves a better fate, and if, by careful writing, acting and producing I can do a little towards reinstating it in its rightful pride, I shall have achieved one of my more sentimental ambitions" (qtd. Morley 1994: xiv). The play was Coward's favourite of the group: he saw it as "the most mature play of the entire sequence, well written, economical and well-constructed" (ibid.: xiv). The play depicts the love affair of two middle-aged and middle-class people, Alec, a doctor, and Laura, a housewife. The pathos of Alec and Laura's secretive and doomed affair is counterpointed with the spiritedly boisterous and uncomplicated relationship of Myrtle and Albert, two of the station staff where Alec and Laura meet.

Still Life is set in the railway buffet where Alec and Laura meet, but the screenplay takes them out of this claustrophobic location, opening out the original play, using many of the possibilities that film possesses. The play is "a classic essay in British understatement and the good old stiff upper-lip", in which two middle-aged, happily-married people "find themselves embarrassingly involved in a great romantic passion that they can do nothing about [...] and the only possible answer is the decent, dutiful one: they must part for good" (Taylor 1984: 4). The relationship remains unconsummated, and as Kramer observes, Laura "gets to be guilty without having been happy" (2007b: 99). David Lean remarked that one chooses "either erotic love and romance or domestic stability, respectability, and the happiness of children; it was far better to choose the latter of the two options if one had to" (Phillips 2006: 96).[8]

Frances Gray suggests that the film script on its own conjures up awkward questions: "With no apparent religious convictions or strong relationships to keep them apart, the lovers seemed simply too timid to violate social norms or even to think well of themselves for upholding them and remaining married", as a 1975 re-make demonstrated, but counters that argument, suggesting that

> their timidity [...] fitted the mood of the thirties and forties and expressed the values implicit in *Tonight at 8.30*. The rich might be silly, the poor might be vulgar, the evening's entertainment implied: but the middle classes, the backbone of Coward's audience throughout this period, were the guardians of order, decency and the family; they could (mostly) control their unfortunate passions and come through to do the right thing. In these lively triple bills, they could even do it in a stylish context. (1987: 66f.)

What Lean and Coward were faced with was unusual in adaptation. Rather than the often drastic pruning needed when turning a novel, a full-length play, or even a short story into a screenplay, they needed to expand the original, opening out the play with scenes that were suggested in the play, and creating a range of new locales. New characters emerge as well, including Laura's

---

8 Jeremy Paxman sees the film as quintessentially English, asking what "does this most popular of English films tell us about the English? Firstly that, in the immortal words, 'we are not put on earth to enjoy ourselves'. Secondly, the importance of a sense of duty [...]. Most of all, the message is that the emotions are there to be controlled [...] there were things which were done and things which were not done" (1999: 5).

husband Fred as well as their two children. Barry Day notes that Coward, in adapting his own play, unlike in previous occasions where he had been "overly faithful to the material with only the occasional embellishment", here uses the story and the characters "confidently as the basis of something created with a totally different medium in mind", and he "manages to keep the narrative simplicity of the original, while extending its emotional complexity" (2005: 102).[9]

The question of strategies in adaptation is raised by Day when considering a later TV version of the material, directed by Alan Bridges, with Sophia Loren and Richard Burton as Laura and Alec. Day acknowledges that a "literary property that exists in one medium has come to be fair game for adaptation into another", but suggests that if producer Carlo Ponti and his team "had given us a new 'take' on *Still Life* – perhaps emphasizing Alec's story rather than Laura's – that would have been one thing, but to tinker with *Brief Encounter*, a story reconceived in purely cinematic terms, is perverse" (ibid.: 115). The later film does not have the linking internalized dialogue so central to the earlier film, and thus loses much of its suppressed, claustrophobic atmosphere. It also brings Laura's husband, Fred, into more prominence, whereas he remains a somewhat ambiguous and peripheral character in the original. Lean's film radically changes the dramaturgy of Coward's play, taking it out of the buffet in Milford Junction Station and considerably expanding its fictional world. Significantly, it presents the doomed relationship in a circular fashion, commencing with the final parting of Alec and Laura, whereas the play follows the events chronologically from their first meeting to their final parting. The film ends with Laura returning home to her husband.[10]

3   Interior Monologue

One of the factors in the well-known emotional impact of the film, and the major transpositional strategy of play to film, is making Laura narrate the events, telling the story from her point of view soon after they have parted and when she is still consumed by grief. What might appear a clumsy narrative device works effectively, with Laura telling us about what is going on inside her. In effect, the whole film, apart from the opening and closing moments, is Laura's

---

9   Day notes that Laura "is a real person of a certain class and time – the film is set in 1939 – which is why so many other women could relate to her and turn her story into one of the perennial 'women's pictures' of all time" (2005: 102).

10   Avron Fleishman notes: "Starting out as the film does at the end of the affair, the ensuing narration generates a vast anachrony, taking us back to the affair's beginning and completing the loop at the close" (1992: 184).

perspective on events. The narrative 'hook' that is used is Laura apparently 'recounting' the events of the affair to her husband; but this is a fully internalized narrative and he does not hear her, although at the end he senses that something profound has occurred. In these moments of narration, her lips do not move, thus signaling to the audience that this is her interior monologue. Laura is the focus of the film and effectively 'controls' the narrative.[11]

Kyle Stevens charts the sometimes fraught position that voice-over occupies in film theory, noting that "it has become common [...] to classify voice-over as 'semi-diegetic', meaning that such sound occurs both inside and outside of the world of the story" (2015: 1). He notes the problematic elements of this device: the "two planes of existence (visual and aural)", suggesting that

> voice-over is not just about the relation of image-body to voice, because we are meant to understand it as precisely *not* of the body before us. *This* voice is defined in opposition to the vocal sound that the body emits to others. In this sense, voice-over is a paradox, a sound which is also not a sound, and a metaphor for the type of linguistic thinking that what we must attribute to a mind [...]. This paradox pictures consciousness as a means of containment and abandon, a non-space in which a character remains isolated from the world yet free to let fly unutterable thoughts. (Ibid.: 2)[12]

Avron Fleishman asserts that *Brief Encounter* is "a drama of consciousness in which desire and unfulfillment themselves become subjects for speculation by the introspective narrator" and suggests that the film dramatizes the active role of consciousness "to a degree rarely seen, before or since, in cinema history" (1992: 182).

One might argue that the operatic aria performs an analogous function to internal monologue in film but is also closely related to the soliloquy in spoken drama. While the sonorous operatic voice is very much of the body we see before us, it is also frequently a sound that is not heard by other characters inhabiting the same world, but a means whereby we, the audience, have access

---

11   Day provocatively asks, on a second viewing, whether this is what "really *happened* or is this a visualization of what she thinks she might have felt? Are we sometimes drifting into her novelization of events?" (2005: 104).

12   Stevens further observes that we "lack vocabulary for referring to this sort of language use [...] and labeling them simply 'inner speech' amounts to a refusal to probe the way *Brief Encounter* [...] relates mind to mind, mind to body, mind to social realm, sound to image, private and public [...]. This division between what Laura's mind and body express is further underlined by the revelation that they exist in different timelines" (2015: 3).

to the thoughts and emotions of the particular character, and is sometimes staged as a form of interior monologue in opera films where a character sings, but their lips do not move.[13] But there is another level of narration in the opera aria where a form of omniscient narration surrounds it in the form of the orchestral accompaniment, so that the character, while allowing the audience access to their innermost thoughts and emotions, is, in turn, 'narrated' by the orchestral narrator (cf. Halliwell 1999: 135–154).

The film is renowned for creating a heightened sense of emotional intensity through its "moody, chiaroscuro camerawork, which makes the most of rain-washed streets, clouds of smoke and steam from the steam trains", with occasional camera work in which "the angles become more and more extreme [...] particularly in the sequence of Laura's temptation to suicide" (Taylor 1984: 5).[14] Alec's removal of the grit in Laura's eye which initiates the relationship, occurs as the express train roars through, and trains play a crucial part in the film. As Day observes: "Without becoming unduly Freudian, it is hard to avoid the interpretation that the unstoppable train symbolizes the male excitement her life misses and which she sedately seeks in novels and films. At later dramatic points of the film the train is used as sexual punctuation, if one accepts this interpretation" (2005: 106).

4   Rachmaninoff

Perhaps what many people remember most about the film is its lush soundtrack. The heightened emotion of the film is supported famously by the extensive use of Rachmaninoff's Second Piano Concerto which creates in the film much of its emotional intensity, particularly when underscoring the frequent conversational exchanges between Laura and Alec where what is not

---

13   Fleishman suggests that "soliloquy and interior monologue are cinematic codes for exteriorizing thought. Their conventions work to the same end in making unspoken thoughts available to the audience, whether the character is alone or in the presence of others [...]. Both are taken to be equivalents of mental language. When this language undertakes to tell a story, we have a narrational activity that calls for a covering term to represent a common mental origin. Thus, *mindscreen narration*" (1992: 175). This mode is closely related to the opera aria.

14   David T. Hansen notes that "the film has a damp, grey feel to it, save at key moments when Laura is bathed in bright light. The dark texture of so many of the film's frames promotes the image of a dimly lit world in which people know very little about each other" (1996: 223). Kramer suggests that Laura in contemplating, but not throwing herself under a train, is a "failed Anna Karenina, second-rate in her tepid modernity" (2007b: 100f.).

said is often crucial; what Harold Pinter described as "the second silence: 'below the words spoken, is the thing known and unspoken'" (2008 online).[15]

The way the music is used supports the narrative trajectory of the film: the opening of the concerto is heard as the opening titles appear, and then elements from all three movements underpin Laura's narrative of her emotional journey, while the closing bars of the concerto are heard at the end of the film. The use of this music is both diegetic (when she turns on the radio at home), and non-diegetic (often 'accompanying' her voice-overs). But frequently these distinctions are blurred: "seemingly playing in the background as she remembers to herself, but yet the use of extracts which are repeated and which are not in their original order indicates that we are not hearing a single diegetic performance of the work" (Cormack 2006: 24).[16]

A crucial, and justly celebrated scene, occurs some time after their first meeting when they are in the station buffet and Alec tells Laura about his passion for medicine. The camera focuses predominantly on her as Alec speaks, and her kaleidoscopic emotional reaction is strikingly visible in her face and eyes, and, of course, is underscored by the swelling Rachmaninoff counterpointing the conversation. Coward commented years later on what he attempted to achieve in this scene through his use of dialogue:

> The thing I like best about *Brief Encounter* is that the love scene is played *against* the words [...]. He's a doctor and he talks about preventative medicine and the different diseases one gets, and all the time he's looking at her. And then she says, 'You suddenly look much younger' – which cuts right through and forces them back to ordinary dialogue.
>
> qtd. DAY 2005: 107

One can speculate how much less effective this scene would be without the music.

---

15   Stevens notes that the music "eases our sonic transition from the space that [Laura] occupies with Dolly, the diegetic objective world, to the soundscapes of her mind. The classic, increasingly tight close-ups collide with Laura's aural liberty, and the black and white optics are in similar tension with the colorful, romantic concerto [...]. Laura often seems caught between the music and the sounds of the train, which again and again punctuate scenes as if with perfect knowledge of her emotional states, or as if she conducts them to suit the vicissitudes of her affective life [...]. In this way, Laura's imagination bestows special powers upon the train – aligned with cinema – as a shaping force for her imaginary retelling" (2015: 3). Kramer suggests that "the (Russian) music retains the Tolstoyan grandeur that Laura renounces" (2007b: 101f.).

16   Kramer notes that "what we see in the film corresponds to Laura's narrative, addressed mentally to her husband; the movie audience hears her unspoken thoughts", the concerto "breaks through on the soundtrack at moments of peak feeling" (2007b: 100).

5   Film to Opera

Is André Previn's operatic adaptation just another example of a glittering literary, or in this case, filmic source, being the attraction where one hopes that
the cachet of the original work will draw the punters in? This is a classic and
well-loved film but perhaps not obvious material for operatic transformation;
not least of potential obstacles is the very centrality of the music of the film as
discussed above.[17] Another large operatic pitfall lies in the fact that the emotional drama in the film is primarily internalized and understated – one reads
it in close-ups of the eyes of the two protagonists as well as in minute facial
gestures – the scene discussed above is a case in point.

Operatic music provides interiority, but a potential danger lies in constructing a libretto which forces the singers to continually announce to the audience
what they are feeling. Despite the swelling Rachmaninoff, the essence of the
film is what remains unspoken, or at least, understated; it underlies much of
the surface banality of the verbal exchanges, but also that which cannot be
expressed in words. As Kramer notes, the music supplies "a language of desire"
that is lacking in the world of the film; there are moments "in which music
and language trade places [...]. At a pivotal moment [...] the Rachmaninoff
concerto drowns out the characters' speech, conveying what their otherwise
banal words express rather than the words themselves" (2007b: 108). Opera is
a magnifying medium, and deals in primal emotions with dramatic but often
unsubtle effects, but it can certainly achieve what Kramer notes occurs in the
film: moments when the textual element of opera retreats or even disappears,
but 'meaning' remains and is expressed even more powerfully in the music
which tells us what the words do not.

Important in the ultimate effectiveness and meaning of the opera are elements of what Kramer describes as "songfulness": the way in which vocal music "works not by what it signifies, but by the material presence of its signifiers,
which address the listener with an unusual, richly gratifying intimacy" (2002:
52).[18] Here the material quality of the voice itself adds meaning where voice,

---

17   Tim Ashley, in an otherwise rather lukewarm review, observes that Previn "mercifully
      avoids referring to Rachmaninoff" (2011 online).
18   Kramer sees "songfulness" as a "fusion of vocal and musical utterance judged to be both
      pleasurable and suitable independent of verbal content. It is the positive quality of
      singing-in-itself: just singing [...]. The one who hears it may not be able to account for it,
      or to say for sure whether it is more an attribute of the music (which seems made for the
      voice), or even of the ear that hears it, but the quality nonetheless seems utterly unmis-
      takable. There is thus [...] a sense of immediate intimate contact between the listener and
      the subject behind the voice" (2002: 53).

as a medium of "meaningful utterance", brings the music "into a space of potential or virtual meaning even when actual meaning is left hanging" (ibid.:
54). The particular singer of a role in opera provides an important, but often
difficult to define, element in the overall meaning of the performance – but so
too do the vocal performances of the actors playing Laura and Alec. Indeed,
the scene under discussion is a prime example of this where the clipped tones,
distinctive intonation and accents of the two film actors tell us a great deal
about the characters and situation, adding an important element of meaning
to the film.[19]

Of course, Previn is vastly experienced as a film composer and understands
the medium intimately. A criticism leveled at this opera, as well as the earlier
A Streetcar Named Desire, is that they both sound like film music.[20] Previn
countered these accusations with the comment: "Writing an opera has nothing to do with writing a film score. A film score is an accompaniment to an
already existing series of images. An opera is a musical extension of the word"
(qtd. Singer 2009: 20). Previn here, perhaps inadvertently, touches on what
one might argue is the literary rather than the visual or even dramatic basis
of opera.[21]

Frederic Döhl argues that Previn's music for the opera is "filmmusikalisch"
('film-music-like'), rather than performing the work of film music, and that
much of the critical reaction to the music remains superficial (2009: 323f.).[22]
He advances a convincing argument that Previn's music functions analogously
to the filmic 'close-up': as he terms it, "akustisches Close-up" (ibid.: 325). Previn
uses particular harmonic gestures to create the sense of a musical close-up on
the emotions of the particular character, and Döhl describes moments where
the music is not an extension of the word, but an extension of the image as
well. He argues that Previn

> created small musical episodes that are not repeated or used as Leitmo-
> tifs in the course of the opera, but that are clearly distinguished from the

---

19   Just how central the vocal aspect of this performance is can be seen in the delightful paro-
      dy of this scene by Victoria Wood (see https://www.youtube.com/watch?v=ajC4Az4wscc).

20   Cf. Frédéric Döhl 2013: 312. Döhl argues that "the sound world of the opera is reminiscent
      of the sound world of Hollywood film music from the 30s to the 50s" (ibid.).

21   Peter Conrad argues that "music and drama are dubious, even antagonistic, partners and
      that opera's actual literary analogue is the novel" (1977: 1; see also Halliwell 1999).

22   Swed observes: "Previn's music does not so much define the opera as enigmatically float
      through it [...]. He may underscore what the characters say or feel, but he doesn't spell out
      time and place. His real genius here is to, like a film composer, set a mood and, like a jazz
      musician, let the music take him where it will" (2009 online).

music that surrounds them. These ephemeral episodes – 'brief encounters', if you will – work like 'affection images' to use a term coined by Gilles
Deleuze. They work like a sudden filmic cut into a close-up. With these
'brief encounters', Previn 'adds meaning' with music in a similar manner
as Lean did with close-up pictures [...]. Previn assures that the spectator
is listening at precisely the moment that he or she should be attentive to
what, from the perspective of the narrative, is happening, to recognize
at all that there is something happening between the main protagonists
when words or actions do not portray this or even contradict the development of the emotions that, in Lean's movie the close-up and in Previn's
opera score his musical equivalents, convey to the audience.

                    DÖHL 2016: 149

One might extend this argument to suggest that these musical strategies also
function as a form of omniscient narration as in a novel. Here the 'narrator' –
the orchestra – is providing a point of view on what is happening, obviously
without the equivalent of the precision available to the director of the film.[23]
In the film it is often the wordless close-up where much of the emotion is
suggested, while in the opera it is the wordless, but musical 'close-up' which
serves a similar function.

Avron Fleishman notes that Laura led a "busy life" on the train – he alludes to the frequent inner narration that occurs there – something which the
opera does not suggest in its staging (1992: 189). But he further observes the
fact that "nothing much happens in this love affair" and that Laura's narration is "largely about psychological events: what she thought and felt as she
had her love affair", revealing a "move toward the full subjectivizing of narrative" (ibid.). This is where the operatic adaptation comes into its own, able
as it is to probe psychological states through its synthesis of text and music.
Fleishman asserts that the filmmakers gave their heroine "a narrational capacity rarely found in films but closely resembling that in the great tradition of
introspective fictional characters" (ibid.). One might argue that Laura becomes
at times an omniscient narrator as in fiction, imagining events or feelings that
she cannot see or experience and it is here where the opera further amplifies
her role as narrator. Opera has the capacity for 'novelising' characters through

---

23   Döhl describes how Previn "changes, for a split second, the instrumentation, pitch, tex-
      ture, and level of dissonance in the chord structure, etc. It works like a sound gesture, a
      blink of an eye, as we see a little smile running across Laura's eyes [...]. What the close-
      up of Laura's eyes achieves in the movie is exactly what the two measures [in the score]
      achieve in lieu of the close-up that the opera house does not reveal due to the distance
      between singers and audience" (2016:151).

its musical suggestion of interiority as well as point of view, but also through its capacity for providing different levels of narration through the complexity of the orchestral music. We listen to the words they are singing but experience their emotions primarily through the music – both vocal line, with its particular individual materiality, and the orchestra – that accompanies them. This 'double' narration occurs as the orchestra is able simultaneously to objectively 'narrate' the characters while they themselves narrate their own feelings and emotions.[24]

While the opera follows the dramatic arc of the film rather than the play, a significant change from film into opera is to shift the focus of the drama from Laura and Alec to include Laura's husband, Fred. He plays a relatively minor role in the film where he is depicted as devoted to her but without the capacity of ever really understanding her dilemma or her deeper feelings and desires. The opening up of this character gives more depth to his relationship with Laura, and consequently, what she has to lose in the affair with Alec. Previn and librettist John Caird decided to "make him growingly aware of Laura's predicament, thereby increasing the tension in the final scenes and, at the same time, giving him something to sing about" (Caird 2011: 10). His aria, "Without you there is nothing", is one of the highlights of the operatic score. His expanded role, like the later film referred to above, significantly shifts the balance away from its primary focus on Laura.

Caird has used the screenplay virtually as a libretto, even retaining some of the stage directions which move from screenplay to libretto. The opera shadows the film in terms of its narrative extremely closely; however, frequently shortening or conflating scenes. The scenes in the film where Laura expresses her own thoughts to the audience as narrator, unheard by the other characters, translate effectively into aria – this is natural for opera – and there are occasional snatches of ensemble where, for example, Laura thinks to herself in the train carriage while Dolly rattles on; Laura moves fluidly in and out of introspective aria into conversational dialogue with other characters, the musical accompaniment smoothing the transitions.[25]

The theme of memory is "embedded in the story's flashback structure, with Laura acting as her own storyteller, remembering the events of the drama

---

24   Conrad suggests that drama is "limited to the exterior life of action [...]. The novel, in contrast, can explore the interior life of motive and desire and is naturally musical because mental. It traces the motions of thought, of which music is an image. Opera is more musical novel than musical drama" (1977: 1).

25   The opera does not stage their frequent visits to the cinema and thus loses the ironic counterpointing of the lurid drama taking place on the screen with the understated, but intense 'drama' of their relationship.

scene by scene as they happened to her" (Caird 2011: 10). Caird noted that musical correlatives for the visual imagery of the film focused "on the themes of time and memory [...]. Alec and Laura are constantly aware of the clock and how little time they have to express their feelings for each other – all made apparent in the music, dramaturgy, and stage sets" (ibid.).[26] Station halls "are halls of Time [...] the life and movement of every person is strongly defined by the passage of time [...]. As Laura watches Alec's train disappearing down the track for the last time, the hall becomes a hall of memory with all the locations of her brief encounter and all the longings and grief engendered by it tumbled together in her yearning, troubled mind" (ibid.: 11).

The opera doesn't attempt to completely match the film's fluid movement between dialogue and overheard interior monologue: the set piece moments are more distinct than in the film, drawing on fundamental elements of operatic dramaturgy – arias, duets, and trios. Another change from film to opera is that in the film Laura's monologues are addressed to Fred, as if she were explaining the reasons underlying her actions, while this focus is not nearly as prominent in the opera where the switching from dialogue to aria, which expresses inner emotion, is naturalised. In musical terms, building up Fred's role also allows more use of a third voice to balance the potentially predominantly duet nature of the opera and there are several moments when the three voices blend in ensemble.

The parting scene between the two occurs at the same point in the narrative as in the film – the first time near the beginning of events, and then as it is replayed near the end.[27] However, a major departure from the film are a series of 'frozen moments' in this final sequence when the action stops: "[...] *the action freezes in time, only Laura remaining animated. In this freeze, as in all subsequent ones, the picture must be an exact replica of the original moment of action in Act One*" (Previn 2011: 88). Here again Laura resumes her role as narrator, explaining what is happening as well as her emotional reaction to the events. It is an effective contrast with the banal conversation of Dolly. Alec places his hand on Laura's shoulder as he leaves to catch his train in the first iteration of

---

26   Without being obvious, there are elements in the music conveying a sense of the passage of time. Fleishman notes of the film that "in the *mise-en-scène*, plotting and dialogue of the main story, time is made an issue. Clocks appear regularly in the railroad station scenes, the lovers' meetings are shaped by a number of temporal orders like the heroine's weekly shopping trips to town, and the dialogue is filled with anxieties about train times" (1992:183).

27   Unlike the linear narrative of the play.

the scene. When it is repeated it carries a strong emotional charge as we now know the pain that lies behind this seemingly innocuous gesture.[28]

However, the opera, unable to provide as precise a point of view as in film where the camera's focus is relentlessly on the face of Laura and Alec, uses a different strategy. The stage direction indicates: "*Alec shakes hands with Dolly. He looks briefly at Laura, then, passing behind her, places his hand on her shoulder* (ibid.). The opera reinforces this by having Laura narrate her emotional reaction as Dolly continues her chatter:

> LAURA: The touch of his hand. A moment of time frozen. (*The action restarts. A train is heard rumbling into the station. Alec leaves the refreshment room and goes out on to the platform. Laura gazes after him as he disappears into the smoke and steam of the platform. Freeze*) Then he walked away out of my life for ever.
> DOLLY: He'll have to run or he'll miss the train. He's got to get right over the bridge to platform one.
> LAURA: Listen for the sound of his train leaving, leaving, grieving (ibid.).[29]

Musically, this is achieved by the contrast between Dolly's fast-moving, rather brittle music as she chatters, and then being interrupted by resounding orchestral chords as the 'freeze' occurs. By freezing the action at the point where Alec places his hand on Laura's shoulder, the focus, like that in the film, is completely on her – in a sense it works both as a visual close-up as well as a musical one as the audience has time to visually register this gesture as Laura (supported by the orchestra), musically describes her reaction to it. As soon as the action restarts, the musical texture and tempo change: this occurs several times – Laura's music has a series of pulsating chords under her vocal line, and the two distinct musical discourses gradually become blurred as their text begins to overlap with Dolly's talk interweaving with Laura's inner monologue. The scene ends with the sound of a train whistle and Laura moving out on to the platform, contemplating suicide, but then shifts to her home:

---

28   Day observes of the film: "The gesture which had seemed too casual earlier now says everything about the pain of saying goodbye – without being able to actually say it. Behind the façade the defenses crumble quietly" (2005: 106).

29   Ironically, there is a reverse influence of the film *Brief Encounter* in the BBC TV 1991 version of *Tonight at 8.30* (with Joan Collins in the main roles). Just as in the film, Alec places his hand on Laura's shoulder as he leaves the buffet. Inevitably, iconic images from the film will influence the way the play is staged.

Fred, Fred I meant to do it. I really meant to do it. I stood there trembling right on the edge. I couldn't do it. Then just in time I stepped back. Was it you that stopped me? You and the children? No it wasn't. I had no thoughts at all for you, for them, for him. Just the overwhelming desire not to be unhappy any more. (*Laura and Fred are both very still. Laura stares into space and Fred watches her closely*). (Ibid.: 90)

Finally Fred rouses her from her 'dream'. The final moments have Alec back at Eden Lock with the sound of his distant voice in duet with her.[30] These last moments in the opera do not have the same level of narration by Laura as in the film, but it is here where the orchestra takes over her role as narrator and the emotion is expressed through the orchestral music. A major change is having the voice of Alec as well as the other two in these final moments in the opera. Laura sings: "I want to be remembered always, to the end of my days" (ibid.: 91) with Alec echoing "always". The film ended with Fred's comment to her: "*with a catch in his voice*": "Thank you for coming back to me" (Coward 1984: 80). The final moment of the opera has Laura alone repeating: "I want to be remembered to the end of my days", as the music fades.

The critical reaction to the opera was muted, though somewhat more positive than in the case of *Streetcar*. Kramer suggests of American operas that, unlike movies,

> the operas are expected to do justice to the works they adapt. No less, but no more [...] [they are] supposed to give something familiar and well loved a fitting home in a new medium. Their success tends to be judged by severe standards [...]. Opera seems to invite [...] severity, perhaps because of its own axiomatic status as high art burdens it with exalted expectations. Even more than the movies, opera tends to provoke the judgment that the book is better. (2007a: 68)

This film is much less of an iconic source than most of the works Kramer alludes to. The opera certainly does not sound like a play with incidental music as was the complaint about the operatic version of *Streetcar*. Previn's knowledge of film and skill as a film composer is apparent here as he is able to create a varied sound world with a wide palette of orchestral colours that suggest a film-music-like quality, but the music has a larger sense of structure that gives

---

30   There is the final return of a prominent musical theme that occurs throughout the opera and which is strongly reminiscent of the melody "Make our Garden grow" from Bernstein's *Candide* – whether an intentional allusion or not is unclear.

a musical coherence to the events. There are points where it blooms into large romantic moments and the vocal writing is grateful, although the role of Laura is somewhat over-written and the singer is forced into the upper register too frequently, adding a somewhat strident quality to the performance which moves it away from the distinctive understated atmosphere of the film. Unlike his earlier opera, Previn's *Brief Encounter* has not gone on to further productions since its premiere.

6   Play/Film to Musical

In 2008, a year before Previn's opera was premiered, another version of this material found its way to the stage. This was an exuberant, highly-successful inter-medial realization of Lean's film by the Kneehigh Theatre Company.[31] Julie Sanders notes that "it is usually at the very point of infidelity that the most creative acts of adaptation and appropriation take place", and on one level this version plays very fast and loose with its source (2006: 20). However, director Emma Rice expressed the desire for "really honouring cinema and really honouring theatre" in the production, justifying the use of the cinema screen, the stagy front cloths as well as the film clips that characterize the production (Radosavljevic 2010: 93).[32] The production exploited the inherited cultural memory of the film and "deftly managed the performance of cliché by respecting [the] audience's shared experience and transcending it through broad but passionate performances and metaphoric, easily-identifiable stage images", displaying a "compassionate humanity that resonated with the audience" (Contini 2009: 131f.). As Claudia Georgi notes, the adaptation "creatively engages with the Coward play and the Lean film; [and] while recalling the historical context in which both texts originated, it creates its own interpretation of the material [...] it freely adapts the historical context of the 1940s, drawing upon both texts as sources of inspiration" (2013: 67).

The production retains some scenes from *Still Life* that are omitted in Lean's film – mainly comic incidents that concern the secondary characters Myrtle, Mildred, Albert and Stanley – but also crucially Laura's memory of childhood

---

31   The production was first staged at the Birmingham Repertory Theatre and the West Yorkshire Playhouse, Leeds, in 2007, and subsequently at the Haymarket Cinema in London in 2008 where the film had its London premiere. It has subsequently been seen in the USA and Australia.

32   Greg Giesekam argues that the use of film in this way lays "bare the making of the performance" and thus lifting the "normal cloak of invisibility that is cast over the [screen] in cinemas and on television" (2007: 250).

ocean swims with her sister which function in the play as a symbol of her desire to escape her humdrum life.[33] In the Kneehigh production, projections
occur with Laura's face superimposed, culminating in scenes of her swimming
in the ocean.[34] The production references the historical context of the film but
omits several of the additional scenes from the film. The circularity of the film's
structure is also avoided, but instead the production has repeated exchanges
between Laura and Fred where he seems to wake her from her day dreams with
the comment: "You've been a long way, haven't you? Thank you for coming
back to me". This shifts the focus towards the idea of possible marital content-
ment rather than the pain and loss experienced by Laura and Alec, while the
representation of their actual affair takes the form of an analepsis, mirroring
the flashbacks in the film (cf. Georgi 2013: 69).

The production is a fascinating blend of different kinds of music: one might
regard it as a musical. It also includes re-enacted film clips with actors in period costumes, recreating in black and white iconic moments from the film,
building upon the comic interludes in play and film that counterpoint the intensity of the drama of the unfolding relationship between Laura and Alec.
The front cloth has openings through which the actors can pass, as if entering
the world of the film, where they suddenly appear in pre-recorded film clips.
Examples include Fred calling for Laura who walks 'into' the film to join Fred
in the film, rather than in 'reality' on stage. The famous sequence alluded to
several times above, where Alec catches his train after the intense scene with
Laura in the buffet, creates a similar effect with Alec seeming to 'catch' the film
of an arriving train through the opening partitions of the screen. We then see a
pre-recorded black-and-white image of Alec as the 'live' colour image of Laura
on stage waves at him. This is a playful blurring of the audience's perception of
what is 'real' and what is fantasy.

The production also investigates the relationship between the stage and
film in the self-reflexive use of film where the actors playing Laura and Alec
take their seats with the audience at the start of the performance as the credits are projected onto the stage screen announcing: "Kneehigh Theatre presents Noel Coward's *Brief Encounter*", thus blurring the boundaries between
the characters in the play and the audience, both watching the performance

---

33   This is reflected in the opera in Laura's aria near the end of Act One where she sings of
      her childhood memories. There are strong musical and thematic echoes here of Blanche's
      aria at the end of *Streetcar*; both arias deal with the idea of escape.

34   Georgi notes that these "childhood memories and longings are not only a means of im-
      plicit characterization, but also serve to allow for occasional glimpses of Laura's state of
      mind which are otherwise denied to the audience" (2013: 69).

about to unfold.[35] This fiction is maintained throughout as actors perform the roles of ushers, programme and sweet sellers, as well as the projection of typical cinema advertisements of the time with the audience being encouraged to sing along to popular songs. These staging devices emphasise the constructed nature of the performance, an effect underlined by having actors play multiple roles as actors, musicians, dancers and stagehands, often with only minimal change in costume, continually underlining the theatricality of the performance and its pervasive self-referentiality.

A parodied and distorted version of a brief section of the Rachmaninoff is used as a leitmotif throughout the performance, sometimes seemingly 'played' on an upright stage piano. However, there are several musical interludes which incorporate Coward's original songs as well as new settings of some of his poems. As well, songs are constructed from individual lines from the film, such as "Like a Romantic Schoolgirl", which comes from Laura's interior monologue on the train after her first kiss with Alec (in this production it occurs during their lunch at the Royal Hotel), and "This Misery Can't Last", which again is derived from Laura's train monologue after her final meeting with Alec. There are two other songs not by Coward – one, "Oh, You Beautiful Doll", from the film adaptation of his review, *Cavalcade* of 1931, and "Goodbye, Dolly Gray", the song made popular during the Boer War, and here sung by soldiers preparing for an air raid. The effect of the music is complex; the use of popular songs of the period of the film express the emotions that people at that time found difficult to express in ordinary life, but at the same time the performative aspect of the production is continually highlighted, drawing attention to the fact that this is a contemporary interpretation of a bygone era.

This production, as well as the opera, both coincidentally appearing almost at the same time, are adaptations of an adaptation itself – part of a process which might be called 'palimpsestuous'. Linda Hutcheon describes such secondary adaptations as "multilaminated"; they are "directly and openly connected to recognizable other works, and that connection is part of their formal identity, but also of what we might call their hermeneutic identity" (2006: 21). Coward's original play underlies these later works, but has undergone a range of transformations into film, opera, and musical. The opera and the musical engage with their forerunners on musical terms, particularly so, of course, in the opera where the intense music recalls the effect, if not the idiom, of the

---

35   Georgi notes that the production "plays with the mediality of stage and screen, sometimes emphasizing their differences, sometimes attempting a convergence. Yet, as smooth as the transitions may be at times, they never permit the audience to confuse the live and mediatized performers" (2013: 7of.).

famous music of the film – and this is affectionately parodied in the musical. The music of the opera expands and explores the emotional content of the play and film, in effect 'novelising' it through the omniscient narration of Laura and the orchestral narrator, while the musical uses a variety of musical and filmic styles to explore the historical contexts out of which the original play and then the film emerged, recreating the film experience of the audiences of the 1940s but with a pervasive element of contemporary self-referentiality.

At play in all these adaptations is memory – the film looks back fondly to the pre-war years of the play; the film's understated drama is underscored by the emotional impact of its music, while the later two adaptations evoke the memory of the film in contemporary terms. The Kneehigh production uses a mélange of musical idioms to provoke the audience's memory of the film, within both a contemporary and period musical sound world. The opera uses a contemporary operatic idiom, sometimes tinged with echoes of the film music of the period of the film, to remind the audience of the suppressed passions of the film and its music, but refracted through the imagination of a composer with an intimate knowledge of a wide range of music, both classical and popular. What might appear a rather slight play, has provoked three fascinating adaptations which investigate the relationship between music and the moving image.

References

Ashley, Tim (2011 online). *Brief Encounter*. Review. *The Guardian* (12 May). http://www.theguardian.com/music/2011/may/12/andre-previn-brief-encounter-classical. [November 26, 2015].

Caird, John (2011). "The Hall of Time". *Brief Encounter*. CD Liner Notes. DGG 00289 477 9351.

Citron, Marcia J. (2000). *Opera on Screen*. New Haven, CT: Yale Univ. Press.

Citron, Marcia J. (2010). *When Opera Meets Film*. Cambridge: CUP.

Conrad, Peter (1977). *Romantic Opera and Literary Form*. Berkeley, CA: Univ. of California Press.

Conrad, Peter (1996). *A Song of Love and Death: The Meaning of Opera*. New York, NY: Poseidon Press.

Contini, George (2009). "Noel Coward's *Brief Encounter*, and *Gone with the Wind*". Review. *Theatre Journal* 61/1 (March): 131–135.

Cormack, Mike (2006). "The Pleasures of Ambiguity: Using Classical Music in Film". Phil Powrie, Robynn Stillwell, eds. *Changing Tunes: The Use of Pre-existing Music in Film*. Aldershot: Ashgate. 19–30.

Coward, Noel (1984). *Brief Encounter: The Screenplay*. London: Lorrimer.

Day, Barry (2005). *Coward on Film: The Cinema of Noel Coward*. Lanham: The Scarecrow Press.

Döhl, Frédéric (2013). "*Brief Encounter:* Zu David Leans Film (1945) und André Previns Oper (2009)". *Archiv für Musikwissenschaft* 70/4: 311–332.

Döhl, Frédéric (2016). "About the Task of Adapting a Movie Classic for the Opera Stage: On André Previn's *A Streetcar Named Desire* (1998) and *Brief Encounter* (2009)". Frédéric Döhl, Gregor Herzfeld, eds. *In Search for the "Great American Opera": Tendenzen des amerikanischen Musiktheaters*. Münster: Waxmann. [Forthcoming].

Fleishman, Avron (1992). *Narrated Films: Storytelling Situations in Cinema History*. Baltimore, MD: The Johns Hopkins Univ. Press.

Franklin, Peter (1994). "Movies as Opera (Behind the Great Divide)". Jeremy Tambling, ed. *A Night at the Opera: Media Representations of Opera*. London: John Libbey. 71–112.

Franklin, Peter (2011). *Seeing Through Music: Gender and Modernism in Classic Hollywood Film Scores*. Oxford: OUP.

Fryer, Paul, ed. (2005). *Opera in the Media Age: Essays on Art, Technology and Popular Culture*. Jefferson, NC: McFarland.

Georgi, Claudia (2013). "Kneehigh Theatre's *Brief Encounter*: 'Live on Stage – Not the Film'". *The Adaptation of History*. Lawrence Raw, Defne Ersin Tutan, eds. Jefferson, NC: McFarland. 66–78.

Giesekam, Greg (2007). *Staging the Screen: The Use of Film and Video in Theatre*. Basingstoke /New York, NY: Palgrave Macmillan.

Gilliam, Bryan (1992). "Strauss's *Intermezzo:* Innovation and Tradition". Bryan Gilliam, ed. *Richard Strauss: New Perspectives on the Composer and his Work*. Durham, NC: Duke Univ. Press. 259–283.

Gray, Frances (1987). *Noel Coward*. Basingstoke: Macmillan.

Halliwell, Michael (1999). "Narrative Elements in Opera". Walter Bernhart, Steven Paul Scher, Werner Wolf, eds. *Word and Music Studies: Defining the Field*. Word and Music Studies 1. Amsterdam/Atlanta, GA: Rodopi. 135–153.

Halliwell, Michael (2012). "Intrusive Narrators: The Representation of Narration and Narrators in the Operatic Adaptations of *The Great Gatsby* and *Sophie's Choice*". *Forum of Modern Language Studies* 48/2: 222–235.

Hansen, David T. (1996). "Finding One's Way Home: Notes on the Texture of Moral Experience". *Studies in Philosophy and Education* 15: 221–233.

Hutcheon, Linda (2006). *A Theory of Adaptation*. New York, NY /London: Routledge.

Hutcheon, Linda, Michael Hutcheon (2014). "The Inward Turn: American Opera Revisits America's Past". *Canadian Review of American Studies* 44/2 (Summer): 178–193.

Joe, Jeongwon (2013). *Opera as Soundtrack*. Basingstoke: Ashgate.

Joe, Jeongwon, Theresa Rose, eds. (2002). *Between Opera and Cinema*. London: Routledge.

Kramer, Lawrence (2002). *Musical Meaning: Towards a Critical History*. Berkeley, CA: Univ. of California Press.

Kramer, Lawrence (2007a). "The Great American Opera: *Klinghoffer*, *Streetcar*, and the Exception". *The Opera Quarterly* 23/1 (Winter): 66–80.

Kramer, Lawrence (2007b). *Why Classical Music Still Matters*. Berkeley, CA: Univ. of California Press.

Lindenberger, Herbert (1984). *Opera: The Extravagant Art*. Ithaca, NY/London: Cornell Univ. Press.

Morley, Sheridan (1994). "Introduction". *Noel Coward Plays: Three*. London: Methuen Drama. vii–xv.

Newark, Cormac (2011). *Opera in the Novel from Balzac to Proust*. Cambridge: CUP.

Paxman, Jeremy (1999). *The English: A Portrait of a People*. Harmondsworth: Penguin.

Phillips, Gene D. (2006). *Beyond the Epic: The Life & Films of David Lean*. Lexington, KY: The Univ. of Kentucky Press.

Pinter, Harold (2008 online). "The Echoing Silence". *The Guardian* (December 31). http://www.theguardian.com/culture/2008/dec/31/harold-pinter-early-essay-writing. [March 23, 2015].

Previn, André (2011). *Brief Encounter*. CD Libretto. DGG 00289 477 9351.

Radosavljevic, Duška (2010). "Emma Rice in Interview with Duška Radosavljevic". *Journal of Adaptation in Film and Performance* 3/1: 89–98.

Sanders, Julie (2006). *Adaptation and Appropriation*. London /New York, NY: Routledge.

Schroeder, David (2002). *Cinema's Illusions, Opera's Allure: The Operatic Impulse in Film*. New York, NY: Continuum.

Singer, Barry (2009). "Encountering Previn". *Opera News* 73/10 (April): 28f.

Stevens, Kyle (2015). "Toward a Theory of Voice-Over through *Brief Encounter*". *World Picture* 10 (Spring): 1–7.

Strauss, Richard (1974). *A Working Friendship: The Correspondence between Richard Strauss and Hugo von Hofmannsthal*. Trans. Hanns Hammelmann, Ewald Osers. New York, NY: Vienna House.

Swed, Mark (2009 online). *Brief Encounter*. Review. *Los Angeles Times*. http://latimesblogs.latimes.com/culturemonster/2009/05/andr%C3%A9-previns-brief-encounter-premieres-in-houston.html. [November 21, 2015].

Taylor, John Russell (1984). "Introduction". *Brief Encounter: The Screenplay*. London: Lorrimer. 4–6.

Weiner, Mark (2002). "Why Does Hollywood Like Opera?". Joe/Rose, eds. 75–92.

CHAPTER 17

On the Intertextual Docks, or, Whatever Happened to Shanghai Lil?

David Francis Urrows

Abstract

"Say, who the heck is Shanghai Lil?" asks one platinum-haired lady of the night in Warner Brothers's 1933 musical film, *Footlight Parade*. Well may she, and also we, ask that question then and today. Even when Lil appears, it is not at all clear just who she is. She is an elusive yet ever-present character, almost a narrative trope, one that crystallizes the essence of the attraction and repulsion of treaty-port era Shanghai (1843–1943) and beyond to the present day. This can be seen from such films as Josef von Sternberg's *Shanghai Express* (1932, where the named character first appears) and *The Shanghai Gesture* (1941), and perhaps all the way to Ang Lee's *Lust, Caution* (2007). Lil is a shape-shifter – ambiguities of ethnicity, persona, and even gender pursue her – and an icon of recontextualization made for intertextual studies. She always appears in a dramatic, and usually musical frame, and here I look at and consider three of her numerous incarnations which involve the narrative intersections of words, music, and the moving image: Dao Hua in Reinhold Glière's socialist-realistic ballet, *Kransnii mak* (*The Red Poppy*, 1927), especially in the abridged version filmed for Czechoslovak television in 1955; Lil in *Footlight Parade*; and her completely rectified persona, Fang Hai-zhen, in the 1964/1973 Chinese 'revolutionary Peking opera', *On the Docks* (*Haigang*).

•••

1 Shanghai Lil: Pretexts

"Say, who the heck is Shanghai Lil?" asks one platinum-haired lady of the night in Warner Brothers's 1933 musical film, *Footlight Parade*. Well may she, and also we, ask that question then and today. My particular interest in her here is not so much with identity, as it is with identification. Out of a repertoire of representations, I have chosen three incarnations of Lil which involve the narrative intersections of words, music, and the moving image: a Soviet ballet, an

American musical film, and a 'revolutionary Peking opera'. While geopolitics for most of the second half of the twentieth century was balanced between the US and the USSR, since 1990 it has shifted to a Sino-US tug of war, and so this brief excursion into Lil's attractive *demi-monde* has resonances on larger levels of global spheres of influence.

The archetypes of Shanghai Lil might be traced back beyond biblical and Graeco-Roman myths of lovely if doubtful sirens, to what Joseph Campbell called "The Meeting with the Goddess". In this encounter, "the ultimate adventure [...] is commonly represented as a mystical marriage of the triumphant soul-hero with the Queen Goddess of the World. This is the crisis at the nadir, the zenith, or at the uttermost edge of the earth" (1949/1968: 109).[1] So it is no surprise to find that, in the far more recent tradition I am discussing, this remote place sometimes turns out to be – Shanghai. More prosaically, Lil is probably a figure made up out of collective memories of the first twenty-five years (1843–1868) of Shanghai's wild and wooly existence as an international settlement, where it was commonplace for male employees of Western *hongs* (corporations) to cohabit with Chinese women. As the city grew, however, so too did public indignation with this free and easy lifestyle, especially in the United Kingdom. When Sir Edmund Hornby (1825–1896) was sent out from London in 1865 to become Chief Judge of the British Supreme Court in Shanghai, he was summoned by Lord Shaftesbury[2]

> to discuss no less a subject than the means to put a stop to the practice of English clerks in the mercantile houses in China keeping Chinese mistresses [...] as I did not see how I could in my judicial capacity prevent the habit, I simply promised to set a good example in not keeping one myself, which I am afraid was looked on as a sign of levity.
>
> HORNBY 1929/1999: 187

When the practice was eventually terminated by "a decree that no one keeping a girl should be allowed to live in the junior hong [staff quarters], the young men, rather than be kicked out of their really luxurious homes [...] gave up their mistresses, with the natural result that they visited the foreign [i.e. Western] women" (ibid.: 188). Thus Shanghai Lil is partly a creation of memory and nostalgia, a shape-shifter, marked by a double existence. Ambiguities,

---

1   The 'goddess' morphs quickly into the 'temptress' in Campbell's exegesis.
2   Anthony Ashley-Cooper, 7th Lord Shaftesbury (1801–1885). A prominent reformer, his memorial in the center of Piccadilly Circus is crowned with the statue of the archer Anteros (often – ironically for this discussion – mistaken for Eros).

of ethnicity, persona, and even gender, surround her, reflecting I think a conflation of memories of a (partial) shift in the 1870s from local to expatriate relationships.

In putting Shanghai Lils technically off-limits, it appears that their stock simply went up. Summary rule-making of this kind had little effect on the growing multi-valent levels of social interaction between Chinese and non-Chinese in the Treaty Ports. Marriages (of greater or lesser validity) were nonetheless contracted. Some accounts even survive from the last quarter of the nineteenth century giving startling details of such relationships and their ups and downs. Among these the various recollections of Charles Halcombe (1866–1933) who went to China and served with the Imperial Maritime Customs (between 1887 and 1893[3]), offer us a window on other aspects of the formation of the Lil mystique. Halcombe frankly detailed two different relationships with Chinese women, with very different outcomes. While extrapolation can be misleading, Halcombe never rose very high in the I.M.C., and may have been a better writer than a bureaucrat. His unexceptional and brief record prior to his resignation points, then, to his typicality rather than the opposite.

The first of Halcombe's liaisons involved a young Soochow (Suzhou) lady who he names as Wang Sêou Jâe (perhaps, *Wang xiaojie*, 'Miss Wang', deliberately vague to preserve her anonymity). Having come into a large sum of money upon the death of her mother (15,000 dollars Mex), this money was held in trust for her by an aunt, whom Halcombe reasoned was interested in the money herself. Miss Wang disappeared shortly thereafter and Halcombe's fears were realized. He could get no help from the Settlement police, and so he hired a former police detective, dressed himself in Chinese clothes, and together they combed the dives and blood alleys of Shanghai searching for her, in vain. Eventually he received a letter from her, telling him that she had been kidnapped and taken in a boat to Soochow. Halcombe followed, but failed to find her, and could only lament that "I left behind me, caged within those somber time-worn battlements [...] one of the best and fairest friends of my roving life in the Far East" (1896: 41).

In late 1888, Halcombe was sent by the I.M.C. to Chefoo (today's Yantai), and here he befriended a cultivated comprador, Liang Ah Tou, who spoke 'pucka English', drank champagne, and smoked Manila cigars. The avuncular Mr. Liang took Halcombe into his home where, at first unbeknownst to Halcombe, his daughter observed the young Englishman surreptitiously from

---

3 He also worked briefly for the *North China Daily News* in 1887, and later became the Chefoo correspondent for the *Shanghai Mercury*. See Bickers (online 2015), who believes Halcombe's tales to be more fictionalized than I do.

behind an embroidered screen. During one of the anti-foreign riots of early 1889, Halcombe was awoken in his house in the middle of the night by foot-steps along the passage to his room. Opening the door,

> I was never more surprised in my life. I was quite mute with astonish-ment, for in walked a decidedly pretty young lady, accompanied by her *amah*, or female attendant [...] Hurriedly opening a bundle the *amah* car-ried, they brought out a complete outfit of Chinese man's clothing, and while the young lady motioned me to at once dress myself in them, the attendant, who could speak a little 'pidgin' English, told me that her mis-tress had come to save my life. There were two or three thousand murder-ous rebels [...] close at hand. (1896: 92)[4]

Halcombe made his escape with the pair and wound up in Liang's house, where he discovered that his heroine was indeed none other than Liang's daughter, "who had trampled upon the rigorous customs of her people, and at the risk of losing her life had saved mine" (1900: 745).[5] Liang was not home; he had gone on a business trip of several days to – Shanghai! Shortly after his return, Liang died, "[b]ut I married his good and faithful daughter, and blessing us, he died peacefully and contentedly, knowing that [...] his little Ah Ghan was safe and happy in the care of one whom he had learned to trust and honour with his friendship" (1900: 94).[6]

After March 1893, when Halcombe left the I.M.C., they lived for a year in Hong Kong where they fairly scandalized the British colonial population. Here Halcombe began to write his successful books including the Taiping Rebellion-themed *The Chung Wang's Daughter* (1894), the autobiographical sketches of *The Mystic Flowery Land* (1896), and the semi-fictional pro-revolution novel, *Children of Far Cathay* (1906). (Indeed, he seems to have been an early exponent of the 'Anglo-Chinese romance', a literary sub-genre that led in time to what is today known in general as 'expat fiction', exemplified by Richard Mason's *The World of Suzie Wong* [1957], among many others.) In 1894, and perhaps for their own safety, they moved back to England where they lived in Kent at Herne Bay

---

4   Halcombe noted that the story had first appeared "in a different form, and under the title of 'Tsing Fong's Screen'" in the newspaper *The Globe* (London), 22 January 1895 (1896: 90).

5   Halcombe's third version (see 1900) presents the story differently in terms of its details from the 1896 book, but is more extensive and in some senses more journalistic. He also reveals here that Liang had been allied with the pseudo-Christian Taiping rebels during the great civil war in China between 1851 and 1864.

6   Ah Ghan (who acquired the English name, Nina) died most symbolically in 1949, in Folkestone.

FIGURE 17.1   The Mother of all Lils? Ah Ghan and Charles Halcombe, ca. 1895 (Halcombe: 1896)

and Dover, and where Halcombe seems to have given up his literary career and held minor, local political offices.

The story of Charles and Ah Ghan Halcombe (see Figure 17.1) explodes a number of myths as well, two of which can be mentioned here. First, the idea that there were no 'proper' (legally recognized) marriages between Chinese and non-Chinese in China prior to the establishment of the Republic of China in 1912 is simply not true. Halcombe was married, at Liang's insistence, "in the Chinese custom and afterwards in the English" (1900: 745). The other is that Edmund Hornby was quite right to disparage the idea that such relationships as Halcombe had could be extirpated from life in the Treaty Ports by some kind of executive fiat. Halcombe was a token of a type, and his racy real-life stories impinge very closely on the dates of the first nostalgic and sentimentalized stirrings of the Shanghai Lil trope and its connections to a violent underworld and the maritime settings of these later tales, all characterized by various themes of drugs, sex, human trafficking, corruption, political crisis, and imperialistic adventure.

2   Shanghai Lil: Texts

'Lil' as a named figure was introduced in the 1932 film hit, *Shanghai Express*, directed by Josef von Sternberg. Here Marlene Dietrich played 'Shanghai Lily', described as "a notorious coaster", blithely glossed as "a woman who lives by her wits along the China coast" (Sternberg 1973: 64).[7] Interestingly, she is accompanied through the film by a *doppelgänger* named Hui Fei, played appropriately enough by Anna May Wong, the outstanding Chinese-American actress of the period and an international celebrity of the day. Thus Lil's ethnic ambiguity is bifurcated between two co-dependent personae in this film. They share the same train compartment for reasons that extend way beyond their profession as 'coasters'. Meeting her old flame, played by Clive Brook, Dietrich mentions that she has changed her name since they last met. "Married?" inquires Brook. And she replies with a shake of her head and the classic line, "No. It took more than one man to change my name to Shanghai Lily." (ibid.: 69) The gramophone which the two women use throughout the film screams late-1920s jazz (including a hepped-up version of Liszt's *Liebestraum* No. 3), an early diegetic use of popular music in film, and one associating Lil with the Jazz Age.

A year later, Warner Brothers brought Shanghai Lil back to the silver screen in a kinder, gentler, more fantastical incarnation in the musical film, *Footlight Parade*; and in 1941, Sternberg brought her back yet again in his film version of John Colton's 1926 play, *The Shanghai Gesture*, where the character is split, bipolar-wise, into a mother (Mother Gin Sling[8]) and a daughter (portentously named 'Poppy'; they are played by the scenery-chewing duet of Una Munson and Gene Tierney). But for the moment I want to turn back to her first important

---

7   In the film, it emerges that her real name is, appositely, Magdalen.
8   For Colton's original Mother God Damn.

musical appearance, which I trace to about five years prior to *Shanghai Express*. This is Dao Hua in Reinhold Glière's groundbreaking socialist-realistic ballet, *Kransnii mak* (*The Red Poppy*, 1927). *The Red Poppy* was proposed to Glière in 1926, composed and first produced in 1927. The plot, developed in a libretto by Mikhail Kurilko, revolves around a politicized love triangle consisting of: Dao Hua, dancer, opium addict and part-time prostitute, who is politically awaked by the events of the story; her 'manager'[9] Li Chanfu, a shady character who runs a restaurant-dancehall-brothel[10] and who is involved with imperialist baddies in drug dealing and arms running; and the captain of a Soviet ship, conveniently docked in Shanghai. Seeing the misery of the coolies toiling on the docks, the captain orders his sailors to help them out in the spirit of prole-tarian internationalism. For this Dao Hua gives him a red poppy, supposedly a symbol of freedom and socialist struggle. The second act is pure spectacle: set in an opium den, Dao Hua hallucinates all kinds of exotica, but the scenes fail to advance the storyline one step. Eventually in Act III, Li and his henchmen plot to kill the captain, but Dao Hua who is now politically awakened sacrifices her own life to save him, passing on her red poppy to a child who will continue the people's struggle.

The background to the whole scenario was probably the 'May 30th Incident' of 1925, in which eight anti-Japanese protestors were killed in Shanghai by Brit-ish concession police. The Incident has been called "the spark which touched off the powder keg of Communist revolution and insured its ultimate success" (Lyall 1979: 45). Then there was the looming expulsion of the Soviet *Comint-ern* advisors from China in April 1927 (the very same year during which Glière [1874–1956] completed the score) by Chiang Kaishek and the *Guomindang* (Kuomintang, KMT) government. The Soviets in turn cast Chiang as an agent of American imperialism, even though the United States had little directly to do with the extraterritorial government of Shanghai or the other China Treaty Ports, although the US did provide arms for Chiang. With its modernist revo-lutionary theme, a ballet about a contemporary political topic was a great in-novation at the time, and it was widely, though not universally, praised after its premiere at the Bolshoi on 14 June 1927. Within 18 months, it had over 100 performances. For the Leningrad production of 1929, ten new numbers were

---

9   In the original libretto he is even called her "fiancé", perhaps prudishly to explain away
      why he obviously has sexual as well as other control over her. Dao Hua is similarly called
      an "actress" (Glière 1933).

10   Identified in the 1955 Czechoslovak film-ballet version (to be discussed below) as the
      'Fairy Palace Dance Hall'.

added by Glière.[11] By 1949, political shifts dictated that the storyline had to change. A Soviet captain was no longer a suitable love interest for a patriotic *communist* Chinese woman, and so a new character, Ma Lizhen, was introduced to give her an alternative, revolutionary, and above all, Chinese lover.[12]

Here we have all the elements of the Shanghai Lil archetype: the beautiful and strong if often helpless temptress at the end of the earth; ethnic confusions and the touchy topic of miscegenation; the life-and-death struggle of good and evil, all played out against a backdrop of the bars, opium dens, and docks of a mythical Shanghai (yet recalling Charles Halcombe's very real experiences in Shanghai, Soochow, and Cheefoo). Musically, the protagonists are represented in stock ways: the KMT and foreign oppressors are only generally treated, with several works approximating contemporary jazz such as the lumbering, decadent Charleston at the start of Act III, with its 'grotesque' orchestration (featuring trombone glissandi).[13] Dao Hua's internal growth and her connection to the people are depicted in two leitmotifs: "The music of one is joyous, delicate, and graceful. It clearly has the national [folk] color [...]. The other leitmotif is a songlike, romantically agitated tune à la Chaikovskii".[14] The Soviet captain and his men have their moment in the popular "Russian Sailor's Dance" (*recte*: 'Dance of the *Soviet* Sailors' [my emphasis]; Glière, 1933: 64), the only part of the ballet commonly heard outside Russia; and there is a large quantity of post-Romantic *chinoiserie* in the score for good measure.[15]

---

11   Including the marvelously named bit of soft-shoe, 'Girls: American Dance' (phonetically spelled Гёрлс).

12   In 1957, the official title was altered to *The Red Flower*, to avoid associations with opium. In the 1955 Czechoslovak television version (still called *The Red Poppy*) most of Act II was recast as a dream sequence, and opium is never referenced.

13   "Professor Thereses regards the American Charleston as a dance full of eccentric steps which he compares to the Shimmy which he condemned in 1920. Then the dancers wriggled with their shoulders: now they wriggle with their legs. The Charleston is very easy to learn, and as in the Shimmy the young men think they should exaggerate and hop about a little bit, like small ponies when they trot". ("Charleston and Other Dances" 1926).

14   "Музыка одного из них жизнерадостна, полна изящества и грации. В нем отчетливо выявлен национальный колорит [...]. Другой лейтмотив представляет собою напевную, романтически взволнованную мелодию в духе лирических тем Чайковского [...]". (Glière, 1966: 146f.) My thanks to Ivan Delazari for his assistance with translation here. Born in Kiev, Glière was baptized Reinhold Ernest Glier. His father was a German wind instrument maker from Klingelthal in Saxony; he had no Belgian ancestry, as is often claimed.

15   The so-called 'complete' recording (see Glière 1927/1994) on Naxos is in no sense complete and contains only about 60% of the original ballet and 1929 additions. Many movements are cut, repeats are taken only randomly and without logic, and the order does not

While we cannot see the ballet in its 1927, 1929, or 1949 productions, for my intertextual reading the 1954 Slovak National Theater production (filmed in an abridged form in Bratislava in 1955 for Czechoslovak television) has turned out to be even more informative, especially given its relationship to the third and last of the examples I will consider.[16] Here, using the 1949 libretto, the target of animosity in the film-ballet shifted: no longer is the central contrast descriptive of "a half-feudal China enslaved by colonial imperialists vs. the young Soviet Russia".[17] By 1954 it morphed into a specifically-targeted vehicle of anti-*American* sentiment in the aftermath of the Korean War of 1950–1953. The Expressionist 'no-dance' opening of the ballet features the coolies stumbling down the 'high plank', unloading a ship in the most arduous manner possible, some with a bamboo 'carry pole'. Overseen by police and whip-cracking supervisors, every huge wooden crate is conspicuously marked "Made in the U.S.A.". Later, when one of these boxes falls and empties its contents onto the quay, it is found to contain rifles destined for the KMT 'bandits'.

Dao Hua, queen and slave, pure goodness and drug-addled prostitute, dominates the entire film-ballet (as a prima ballerina, here the stunning Jarmila Mansingrová, should). Having met the Soviet captain (in uniform), and seen to it that he's friendly with her sweetheart, Ma Lizhen (dressed in green), she is torn between the two of them; and then she has the bad luck to catch the eye of the 'Harbormaster' (probably meant to be the head of the Shanghai office of the I.M.C., presented here as an American although this is historical nonsense). Her mixture of mythical and political message is best viewed in the scene in Act I in which she struggles with her controller, Li Chanfu, who wants her to serve the American. Dressed in red and black they dance out a cosmic battle between socialism and capitalism, in full view of the oppressed coolies, Soviet seamen, and wicked imperialists, all 'on the docks', while fragments of *The Internationale* (interwoven into the otherwise romantic leitmotifs of Dao Hua's music) hint at ultimate victory, though for the moment Li is triumphant in his brutal subjugation of Dao.

---

follow the 1933 piano score. It probably reflects only the way the ballet was given in an abridged form in Leningrad in the 1980s. The 1955 Czechoslovak television version is cut and reordered to an even greater extent, but not in the same way, and contains sections that the Naxos recording omits.

16   The opening titles in the 1955 film-ballet situate the action in "China, 1925", that is, before the break between the Soviet and KMT governments, and presumably prior to the May 30th Incident.

17   "полуфеодального Китая, порабощенного колонизаторами-империалистами, и Советской России – молодой страны социализма". (Glière 1966: 143).

All the while, the Soviet sailors pay not a moment's attention to what is going on. But it is not so when the American Navy comes to town! Dao Hua may meet a heroine's end – after all, the finale of *The Red Poppy* is specifically an apotheosis – but her followers, perhaps the girl to whom she gave the red poppy in 1925 – are more practically minded, as noted with the 'coasters' of Marlene Dietrich and Anna May Wong. In 1933's *Footlight Parade*, which ends with three spectacular musical *prologues* staged by Busby Berkeley, Lil reappears as the elusive love interest of James Cagney, cast against type as a happy-go-lucky Navy man who is looking high and low for his 'Shanghai Lil'. (The archetype of the quest runs backwards through Halcombe's Suzhou beauty, to Campbell's distant Goddess.) This is, of course, the Shanghai Lil that gets remembered, not least through Harry Warren and Al Dubin's torch song standard, composed for the film.[18] Lil here again appears in her trickster guise.[19] To us today Cagney's desirable Lil is played by Ruby Keeler; but to film audiences in the theater (and diegetic audiences in the film) she is 'Bea Thorn', one of Cagney's secretaries who gets her big break in the prologues which are the topic of the film. Thus the *mise-en-abyme* is much deeper than a short film clip will show, and Keeler is her own *doppelgänger*.[20] The film is in fact one of the most notorious of the pre-Hays Code enforcement productions, openly showing interracial relationships, (married?) couples in bed, endless coy and not-so-coy references to sex, and a degree of racial integration that would not return to American screens

---

18   Warren (1893–1981, born Salvatore Guaragna) appears briefly in the film as the conductor of the orchestra in this sequence. After Irving Berlin he was the most successful popular song writer of his time, and actually had more songs listed on the Hit Parade than Berlin, including *Chattanooga Choo Choo* (1941, with Mack Gordon), the first song ever to go 'gold'.

19   In the previous year's *Shanghai Express*, Dietrich's Lily had all-but submitted to her tormentor, the warlord Chang (Warner Oland), who in a twist was subsequently killed by her alter ego, Anna May Wong's Hui Fei.

20   This vital aspect of the story creates more depth to the complex issue of ethnicity and identity than might appear evident at first. In addition to the fact that in the 1930s actors were usually under contract to studios and had little say in which roles they played, this is a case of understood and inevitable 'impersonation' by a *diegetic* character in the developing narrative of the film, and not one of so-called 'cultural appropriation'. Nor is Keeler's impersonation of an Asian woman a case (so deplored today) of overlooking an available Asian actress, much less is it, for example, equivalent to the case of Anna May Wong, who lost out to Luise Rainer for the role of O-Lan in the 1937 MGM version of *The Good Earth*. That occurred because Paul Muni had been cast in the role of Wang, and the Hays code (properly the Motion Picture Production Code, originally adopted in 1930 but only rigorously enforced after 1934) had banned 'interracial' couples on screen. Shanghai Lil only exists in an environment rife with ambiguities.

until the late 1960s.[21] In a Shanghai dive, a drunken Cagney searches for Lil down the length of a 'long bar'[22] which features Chinese and Western prostitutes, British, French, American, and African-American servicemen, a wealthy Jewish gentleman from 'Palestine', and locals, with the Asian characters mostly played by the diegetic chorus members of the film in yellowface. While today the gatekeepers of cultural capital may frown on these stereotypes, at the time they were cutting edge of frankness and inclusivity.

When Cagney finally catches up with Keeler, it takes only one chorus for her to go from playing hard-to-get in a rather treacly version of pidgin English, to one of the most surprising moments in Cagney's early film career: his bar-top soft-shoe and tap dance number with Keeler (Cagney had started as a child star in vaudeville; he sings the famous Shanghai Lil number himself in the film). The sequence (and the film) ends with Cagney and Keeler both dressed as Marines (a recurrence of military uniforms, as in the Soviet sailors of *The Red Poppy* and the highly-militarized scenario of *Shanghai Express*), marching off to their future. So in the American version nobody dies and, unlike Dao Hua, Lil manages to snag her sailor beau and a happy ending is arranged. But then this is Hollywood, and such things happen there.

For my third representation, we must now move to 1949: Mao Zedong and his Communist Red Army are victorious, Chiang and the KMT flee to Taiwan, prostitution is outlawed, and the third of the Chinese population addicted to opium are given one year to sort themselves out or be shot. Poor Shanghai Lil! Needless to say, she didn't really die in *The Red Poppy*, or marry her handsome doctor in *Shanghai Express*, or stowaway on a troop ship at the end of *Footlight Parade*, or even wind up being shot by her own mother as in *The Shanghai Gesture*. No, it appears she gave up her decadent lifestyle, overcame her addiction, joined the Communist Party, and by the early 1960s she is to be found in the character of Fang Haizhen, Secretary of the Communist Party Branch of the dockers brigade, in the 'model work', *Haigang* (*On the Docks*).[23] The opening

---

21 Even more explosive than the 'Shanghai Lil' segment was the scandalous 'Honeymoon Hotel' sequence, backed up with another Warren and Dubin hit of the same name, and set in a Jersey City hostel patronized by couples who all have the surname, Smith.

22 The pre-1949 American Club in Shanghai was famous for having the world's longest contiguous bar.

23 In the traditions of Beijing opera, Fang is supposed to be a male lead character only played (due to casting exigencies in 1966) by a woman. But in the performative context it is hard to understand this as a case of travesty, and not to see 'him' as 'her'. The female side of Fang's rather androgynous persona was much enhanced by the removal from the script of a strong female character (Mother Han) in the play on which the opera was based. The resulting gender ambiguity may just be the intertextual ghost of the ethnic ambiguity in

of the work is especially telling in its obvious remodeling of the 1955 Czecho-slovak *Red Poppy*: the 'no-dance' opening of the ballet is recast as a 'no-sing' opening of the opera. The docks are now completely mechanized though fully staffed:

> A summer morning, 1963. A dock on the Huangpu River in Shanghai. Red flags flutter gaily on numerous ships. Sunlight shimmers over the fluctuating current. The slogan 'Long Live the General Line for Socialist Construction' hangs from a tall derrick. To the sound of steam whistles, the curtain rises [...] dockers are loading a ship. Cranes are in operation, carts shuttle to and fro. A scene of bustling activity. [Workers] unload sacks of rice from a net onto a platform truck and they hook the crane to another net on the ground [...]. A group of dockers dance across the stage. A worker waves towards an incoming boat. Two workers haul in a cable [...]. Three workers enter, jump over the cable, and perform a cable dance. They strike a pose and loop the cable over a capstan [...].
>
> *On the Docks* 1973: 1

Powerful cranes effortlessly move huge crates around which now proudly pro-claim "Made in the People's Republic of China", and the first words sung in the drama are a humorous "Rest break!" as the dockers scramble for a bottle of soda pop. The grim opening of *The Red Poppy* has not been forgotten; but the point of the opening sequence of *On the Docks* is manifestly to show just how much things have changed since the bad old days of Glière's socialist-realist ballet, specifically, I think, as portrayed in its 1955 film-ballet version.

Fang, the rectified Lil, is like most converts a zealot, and while not boss-ing the men around she clutches her talisman, the 'Communiqué of the Tenth Plenary Session of the Eighth Central Committee of the Chinese Communist Party'. The plot of *On the Docks* revolves around two problems: first, how did fiberglass get mixed into a shipment of seed rice headed for an unnamed Af-rican nation?[24]; and second, what to do about Han Xiaojiang, a docker who thinks he's cut out for better things than being a stevedore. Fang is assisted in this latter problem by kindly old Uncle Ma. But who is this? Surely, he is Dao

---

earlier incarnations of Shanghai Lil. See the section on the work, *"Haigang* [translated here literally as 'The Harbor']", in Liu 2010: 399–404.

24   China had an active policy of supporting African nations in the post-colonial era and the early 1960s in particular, as with the railway built with Chinese funding between Tanzania and Gambia, as well as support to Ghana, and Algeria. In some cases China set up guerilla training movements that overthrew the very governments China supported. See Westad 2012: 334, 352. Today, China is often itself seen as a neo-colonial power in Africa.

Hua's old boyfriend from *The Red Poppy*! Now aged forty years and retired, Ma takes Han in hand and tries to correct his political ideology through a tour of the "class education exhibition hall in the office building of the former American bosses" (*On the Docks* 1973: 32). He rages, practically narrating the opening sequence of the 1955 *Red Poppy*:

> Who snarled and bared their claws like wolves?
> Who worked like horses and toiled like oxen?
> Who set up the steep and narrow 'high plank'?
> Who trudged on endlessly in sheer exhaustion?

He tells Han:

> Compare before liberation and after,
> Look at the carry pole, 'high plank' and tattered clothes,
> The foreman's whip and manacles ...
> Look carefully at every one.
>   Ibid.[25]

Mulling over their former lives, Fang asks Zhao Zhenshan, the chief of the dockers brigade, to recall their pasts as child laborers in the era of *The Red Poppy*:

> Don't you remember when we were both no higher than a shovel when we came to this dock to shovel coal? That was before liberation. Think of all the sufferings we went through. Think of the millions on this globe who are still leading a life worse than beasts of burden [...] we must not forget to be vigilant. We mustn't let the whir of machinery drown out the sound of the class enemy sharpening his sword.
>   Ibid.: 17

Fang is a Lil purged of (most) controlling influences. While all difficulties are resolved in the end with the same type of *Internationale*-accompanied apotheosis that concludes *The Red Poppy* (here, the object of desire is the "Marxism-Leninism-Mao Tsetung thought in our minds"; ibid.: 41), Fang's final words nonetheless hint at the undercurrent of violence that accompanies Shanghai

---

25   First performed in 1966, the action of the opera is set in Shanghai in 1963, the only one of the 'model works' (*yangbanxi*) set in then-contemporary China. For a summary of the history of these works, see Melvin/Cai 2004: 250–255.

Lil everywhere she goes: "The Pacific is far from pacific and Shanghai port is not a harbor of refuge". (Ibid.: 40)

Now, what does all this have to do with intertextuality?

3   Shanghai Lil: Intertexts

In the examples I have adduced here, I have identified Shanghai Lil as a figure who exists, where she exists at all, at an intersection of words, of music, and of the moving image. However, descriptions of these appearances in (mostly) films may have raised more questions than they have answered. How is Ruby Keeler's ingénue hoofer in some sense the 'same' Lil as Dietrich's icy courtesan Lily? Isn't Dao Hua more closely related to the 'faithful slave' trope, more akin to Liu in Puccini's *Turandot*, almost exactly contemporary (1926) with Glière's ballet? What has Fang Haizhen, who after all in the Beijing opera tradition is supposed to be a *male* character, got to do with any of them? The answer to this lies, I think, in certain theoretical approaches in the repertoire of intertextual studies.

The funhouse of intertextuality is a place where a musicologist probably has no business going. But, having bought my ticket I enter at my peril and offer the following analysis. All three Lils I have mentioned are different, radically different in some cases, from each other due to what literary theorist Laurent Jenny called "perturbation". "Intertextuality is [...] a mechanism of perturbation", he wrote:

> Its function is to prevent meaning from becoming lethargic – to avert the triumph of the cliché by a process of transformation. Cultural persistence indeed provides nourishment for all texts, but it also poses a constant threat of stagnation, if the text yields to automatism of association, does not resist the paralyzing pressure of increasingly cumbersome stereotypes. (1982, 60)

Jenny goes on to explain what he thinks is significant in the intertextual process. It is, he maintains,

> [t]o spotlight the clichés (the 'mythologies') which have become ossified in the sentence, to distance ourselves from their banalities, by overdoing them, and finally to free the signifier from the waste that encrusts it in order to launch it *on a new career*. (Ibid.; my emphasis)

Understood in this way, we can expect every Lil to be different: Ruby Keeler's Lil may be specifically a parody of Dietrich's (which Jenny would characterize as 'explicitly intertextual'), or she may be understood at one and the same time as only referring to an 'architextual' model, in the persons of Dietrich's Lily or even Glière and Kurilko's Dao Hua. As Graham Allen has explained it, with reference to both Jenny and Gérard Genette:

> When a work enters into a relation of intertextuality with a genre, what was, in that architextual genre, a code (a generic structure) can become part of the text's or hypertext's message [...]. We move, in such cases from general codes within a genre to a meaningful element of a particular text. (2011: 109)

It is this which I think links and explains the dissimilarities of the different Lils, making it comprehensible (and realistic) to see them as versions, or – to use the word loved by intertextual scholars – *palimpsests* of each other.

An objection might be raised at this point, that the screenwriters of *Shanghai Express* and *Footlight Parade* probably had no clue about *The Red Poppy*. And while Jiang Qing ('Madame Mao', 1914–1991) and her gang probably used of lot of details from the 1955 Czechoslovak film of the ballet in their 'model works' of the 1960s, it's unclear whether they knew either of the Hollywood films. The pre-1949 KMT government had objected to both of them for their problematic portrayal of China and the Chinese. But before she married Mao in 1938, Jiang Qing was a minor film actress – in Shanghai, in fact – and may well have known them. It is also interesting to consider the possibility that Fang's character in *On the Docks*, understood as a version of Shanghai Lil, may actually reflect Jiang Qing's own transformation from Shanghai movie starlet (a Lil-in-Training) in the 1930s to Chinese Communist Party luminary. Considering who knew what, raises unanswerable questions; but I will refer again to Genette and his discussion of what Graham Allen called the "missing or forgotten hypotext" (Allen 2011: 108). Genette pointed out, as Allen puts it, that "sometimes the existence of a hypotext is too uncertain to be the basis for a hypertextual reading" (ibid.) and that "this is the most irritating palimpsest of all, which reduces me to hunches and to questionings" (Genette 1997: 383; qtd. ibid.). In Allen's view, however, "it is precisely in that critical act of interpretation of the text [...] that such hunches and questionings are positively embraced" (ibid.).

Thus I 'positively embrace' my abductive hunches about Shanghai Lil, and find her even in the character of Fang, launched, as Jenny put it, "on a new career". "Each intertextual reference", for Jenny, "is the occasion for an alternative:

either one continues reading, taking it only as a segment like any other, or else one turns to the source text, carrying out a sort of intellectual anamnesis where the intertextual reference appears like a paradigmatic element that has been displaced, deriving from a forgotten structure" (1982: 44). Allen then expands on this by explaining that for Jenny, texts "can, at one of the same time, have their intertextual determinants directed towards a specific text (hypotext) or towards a model of a kind of textuality such as parody or montage, à la Genette's architextuality" (2011: 109).

'Displacement' and 'forgetting' are in fact what allowed Lil, in the persona of Fang, to reappear on the docks in Maoist Shanghai, her love interest now a little red book issued by the Central Party Committee. In this palimpsest (or parody, or montage) she certainly has what Jenny called "a new career", as for example has Uncle Ma (in retirement, his new job is political re-education). And her career extends into the present day, for instance (possibly) in Ang Lee's 2007 film version of Eileen Chang's novella, *Lust, Caution*[26], where although for once actually played by a Chinese actress (Tang Wei), the diegetic character herself, Wang Jiaji, is a university student and an amateur 'actress' only playing at being, partially, a Lil-type figure (as 'Mrs. Mak'). Thus the 'displacement' Jenny predicted, that arises from 'overdoing' the character, appears to be in some senses fulfilled, and we recognize this through an intertextual reading of the story (and the film) against the architextual tradition I have briefly summarized here.[27] Musical intertextuality, still an infant concept at present, hardly applies here except to point out that as a creature of the period 1925–1935, the cinematic Shanghai Lil is 'accompanied', as it were, by jazz. Jazz appears to be 'absorbed' in subsequent reappearances of Lil (just as the opening of the film-ballet version of *The Red Poppy* was absorbed in the first scene of *On the Docks*). In the 1960s, of course, this 'decadent' music was replaced by a repertoire more 'politically correct' for the times, something adumbrated by Glière in 1927, who nonetheless managed to combine jazz, post-romanticism, and expressionist realism in his score.[28] (Indeed, if one wished to explore

---

26   Begun in the 1950s, but not published until 1979.
27   I remain ambivalent as to whether 'Mrs. Mak' is a real instance of Shanghai Lil. Though
      the time and the setting are correct, she is well-educated and not herself part of a social
      underclass or a moral underworld, nor is she found 'on the docks'. While Lil may always
      be a femme fatale, it does not logically follow that all *cheungsaam*-clad femmes fatales are
      Shanghai Lil, even in Shanghai. There is an imperative need to avoid a racial stereotype
      here. However, it is worth recalling once again that in the score of *The Red Poppy* Dao Hua
      is also called an 'actress'.
28   It would overstate things to treat jazz generically as an indexical sign of Shanghai Lil.
      Along with Manila, Shanghai was the great center in Asia for jazz in the 1930s, and even I

purely musical intertextuality further in this case, it would be interesting to know if while composing his score Glière knew, or knew anything about, Ernst Krenek's sensational 'Jazz-Oper', *Jonny spielt auf*, first performed at the Leipzig Stadttheater on 10 February 1927. *Zeitoper* is not that far removed, really, from socialist-realism.)

Marshall McLuhan once said that "recognition is a more profound and deeper experience than mere cognition"[29]. Shanghai Lil is a character who endures endless recontextualization, and thus when we encounter her, we re-cognize her on that deeper intertextual level which allows us to remove her from her context and consider her alternatives. Freed from 'the waste that encrusts her', 'that little devil', as James Cagney might say, 'she's just a butterfly'.

References

Allen, Graham (2011). *Intertextuality*. 2nd ed. London: Routledge.

Bacon, Lloyd, Busby Berkeley, dirs. (1933/2006). *Footlight Parade*. Film [DVD]. USA/UK: Warner Brothers.

Bickers, Robert (online 2015). "From the Mystic Flowery Land [...] to Herne Bay". Online. http://robertbickers.net/2015/02/22/from-the-mystic-flowery-land-to-herne-bay/ [02/11/2015].

Campbell, Joseph (1949/1968). *The Hero with a Thousand Faces*, 2nd ed. Princeton, NJ: Princeton Univ. Press.

"Charleston and Other Dances: A Local Cicerone on Foibles and Fashions of To-day" (1926). *The North China Herald* (Shanghai). 20 February: 336.

Elder, Chris, ed. (1999). *China's Treaty Ports: Half Love and Half Hate*. Hong Kong: OUP.

Genette, Gérard (1997). *Palimpsests: Literature in the Second Degree*. Trans. Channa Newman, Claude Doubinsky. Lincoln, NE: Univ. of Nebraska Press.

Glière, Reinhold Moritzevich (1933). *Le pavot rouge: Ballet en 3 Actes et 8 Tableau avec Apothéose*. Piano Score. Moscow: Édition de Musique de l'État.

Glière, Reinhold Moritzevich (online 1955). *Červený Mak*. Film-Ballet. Československý Štátny Film. https://www.youtube.com/watch?v=DkTm5OVKyKc [28/10/2015].

Glière, Reinhold Moritzevich (1966). *Reingold Moritzevich Glier* [sic]: *Statii. Vospominaniia. Materialy* [*Essays. Reminiscences. Materials*]. Vol. 2. Leningrad: Muzika.

---

had the opportunity to hear the legendary, though geriatric, 'Peace Hotel Jazz Band' on my first visit to the city in the spring of 1990. The old members had practiced in secret during the years of the Cultural Revolution (1966–1976).

29 The only reference I can cite is having heard him say approximately this myself on a re-run of an episode of *The Fulton Sheen Program* (ran 1961–1968) to Bishop Fulton J. Sheen. There seems to be no online index of this program, its guests, or broadcast dates.

Glière, Reinhold Moritzevich (1927/1994). *The Red Poppy: Complete Ballet*. St. Petersburg State Symphony Orchestra, André Anichanov, conductor. 2 CDs. Naxos 8.553496-7.

Halcombe, Charles J.H. (1896). *The Mystic Flowery Land: A Personal Narrative*. London: Luzac & Co.

Halcombe, Charles J.H. (1900). "My Mysterious Protector: A Romantic Story of Real Life. How a Chinese Girl Saved the Author's Life, and Afterwards Became His Bride". *The Wide World Magazine* 2/82 (April): 741–745.

Hornby, Sir Edmund (1929/1999). *An Autobiography*. New impression. London: Constable & Co.

Jenny, Laurent (1982). "The Strategy of Form". Tzvetan Todorov, ed. *French Literary Theory Today: A Reader*. Trans. R. Carter. Cambridge: CUP. 34–63.

Liu Ching-chi (2010). *A Critical History of New Music in China*. Trans. Caroline Mason. Hong Kong: Chinese Univ. Press.

Lyall, Lesley (1979). *New Spring in China?* London: Hodder and Stoughton.

Melvin, Sheila, Cai Jindong (2004). *Rhapsody in Red: How Western Music Became Chinese*. New York, NY: Algora.

On the Docks: A Modern Revolutionary Peking Opera. Revised by the 'On the Docks' Group of the Peking Opera Troupe of Shanghai (January 1972 Script) (1973). Beijing: Foreign Languages Press.

Sternberg, Josef von, dir. (1932/2012). *Shanghai Express*. Film [DVD]. USA/UK: Universal Studios.

Sternberg, Josef von (1973). Morocco *and* Shanghai Express: *Two Films by Josef von Sternberg*. London: Lorrimer.

Westad, Odd Arne (2012). *Restless Empire: China and the World since 1750*. New York, NY: Basic Books.

Xie Tieli, dir. (1973/2004). *Haigang* [= *On the Docks*]. Film [DVD]. People's Republic of China: Qi Lu Yin Xiang Chu Ban She .

Figures

Notes on Contributors

Frieder von Ammon

(frieder.von_ammon@uni-leipzig.de) is Professor of German Literature at the University of Leipzig. He is co-editor of *Arbitrium, Goethe-Jahrbuch, Mikrokosmos*, and *Münchner Reden zur Poesie*, as well as author of numerous articles and *Ungastliche Gaben: Die 'Xenien' Goethes und Schillers und ihre literarische Rezeption von 1796 bis in die Gegenwart*. His book *Fülle des Lauts: Aufführung und Musik in der deutschsprachigen Lyrik seit 1945. Das Werk Ernst Jandls in seinen Kontexten* appeared in 2018.

Alla Bayramova

(bayramova_alla@mail.ru) is director of The State Museum of Musical Culture of Azerbaijan; graduated from Azerbaijan State Conservatoire, Musicology Faculty; got her PhD in musicology. Honoured Culture Worker of Azerbaijan, Assoc. Prof. of Western University, Baku. A member of the International Council of Museums (ICOM), where she is a member of the board of the International Committee for Literary and Composers Museums (ICLM) and a member of the advisory board of the International Committee for Museums of Music and Musical Instruments (CIMCIM). A member of Word and Music Studies Association (WMA). Her postdoctoral research is focused on the interrelationship of music and literature in the Azerbaijani culture, as this field and intermediality on the whole has not been studied enough in Azerbaijan. To fill this gap, Alla Bayramova initiated two international conferences on the problems of intermediality organized in Baku (2014, 2016). She is the author of numerous publications on relations between music and literature, including her monograph *Nizami Ganjavi's Poems in the Context of Interreflection of Arts* (2014).

Walter Bernhart

(walter.bernhart@uni-graz.at), retired Professor of English Literature at the University of Graz, Austria, is the founding and current president of The International Association for Word and Music Studies (WMA) and was the founding director of his university's Centre for Intermediality Studies in Graz (CIMIG). His collected *Essays on Literature and Music (1985–2013)* were published in 2015, and his most recent intermedial publications include "From Orpheus to Bob Dylan: The Story of 'Words and Music'" (2017) and "Absence of Words and Absence of Music in Opera" (2019). He is executive editor of the book series Studies in Intermediality (SIM) and Word and Music Studies (WMS), both published by Brill | Rodopi (Leiden, Boston, MA), and has (co)edited numerous individual volumes.

Christopher Booth

(topher.booth@gmail.com) earned a PhD in Musicology at Catholic University in Washington DC in 2018, having completed his masters in Music Theory at SUNY Potsdam. He has presented papers at American, Canadian, and British music conferences. His dissertation, titled *Preexisting Music in Historical Fiction Film*, primarily addresses hermeneutic considerations involving the intersection of music and film as it relates to narrativity and critical theory. He teaches music history at Old Dominion University and is working on several publications relating to film music and cinema studies.

Peter Dayan

(Peter.Dayan@ed.ac.uk) is Professor of Word and Music Studies at the University of Edinburgh, and Obel Visiting Professor at the University of Aalborg, where he works with the Centre for Research in Contemporary Poetry. He is a regular contributor to WMA conferences and publications. His third book on word and music studies, *The Music of Dada: A Lesson in Intermediality for Our Times*, was published in 2018.

Axel Englund

(axel.englund@littvet.su.se) is a Wallenberg Academy Fellow in Literature at the Department of Culture and Aesthetics, Stockholm University. He is the author of *Still Songs: Music In and Around the Poetry of Paul Celan* (2012), the first book-length study to approach the topic of Celan and music. Englund's articles on poetry and musico-literary intermediality have been published in *The German Quarterly*, *German Life & Letters* and *Perspectives of New Music*, as well as in numerous anthologies. Together with Anders Olsson, Englund has also edited *Languages of Exile: Migration and Mutilingualism in Twentieth-Century Literature* (2013). In 2011, he was an Anna Lindh Fellow at Stanford University, and he has held visiting scholarships at Columbia University and Freie Universität Berlin.

Michael Halliwell

(michael.halliwell@sydney.edu.au) studied music and literature at the University of the Witwatersrand in Johannesburg, at the London Opera Centre with Otakar Kraus, and in Florence with Tito Gobbi. He was principal baritone with the Netherlands Opera, the Nürnberg Opera, and the Hamburg State Opera, singing over fifty major roles as well as several world premieres and appearances at international festivals. He has published widely on words and music; his books include *Opera and the Novel* (Rodopi, 2005) and *Myths of National Identity in Contemporary Australian Opera* (Routledge, 2018). He is currently on the staff of the University of Sydney Conservatorium of Music, serving in a variety of teaching and administrative roles. His recordings include a double CD of Rudyard Kipling's *Barrack-Room Ballads* and Boer War songs, *When the Empire Calls* (ABC Classics 2005); *O for a Muse of Fire: Australian Shakespeare Settings* (Vox Australis 2013); *The Oriental Song-Cycles of Amy Woodforde-Finden* (Toccata Classics, 2014); *That Bloody Game: Australian World War One Songs* (Wirripang 2016).

Heidi Hart

(heidi.hart@usu.edu) holds a PhD from Duke University and teaches German and culture courses at Utah State University. She has resently published two monographs, one on Hanns Eisler's art songs and another on music and the environment in dystopian narrative.

Ruth Jacobs

(s1271487@sms.ed.ac.uk) is a PhD Candidate in Comparative Literature at the University of Edinburgh. Her thesis explores the relationship between music and traumatic memory in the work of Arnold Schoenberg, focusing on his String Trio and *A Survivor from Warsaw*. She is also interested in the way live performance intersects with academic research and discussion. Most recently, she co-organised a study day as part of the Edge of Words Research Project at the University of Edinburgh titled: "Performing Memory: The Holocaust in Music and Poetry". At this event she performed Gideon Klein's String Trio with cellist Gage Ehmann and violist Tom Widdicombe in order to promote a discussion of music's role in transmitting Holocaust memory.

Saskia Jaszoltowski

(saskia.jaszoltowski@uni-graz.at) is Assistant Professor at the Department of Musicology of the University of Graz. Her research focuses on the history and aesthetics of music in the 20th and 21st centuries, concentrating on audiovisual and intermedial phenomena as well as social and political implications of musical life. She was awarded a doctorate 'summa cum laude' at the Free University of Berlin for her PhD thesis on the soundtracks of animated cartoons (*Animierte Musik – Beseelte Zeichen: Tonspuren anthropomorpher Tiere in Animated Cartoons*, Stuttgart 2013) while working as a research assistant at the Cluster of Excellence 'Languages of Emotion'.

Lawrence Kramer

(lkramer@fordham.edu) is Distinguished Professor of English and Music at Fordham University in New York City. He is the author of many books, most recently *The Thought of Music* (University of California, 2016) – the third installment, with *Expression and Truth* (California 2012) and *Interpreting Music*

(California, 2010), of a trilogy on musical understanding –, and *The Hum of the World* (California 2019); the long-time editor of *19th-Century Music*; and a prizewinning composer.

Bernhard Kuhn

(bkuhn@bucknell.edu) is Professor of Italian Studies at Bucknell University, where he coordinates the Italian Studies Program and teaches Italian language, culture, and cinema. His current areas of research include Italian cinema, intermediality, and, in particular, the relationship between opera and cinema. He is the author of a book entitled *Die Oper im italienischen Film* (*Opera in Italian Cinema*) and several articles concerning intermedial aspects of the relationship between stage media and film.

Emily Petermann

(Emily.Petermann@uni-konstanz.de) is the author of *The Musical Novel: Imitation of Musical Structure, Performance, and Reception in Contemporary Fiction* (2014) and of several articles dealing with various facets of intermediality studies, such as the *Bildgedicht*, jazz novels, and film musicals. She is the co-founder of the Word and Music Association Forum (2009) and since 2017 has been a member of the Executive Board of the International Association for Word and Music Studies. Other research interests include children's literature and forms of nonsense across media.

Marion Recknagel

(mail@marion-recknagel.de) is a freelance musicologist and literary critic, who studied musicology, comparative literature, and theatre at Leipzig University, where she received her PhD in 2006. From 2002 to 2004, she was Research Fellow for the project Musikstadt Leipzig at the Institute of Musicology at Leipzig University. She was a Research Associate in comparative literature at Leipzig University's Institute of Classical Studies and Comparative Literature from 2009 to 2013. Her research interests focus on musical and dramaturgical concepts of opera in the nineteenth and early twentieth centuries, the life and works of Leoš Janáček, nineteenth-century musical aesthetics, and the relationship between music and literature. Her current research project focuses on the history of rhythm and metre in eighteenth-century music and literature.

Jordan Carmalt Stokes

(jstokes@wcupa.edu) received his PhD from the CUNY Graduate Center, where his dissertation, *Music and Genre in Film: Aesthetics and Ideology*, was co-recipient of the Barry S. Brook Award. His research and reviews have been published in *Music and the Moving Image, The Journal of Musicology, American Music*, and

American Music Review. He currently teaches at West Chester University, and hosts the podcast "New Books in Music" on the New Books Network.

David Francis Urrows

(odresel@hotmail.com) is a historical musicologist and composer. Between 1989 and 2018 he taught at Hong Kong Baptist University, where he established The Pipe Organ in China Project (www.organcn.org). He has also taught at the University of Massachusetts, the Hong Kong Academy for Performing Arts, and Eastern Mediterranean University. He is editor of the critical edition of the works of Otto Dresel (1826–1890) and has also written on topics ranging from Hildegard of Bingen to nineteenth-century émigré studies to twentieth-century choral music to Andrew Lloyd Webber. His book *Keys to the Kingdom: A History of the Pipe Organ in China* was published in 2017. He has been a member of wma since 2003 and is Secretary of the Association.

Werner Wolf

(werner.wolf@uni-graz.at) is Professor and Chair of English and General Literature at the University of Graz, Austria. His main areas of research are literary theory (aesthetic illusion, narratology, and metafiction/metareference in particular), functions of literature, 18th- to 21st-century English fiction, as well as intermediality studies (relations and comparisons between literature and other media, notably music and the visual arts). His publications include, besides numerous essays, reviews and contributions to literary encyclopedias, the monographs *Ästhetische Illusion und Illusionsdurchbrechung in der Erzählkunst* (*Aesthetic Illusion and the Breaking of Illusion in Fiction*, 1993) and *The Musicalization of Fiction: A Study in the Theory and History of Intermediality* (1999). He is also (co-)editor of volumes 1, 3, 5, 11 and 14 of the book series Word and Music Studies (1999–2015) as well as of volumes 1, 2, 4–6 and 11 of the series Studies in Intermediality: *Framing Borders in Literature and Other Media* (2006); *Description in Literature and Other Media* (2007); *Metareference across Media: Theory and Case Studies* (2009); *The Metareferential Turn in Contemporary Arts and Media: Forms, Functions, Attempts at Explanation* (2011); *Immersion and Distance: Aesthetic Illusion in Literature and Other Media* (2013); *Meaningful Absence Across Media: The Significance of Missing Signifiers* (2019).

Printed in the United States
By Bookmasters